GOOD FAITH AND TRUTHFUL IGNORANCE

D1051768

GOOD FAITH AND TRUTHFUL

IGNORANCE *A Case of Transatlantic Bigamy*

Alexandra Parma Cook & Noble David Cook

Duke University Press   Durham and London 1991

© 1991 Duke University Press
All rights reserved
Printed in the United States of America
on acid-free paper ∞
Library of Congress Cataloging-in-Publication Data appear on the
last printed page of this book.
The publisher and authors gratefully acknowledge the support of the
Program of Cultural Cooperation
between Spain's Ministry of Culture
and United States' Universities.

to doña Beatriz

I think it's a good thing that important events which quite accidentally have never seen the light of day, should be made public and not buried in the grave of oblivion. It's possible that somebody may read them and find something he likes and others may find pleasure in just a casual glance; and as a matter of fact, Pliny says there is no book, however bad it may be, that doesn't have something good about it, especially as tastes vary and one man's meat is another man's poison. I say this because I think that nothing should be thrown away or given up completely so long as it's not really disgusting. —Prologue to **Lazarillo de Tormes** *(anonymous, 1554)*

Contents

❧

List of Illustrations and Maps

➤●◀

Preface

❧◆❧

We did not set out to write biographical narrative as we began research in the General Archive of the Indies in Seville in the early months of 1985. Our subject was the history of an entire people, the native inhabitants of the Colca valley of Peru, from the time of the European conquest in the 1530s. During the course of research we came across a bundle of documents relating to first one, then more, legal claims against one of the settlers of the valley. We found no good information to complete the intended ethnohistory in these *legajos*, but we did become more and more engrossed by the court case that daily unfolded before our eyes. As we read, we became slowly convinced that the story of the protagonists deserved a hearing.

The rise of Spain, beginning with the marriage of Ferdinand of Aragon and Isabella of Castile in 1469 to the death of Philip II in 1598, is stunning. Many important events took place in that span of time, but perhaps the most significant was the discovery of a new continent in 1492 by Christopher Columbus. The exploration and conquest of that distant and vast territory, and the hitherto unimaginable quantities of silver and gold found there, helped support Spain's pretentions to European hegemony. During the sixteenth century thousands of young men from all sectors of Iberian society, often born far from the seacoast, took to the waters of the Atlantic. With the exception of the major conquistadores, men such as Cortés, Ponce de León, de Soto, Orellana, the Pizarros—the leaders whose exploits were described meticulously by contemporary chroniclers—we know precious little of the less illustrious men and women who settled in the colonies.

Why did so many break roots in Spain, leave their homes, their mothers and fathers, their sisters and brothers, and risk the voyage to the unknown lands in the west? The promise of riches was often one of the reasons, but there were other, more complex, and at times personal motives. How did they pay for the passage, who did they associate with, and how did they establish themselves in the New World? What of the women, generally ignored in the primary accounts of the events of discovery and conquest? We know that although many remained in Spain, there were enough courageous women who ventured to the Indies in the early expeditions to leave an indelible mark on colonial

Hispanic society. How did the men who succeeded overseas invest their wealth, and how did those who returned to Europe early, the men known in Spain as *indianos*, fare in the land of their birth?

Francisco Noguerol's story provides tantalizing answers to many of these questions, and much more. We hope that through him and his wives, doña Beatriz de Villasur and doña Catalina de Vergara, as well as the men and women who surround them, we can understand the mentality and ambitions of sixteenth-century Spaniards, especially those who embarked on the exploration, conquest, and settlement of the New World. The book is written from the point of view of the conquerors, not those vanquished in the brutal clash of two hitherto separate worlds. Here we have tried to see events through the eyes of the Europeans, not the people who inhabited the Americas and whose sometimes ruthless exploitation and decimation is a theme of past and future inquiry.

This book tells the tale of a man and his two wives, and of the labyrinthine legal world that ultimately entrapped a successful conqueror. The case, argued before the august Council of the Indies, has special appeal and takes on a life of its own. Fortunately for historians, every action and reaction, numerous questionnaires prepared by all parties in the lawsuit and conscientiously answered by many witnesses, in short, every minute detail was recorded by the busy scribes of the court and survive as a testament of not only the lawsuit itself but also as a window into the operation of the sixteenth-century legal system. The day-by-day maneuvers of the lawyers, and the charges and counter-charges of the litigants, all come to life, and we have attempted to recreate the excitement, the slow building of tensions, as the lawsuit progressed. As we followed the daily litigation in the records, reviewing hundreds of pages, the protagonists and their lives took on reality from the dust and fading ink of the deteriorating papers. Litigations often took years, and they did not always proceed in a logical sequence, making a modern reader puzzled over certain actions and perhaps impatient with the questions and answers of the witnesses. We have included only a fraction of the multitude of details, yet we feel that in order to illustrate the complexity, slowness, and repetition involved, it is necessary to let the readers get a small taste of the surviving documents.

The story of Francisco Noguerol de Ulloa and his two wives is intended to be a mirror of a segment of Spanish society in the sixteenth century, the middle class and minor nobility. Francisco dominates the book, but through him and his interaction with others the general milieu of the period, on a familial rather than global level, springs into view. As Noguerol's adventures and tribulations unfold, we can glimpse the world he lived in: the religious and moral values of the period, and the surprising degree of freedom and openness that existed in spite of the highly structured and hierarchical society under the shadow of the Inquisition.

It is difficult enough to piece together the lives of the sixteenth-century elite, the monarchs, members of the aristocracy, the major military and clerical leaders. It is doubly arduous to reconstruct the careers of those of the lower rungs of the social order. The *legajos* of litigation assisted us in the quest for the personalities of our figures. The court cases involving Noguerol filled much of the middle block of our history, and part of the first as well. But for the initial activities in the Indies, we were forced to review the published materials on the conquest of Andean America, then go to the service report filed by the man as he petitioned for royal favors. The search resembled a detective's slow and methodical investigation. We were surprised often by new twists, some with unexpected resolutions. At times working as genealogists, we consulted the parish registers, unfortunately with less than hoped-for success, for the years of our protagonists were missing from the record. But we were able to trace descendants into the seventeenth century. In contrast to the church rolls, the notarial information abounds. But anyone who has used these documents for tracing individuals knows well the pitfalls of such research. The scribal script is often the most difficult of all for even the most adept paleographer. Thousands of pages of transactions, contracts, or wills, for example, might be included in a notarial bundle for a single year, especially in a major city, and there are usually no indexes. Notarial research is monotonous; a clue may be followed by hundreds of pages of irrelevant entries. By educated guesses, and often just luck, we were able to finally locate the key materials to complete the puzzle of the later years of the lives of our principals.

Professor Woodrow Borah, kindly commenting on an early version of our manuscript, pointed out its striking similarity with Spanish picaresque novels of the period. That is true. The novelists created parallels to the real world that surrounded them. But we are not novelists. We have not strayed from what we can prove or reasonably assume on the basis of the documentary evidence. If we describe the seasickness of the protagonist, for example, it is because he more than once complained of its agonies.

We not only followed Francisco Noguerol de Ulloa through the extant documentation, but we also visited all the places, with the exception of Chile, that our often infamous conquistador trod. We contemplated the same countryside and surveyed the vestiges of the sixteenth century in the villages and cities that figure in the narrative. More often than not, however, we were forced to use our imagination as we tried to visualize the sites as Noguerol and his two wives saw them. The present work, however, is not the product of imagination; rather, it is a tribute to the Spanish record keepers who made it possible to reconstruct the lives of ordinary people who lived in an extraordinary age. Francisco Noguerol and doña Catalina de Vergara attempted in manifold sixteenth-century ways to assure a legacy of remembrance. But a fatal series of events effaced that memory. In these pages we hope, assisted by doña Beatriz de Villasur's search for justice, to resurrect the couple from the abyss of oblivion to which they have been assigned.

Acknowledgments

Many people and institutions have helped us during our research and writing. To name all who have contributed in one way or another would require a small monograph. We simply wish to say "thank you for your patience" to all who have been, over the past five years, subjected to our enthusiastic recounting of details on the latest developments of the "Noguerol Saga."

The research would not have been possible without the following grants: the Comité Conjunto Hispano Norteamericano para la Cooperación Cultural y Educativa, and we would especially like to thank María del Carmen Rodas of the committee for her help; and a Mellon Foundation Grant administered by the University of Bridgeport. Supplementary material on Francisco Noguerol had been collected during earlier research. The most important support was provided by the Fulbright Commission in Peru, the Wenner-Gren Foundation for Anthropological Research, and a National Endowment for the Humanities Summer Grant.

The Archivo General de Indias, in Seville, under the direction of Rosario Parra, is a wonderful place to work, in large part because of the courtesy and warmth of the staff. We appreciate the efficiency and speed of the personnel of the Archivo Provincial de Valladolid, given the limited time at our disposal, and we especially thank director María Jesús Urquijo Urquijo and her assistant Raquel García González. Above all, we are truly grateful to María Consuelo Sendino González, the Head of the Municipal Library of Medina del Campo, where the town papers were temporarily housed. She and her husband, José Luis Núñez Baticón, postponed their August vacation to allow us to finish examining the documents. We also thank the directors and personnel of the following depositories, whose courtesy and helpfulness made our research easier and quicker: in Spain, the Archivo General de Simancas, the Archivo Provincial de Salamanca, the Archivo Diocesano de Valladolid, the Biblioteca Nacional, the Biblioteca del Palacio, and the Royal Academy of History; in Peru, the Archivo Nacional del Perú, the Biblioteca Nacional, the Archivo Histórico Provincial of Arequipa, and the Archivo Parroquial of Yanque. We thank also the staff of the Inter-Library Loan Department of the University of Bridgeport, and the

History Department of Yale University. Appointment as a Visiting Fellow and then Visiting Professor at Yale provided easy access to the excellent holdings of their collections.

We would like to express our gratitude to several scholars who took time from their own work and read and commented on the manuscript: Woodrow Borah, George Lovell, Franklin Pease, Nicolás Sánchez-Albornoz, and John TePaske. Jonathan Spence's request to be kept posted on "the case of the transatlantic bigamy" inspired the title. We are indebted to John Lynch for his kind encouragement and timely counsel. We owe a clear intellectual debt to several others whose work influenced the direction of our approach: Emmanuel Le Roy Ladurie, Carlo Ginzburg, Natalie Zemon Davis, Judith C. Brown, and James Lockhart.

Frank Smith's invaluable professional suggestions have helped to shape this volume and we are grateful for his candor. We also thank María Rostworowski de Diez Canseco, Rafael Varón, Margarita Suárez, and John Casey for important leads, Andrew Urbansky for his translation of two Latin documents, and Mariana Mould de Pease for her generous encouragement at a time we needed it most. Two evaluators of the manuscript and our editor at Duke University Press, Lawrence J. Malley, made several excellent comments on the final version. We thank Marcia Harrington for her fine maps. Jarmila and George Parma have our unlimited gratitude for taking care of Karoline and Vincent during those long summer weeks of 1986. Their "sacrifice" enabled us to complete an important segment of the research in order to bring the story of Francisco Noguerol and his two wives to an end. The research, writing, and revising caused us at times to neglect our roles as parents, and we are thankful for the patience and understanding of the younger Cooks.

Prologue
Justice Be Fulfilled

Let justice be fulfilled.—*Doña Costanza de Espinosa*

The story of Francisco Noguerol de Ulloa begins not at the time of his birth, but rather a few years later, when an incident took place that changed the circumstances of his family. It was the first in a chain reaction of events that marked his life.

Francisco's father, Mendo Noguerol, was posted as *alcaide* (governor) at the royal fortress of Simancas. We find him there in 1520 during the revolt of the *comuneros* against the young Emperor Charles V. The uprising, though widespread and passionate, was crushed within a year, and its leaders, Juan Padilla and Juan Bravo, were executed. One of the defeated insurgents, don Antonio de Acuña, bishop of Zamora, was captured while attempting to flee to France. Bishop Acuña posed a dilemma for the victorious Charles. As a churchman, he was protected by ecclesiastical immunity, yet his role during the rebellion was too crucial to let him go unpunished. Thus, while the emperor and the pope were negotiating an appropriate treatment of the renegade bishop, Acuña himself was locked up in a small cell of Simancas. The emperor commanded Mendo Noguerol to keep the controversial inmate well guarded and not to permit any visitors, except a priest and a royal interrogator. Furthermore, he instructed Mendo always to be present during such meetings.[1]

The energetic clergyman, one of the last warrior bishops of the Middle Ages, was not resigned to languish in prison, and he schemed to escape. It was Sunday, 26 February 1526, about ten o'clock in the morning. The townspeople and some of the soldiers in the fortress were attending Mass in the cloister of the church of El Salvador, because the temple itself had recently collapsed and was being rebuilt. The bishop, normally an early riser, did not appear as usual, and Mendo Noguerol, wondering if something was amiss, went to see the prisoner.

Acuña was waiting for his jailer. Following a brief conversation, he suddenly hurled a leather pouch containing a heavy stone at Mendo, striking him in the face. The unfortunate man, stunned by the impact, had no time to recover, for the clergyman stabbed him, with several sharp thrusts in the throat, using a makeshift spear. Mendo Noguerol fell dead, and the bishop rushed from the cell. The illustrious inmate, however, did not escape. One of Mendo's sons, alerted by the commotion, shut the main gate, and Acuña, realizing his only chance to flee was to jump from the high ramparts of the fortress, a feat that would have meant a severe injury if not death, surrendered.

A thorough investigation followed, and an intricate plot involving a chaplain, a muleteer, and Mendo's slave girl, Juana, was uncovered. All, with the exception of the muleteer who was never found, were tortured and punished. Antonio de Acuña was garroted in the courtyard of Simancas castle on 23 March 1526, with the emperor's authorization. The cold-blooded murder of a royal official provided the needed pretext to be rid of the bellicose bishop. Nevertheless, Charles V abstained from Holy Communion until he received papal absolution. The papal nuncio at the imperial court and later author of *The Book of the Courtier*, Baldassare Castiglione, commended the emperor's piety and excused his unusual action against a churchman because Acuña was "so wicked a man, who so often and with such extreme criminal acts made himself unworthy of enjoying the privileges and favors that are granted to bishops."[2]

Mendo Noguerol's death marked the beginning of Francisco Noguerol's recorded life. Francisco was sixteen years old when his father was assassinated. He was shocked and saddened by the murder, and must have echoed his mother's reputed cry, "let justice be fulfilled."[3] Until he reached majority of age, at twenty-five, Francisco's fate would be directed by his mother, doña Costanza de Espinosa, a strong-minded and forceful woman who took charge of property and her children's lives.

Following Mendo's death, doña Costanza made a claim on the sparse estate of the bishop of Zamora. The family also expected compensation from the monarch; after all, Mendo perished in His Majesty's service. The royal secretary, Francisco de los Cobos, promised in the king's name that "with regard to the children of Noguerol, when the time comes, and when there is an appropriate occasion, that which is called for will be done."[4]

Mendo Noguerol, a native of Galicia and an *hidalgo* of "buena sangre," did not leave his family without resources, and his widow commanded a modest fortune. Mendo's brother served as paymaster general to the king, and doña Costanza as well as the siblings fully exploited such connection. Two daughters, Ynés and Francisca, had entered the Benedictine order in 1522 while their father was still alive, and they were well provided for. The children who were still under their mother's tutelage, however, needed to be settled. Doña Costanza strove to arrange suitable marriages for them, and her intransigence in her choice of bride for Francisco shaped the future of her oldest son.[5]

THE INDIES

I

She Who Died

God has been served to carry from this world she who died.
—*Doña Ynés Noguerol de Ulloa*

As darkness fell on Valladolid on the penultimate day of March 1557, a
man sat alone in an oppressive cell of the royal jail. Francisco Noguerol
de Ulloa had just given a thorough deposition to the Licentiate Santander, the court reporter of the Council of the Indies. He had been
charged with bigamy and illegal shipment of treasure from Peru by a
woman he had believed dead and by an ambitious agent of the king. In
his solitude Francisco must have wondered how a once powerful *encomendero* and a prominent citizen of Arequipa could have fallen into
such disgrace. He who fought numerous battles defending royal interests in Peru and whose body was forever marked with painful me-
mentos of his loyalty—how did he incur His Majesty's wrath? It was on
King Philip II's order that he had been imprisoned. And neither his
status nor his pleas caused the court to relent and allow him house
arrest.[1] Noguerol's thoughts might have shifted to his youth, his life in
the Indies, but most of all he must have cursed the letters his sisters had
written to him eleven years earlier, letters that were, in part, the cause of
his present downfall.

Doña Ynés and doña Francisca, nuns in the Benedictine convent of
San Pedro de las Dueñas, had corresponded occasionally with their
brother who resided in Peru. But the mail was slow and undependable.
This time they wrote to tell Francisco that his wife, doña Beatriz de
Villasur, had died, and to reprimand him for neglecting his own family.
They desired, above all else, his return.[2]

"Very magnificent señor. We, all your brothers and sisters, are at your
service. We are very surprised at the little concern and account that you
have shown us, and especially my señora our mother, to whom you
should come. None of all her children come to see her, to provide her
with a pleasant old age and end. Although letters will hurt you, and we
do not know what this one will do, let it be done. We all know that you
do not plan to come, and that you are rich, as all those who come from
there say you are.

"It was because of doña Beatriz de Villasur, and certainly to you there was more than enough reason, but now there can be no excuse, because God has been served to carry from this world she who died of *dolor de costado* [chest pains] after seven days.[3] And thus it is by the love of God. You should pay attention to the advanced age of our mother, and to how much she has always loved you. Come to give her a pleasant old age, for there is not another thing in this life that she more desires. The señora doña Francisca and I are well, although you should already know in how much need we live, because my señora has much work with having so many children with whom to fulfill her obligation. . . . There is not enough space to take care of those we have at present, but it is necessary to make the most of what one has, and thus we all hope for your arrival as our salvation, as the solution to all. I pray to Our Lord that he puts the thought in your mind, and that you will do it, that you will put it into effect. In the meantime, whatever gift or alms that you send to us would be a very great gift, and we would have an even greater obligation than we now have to supplicate Our Lord to bring you well before our eyes.

"My señora is very old and ill. For the love of God come to see her before God carries her away, because you know that she does not want or desire anything more in this life than to see you, whose very magnificent person may God guard. From this house of San Pedro de las Dueñas on the seventh day of June of the year of Our Lord 1546. I kiss your hands. Your servant and sister, doña Ynés Noguerol de Ulloa."[4]

Doña Francisca's letter was equally to the point, although somewhat shorter than that of her sister. "Very magnificent señor. I do not know where to begin to scold you for the great inconsideration in not coming to see my señora and give her a pleasant old age, because you now have the possibility of doing it.

"According to all here who tell us of you, you did not return because of doña Beatriz de Villasur, and now she is dead. Although that has given us little contentment, it has removed this embarrassment. For the love of God, come, and give us this pleasure. All of us have no other worldly father to have been favored with except you. We will not cease to pray to God until He grants our wish. I pray to His Divine Majesty to put this thought into your mind, and that we will see this much desired day.

"My señora is already very old and desires greatly to see you before she dies. For the love of God, give her this contentment, because when God wills nothing stands in the way. May Our Lord guard and prosper your very magnificent person, and bring you to this land, for our rest and the solution to the needs that we suffer from. From this Monastery of San Pedro de las Dueñas, the seventh of June of 1546. Your servant, who kisses your very magnificent hands, doña Francisca Noguerol."[5]

These crucial missives had reached Francisco during a bloody up-heaval in Peru, a civil war between the rebel forces of Gonzalo Pizarro and the Crown. The wounds that Noguerol had sustained then were still aching; they had never quite healed. Noguerol had spent more than twenty years in the Indies, living a turbulent existence he relished at first; and yes, his sisters were right, he had become rich and the name Noguerol de Ulloa was well known in Peru. Perhaps as Francisco tried to ignore the clamor from the adjacent cells, noise that aggravated his chronic headache, he pondered his past.[6]

II

Hardship and Risk

You . . . have served His Majesty in these parts at your cost with your horses and arms with much hardship and risk. . . . And you are a caballero.*—Francisco Pizarro*

Tales filtering into Spain in the late 1520s about Francisco Pizarro's discovery of fabulously wealthy lands had created ripples of excite-ment. Francisco Noguerol de Ulloa had many occasions to hear the most recent news from the Indies. The young man had served Charles V as a palace guard in the company of don Alvaro de Luna in the strategically important fortress at Fuenterrabía. For a while he had been in the retinue of the Count of Benavente. Later, Noguerol had entered the service of the Duke of Medina Sidonia, who had invested in some of the ventures in the exploration of the New World. Francisco had stayed in the duke's "house and service" for two years, and he embarked for Peru while still in his employ.[1]

Francisco Noguerol had various positions available to him in Spain, partly because of his family connections. But such posts did not provide the independence and opportunities he dreamed about. Following his father's death, Francisco had been living under the domination of his mother, doña Costanza de Espinosa, a woman he loved, but the young man's devotion and obedience also bred resentment of doña Costanza's uncompromising hand. Francisco was dissatisfied, and life in the New World had become alluring, especially as the opportunity arose to travel to Peru in the service of the Duke of Medina Sidonia. In the Indies young Spaniards of moderately affluent families could, if they were persistent, talented, and fortunate acquire wealth, power, and prestige. Furthermore, in the Indies a man could escape the constraints of an unwanted marriage. Doña Costanza had forced Francisco, threatening to curse him unless he agreed, to marry doña Beatriz de Villasur, but she could not stop her son from abandoning his bride and setting out for a world that promised riches as well as freedom.[2]

Noguerol embarked for the New World sometime in 1534. The voyage from Seville to Panama, a passage of several months, had seemed endless to Francisco, who suffered from seasickness. But he had forgotten the discomfort after he disembarked in the bustling port of Nombre de Dios. The rugged terrain, the wild tropical rainforest of the isthmus, were unlike anything he had ever seen in Spain. As Noguerol trudged across the narrow strip of land to the Pacific harbor of Panama in the company of other travelers, some of whom had probably participated in the conquest of the Antilles and Mesoamerica, his excitement must have grown. Rumors took on realistic proportions in Panama City, buzzing with fresh details of Pizarro's progress to the south.[3]

Early association with an explorer was important when the booty was divided. Francisco Noguerol de Ulloa was not among the lucky soldiers attached to Francisco Pizarro in the first stages of the conquest of Peru who had benefited from the enormous treasure that had been collected as ransom for Atahualpa, the captured ruler of Tawantinsuyu, the Inca empire. But the vivid descriptions of the marvelous hoard of precious metals surely conjured up images of similar fortune to come.

The captive Inca, in a desperate effort to satisfy the Spaniards' greed, had ordered large quantities of silver and gold to be brought to the north Peruvian highland city of Cajamarca, hoping to win back his freedom. The expertly crafted objects had filled two rooms. After they had been recorded, the irreplaceable articles were melted down and the ingots officially marked. A fabulous distribution of riches had followed: everyone from the king of Spain down to the lowest foot soldier had received a share. Meanwhile, the Inca had continued a prisoner. Many Spaniards, apprehensive about setting the powerful chief at liberty, had argued that he should be put to death. Francisco Pizarro at first had protected the captive but later backed down, persuaded by the group that advocated execution of the ruler. On 26 July 1533, the Inca Atahualpa was garroted, only shortly after he had converted to Christianity.[4]

By the time Noguerol had reached his final destination, sometime in

1535, Pizarro's early followers had already plucked the bulk of the rewards, along with the Indian grants at San Miguel de Piura, Cajamarca, Jauja, then Cuzco. Furthermore, festering animosity between the chief leaders of the venture, Francisco Pizarro and Diego de Almagro, was corroding unity among the Europeans.

The partners, along with the priest Hernando de Luque, had begun preparations in 1524 for exploration of the region south of Panama, and later they signed a formal agreement of cooperation. Francisco Pizarro had returned to Spain to herald the promising territories and to recruit fresh soldiers. He had secured for himself the title of governor and captain-general of Peru, leaving Diego de Almagro the insignificant post of commander of Tumbez, while Luque was named bishop of the city. Almagro, incensed, had sent complaints to Spain and had remained a partner only because he was promised the governorship of lands to the south of Pizarro's domain. In 1535 Almagro, while acting governor in Cuzco, had learned that the emperor had confirmed Pizarro's control over the north and had authorized his jurisdiction of the south. It seemed that the Inca capital fell within Almagro's sphere, but no one was yet certain of the boundaries. The uneasy partners had signed a truce in Cuzco in June of 1535, and Almagro at once began preparations for a large expedition to explore his southern domain, rumored to abound with flourishing cities. Pizarro, hoping for respite from a pestering rival, liberally contributed to the effort. Francisco Noguerol and dozens of other recent arrivals in Peru, as well as veterans disappointed with their share in the spoils, flocked to Almagro's banner.

Diego de Almagro had become friendly with the Inca Manco Capac and before leaving Cuzco asked him advice. The Andean chieftain readily obliged and even promised to send his brother, Paullo Tupac, and the high priest, Villac Umu, along with Indian porters, to accompany the explorers. It served Manco Capac's purposes to aid Diego de Almagro and ensure his long absence from the Inca capital.

Diego de Almagro with about fifty Spaniards set out from Cuzco on 3 July 1535. The contingent joined in Paria an advance party of one hundred men led by Captain Juan de Saavedra, and together they marched on to Lake Poopó. The soldiers reached Tupiza in October of that year. There the Europeans were met by a group of friendly Indians who offered them gifts from Chilean chieftains: two large gold nuggets, one weighing fourteen pounds, the other eleven. These overwhelming presents stimulated the Spaniards' appetites, as they had visions of a Chile as rich as Peru had been. Thus encouraged, the conquistadores pushed southward, ruthlessly looting Indian settlements along the way to replenish food as they searched for treasure.[5]

In Chicoana, Francisco Noguerol de Ulloa, who had brought fresh supplies and fifty more Spaniards from the north, joined the expedition. The group also included several thousand Indian porters and warriors sent by Manco Capac. Francisco, though a comparative newcomer, was not entirely inexperienced in the art of war. After all, while he had been stationed at Fuenterrabía he did engage in "battles and skirmishes and attacks alike" not only there, but "in other forces that at the time they offered." Diego de Almagro trusted Noguerol's capabilities enough to rely on him to lead the reinforcement.[6]

The Spaniards and their Indian retinue reached the snow-covered pass of San Francisco at the end of March of 1536. As the soldiers and native porters plodded through the icy and windy mountain pass, many succumbed in the freezing temperatures. Reports on the number of Indians who perished vary widely, from 2,000 to 10,000, and approximately 170 horses froze. Francisco Noguerol, cold and worn though he was, survived the treacherous passage. He was young and strong, and perhaps images of gleaming gold and silver helped to warm his shivering body.

The expedition reached Copiapó, and by mid-1536 it arrived at the Maule River, where the dwindling and tired group was attacked by the Araucanian Indians. The native warriors fought with fierce determination and killed many of the would-be conquerors. Diego de Almagro and his men finally had to admit the futility of the venture. They found neither wealthy cities nor the gold they searched for, and they began to suspect that the two huge nuggets presented them in Tupiza were enticements that had led them into a dangerous trap. Exhausted and without any treasures to compensate for the hardships, the disappointed soldiers decided to return to Cuzco. Almagro, hoping for a less perilous route, chose to follow the coast, through the Atacama desert. He ordered that an advance company of eighty men, led by Francisco Noguerol de Ulloa, embark ahead in order to shield the progress of the rest of the troop from Indian ambush. A few days later squads of six to eight men, about one day apart in order to assure adequate water from the sparse and deficient desert springs along the trail, forged ahead toward Atacama, where all were reunited. After an odyssey of almost two years, the failed and decimated expedition reached Cuzco in early 1537. Francisco Noguerol was among the fortunate survivors.[7]

Diego de Almagro had returned to a Cuzco devastated by an Indian siege led by Manco Capac. The Inca, taking advantage of Almagro's absence as well as the continuous strife among the Spanish settlers, had assailed the old capital of Tawantinsuyu, and the sacred burial site of his ancestors, with thousands of Indian warriors. Following months of violent fighting and deprivation, Manco's stranglehold on the city had been loosened.

Hernando and Gonzalo Pizarro, exhausted from the long siege, put up only a feeble resistance to Almagro's reassertion of his claims to Cuzco, and they were captured and imprisoned. Diego de Almagro was adamant about winning back the governorship of the Inca capital, which he felt had been usurped by Francisco Pizarro. When armed conflict broke out between the two factions, Francisco Noguerol de Ulloa, along with the other "men from Chile," supported Almagro.

In July 1537 Almagro's forces met and defeated at Abancay an army that Francisco Pizarro had sent from Lima. Realizing his weaknesses as his brothers remained captive, Francisco Pizarro entered into negotiations with his foe. The dispute was to be arbitrated by Friar Francisco de Bobadilla. The Almagrists, however, distrusted the cleric, a known Pizarrist, and refused to honor his decision. In the meantime Gonzalo Pizarro had escaped from captivity; nevertheless, Francisco Pizarro acquiesced to Diego de Almagro's demand and ceded to him the administration of Cuzco until a judgment was pronounced in Spain.

Mollified, Diego de Almagro released Hernando Pizarro, who instead of setting sail for Spain as he had promised, organized a new military force against Almagro, and in a battle at the Pampas de las Salinas near Cuzco on 6 April 1538, won a final victory. Diego de Almagro fled back to Cuzco, where he was seized by Pizarro's soldiers and later executed.

Francisco Noguerol de Ulloa did not fight in the battle of Salinas. He was in Cuzco, entrusted by Almagro with guarding some thirty Pizarro supporters.[8] The result of the conflict was less than favorable to anyone on Almagro's side, and indeed Noguerol, as had his father, could have perished while serving as a jailer. Yet the adroit *hidalgo*, in spite of the compromising association with a loser, not only lived but less than two years later received from the Governor Francisco Pizarro, anxious to win over former Almagrists, what he had hoped for all along, an *encomienda* of Indians.

The *marqués* bestowed on his new ally 1,030 Indians scattered in nineteen villages in the area of Los Ubinas, a region to the west of Lake Titicaca, in the direction of the Pacific coast. Francisco Pizarro set forth within the prescribed formula Noguerol's merits: "You, Francisco Noguerol de Ulloa have served His Majesty in these parts at your cost with your horses and arms with much hardship and risk, and in this cause you have become indebted; and in the kingdoms of Spain in the wars that His Majesty has had with his enemies on the frontiers. And you are a *caballero*, a person of much honor and a servant of the king."[9]

As he joined the ranks of the *encomenderos*, Noguerol was also called upon to Christianize his Indians: "you have to serve in conformity with the royal orders and ordinances for the good treatment of them, and further, you are obligated to indoctrinate them and teach them in the matters of our Holy Catholic Faith, and in all treat them well as His Majesty orders."[10]

Francisco Noguerol de Ulloa must have been jubilant. Although he had suffered many setbacks since he arrived in Peru, he had finally reaped the long-desired prize: a profitable *encomienda*. Francisco was correct to abandon the hopeless cause of Diego de Almagro that had been carried on by Almagro's *mestizo* son. He had much more to gain in Francisco Pizarro's employ. Perhaps he shared the views of another former Almagrist, Alonso Enríquez de Guzmán, who slyly explained "at the present the said Hernando Pizarro and I have become friends, because he is alive and the other [Almagro] is dead, and to treat with the dead is most vile."[11] It was not unusual that the *marqués* rewarded a former enemy; after all, it was in Pizarro's interest to appease and win over Almagro's supporters and thus weaken the potential threat posed by the son of his executed enemy. But Francisco Pizarro went even further in his trust; when he composed his last will, Francisco Noguerol acted as one of the witnesses.[12]

III

Neither Rectitude nor Tranquility

Where there is no justice, there is neither rectitude nor tranquility.—Francisco Noguerol de Ulloa

Francisco Pizarro was assassinated by a group of disgruntled Almagrists in Lima on 26 July 1541, and Diego de Almagro the Younger was proclaimed governor. Pizarro's murder left Noguerol in a very vulnerable position. His former Chilean companions would have been tempted to punish the deserter had they captured him. Luckily he was neither in Lima nor Arequipa at the time, but sailing between the two cities, on board a ship carrying precious metals to the *marqués* in the capital. Francisco departed from Arequipa on Thursday, 1 July 1541. The vessel made slow progress northward and stopped several times to take on further goods. Noguerol, as usual, became "distempered by the sea" and was glad to step on solid ground in Nazca to help the captain load the needed provisions.[1]

While in Nazca, a servant of the Veedor Saucedo told the two men that Pizarro had been murdered in Lima. Francisco was somewhat taken aback and inquired how the *veedor* knew about the assassination. The informant revealed that a man named Espinal had intercepted and read a letter carried by a slave from Lima to his master, who was outside the city with his Indians. In a hastily scribbled note the *encomendero*'s wife had begged her husband: "Señor, come quickly and take charge of your house and hacienda, because you must know that the men of Chile have killed the Marqués Don Francisco Pizarro, and have raised up as governor don Diego de Almagro."[2]

Noguerol feared reprisals at the hand of the Almagrists. He knew he could not return to his estate in Arequipa or even safely remain in Peru. As Francisco was considering his options, four mysterious figures arrived "in coats of mail and helmets and armed with swords, daggers and lances on horseback." One of the riders was a cleric, and Noguerol started a conversation with him. When he ascertained that the horsemen had come from Lima, Francisco innocently asked the priest in armor, "How is the *marqués*?" The man replied sarcastically, "He is very well; he was never better than now." The clergyman then informed Noguerol that "don Diego has risen for governor of all the realms and has been received by the cabildo of Lima."[3] Furthermore, he showed Francisco letters and orders from Almagro the Younger, and asked him to help capture the captain and the valuable cargo originally destined for Pizarro.

Noguerol had no intention of assisting the priest, but he did need to reach the vessel anchored off the shore. While Francisco was talking, the captain, fearing for his safety, had decided to return to his ship, thus leaving Noguerol stranded among the enemy. When the cleric queried how the captain might be taken, Francisco, "seeing that God was providing me with the way to salvation [I] told him [the cleric] that if the boat turned around toward the coast, it seemed like a good idea to me that he and one of his men should come with me and my companions and we would board a small boat, and go out to talk to the captain." The cleric accepted Noguerol's plan. When they reached the ship, the captain, unsure of Noguerol, asked what he wanted, "and without responding, I left the small boat and jumped on board, along with my companions, and I winked at the captain three or four times and told him, 'You know that the Marqués Don Francisco Pizarro is dead and what it means?' The reason I winked at him rather than tell him directly what I wanted was because I was not sure if he would do what we afterwards did."[4]

The captain refused to negotiate with the cleric and set sail, shouting, "I will go to Lima or wherever else I deem better." The vessel headed north, but far to sea in order to avoid Almagro's patrol boats. It did not take long before Noguerol had to be confined in bed because "the sea once again made me ill disposed." Francisco, unsure of the ultimate destination, had invited the captain to come and see him. At first the suspicious seaman ignored the invitation, but eventually he did descend below deck, and after initial mistrust, the two men agreed to "come to this Royal Audiencia of His Majesty [Panama] to inform [him] of what had happened."[5]

Francisco reached Panama in the beginning of August 1541, and shortly thereafter, on the thirteenth of the month, wrote to Charles V giving him an account of the events in Peru, "acting speedily in this regard, so that the problem may be remedied, without delay, because with brevity one can quickly remedy it and with tardiness great evil and damage can result, both for the natives as well as for the Spaniards." After describing his whereabouts at the time of Pizarro's assassination, Noguerol reiterated to the king a proposal for a solution to the upheaval in Peru, a plan he had already submitted to the members of the Audiencia of Panama. Noguerol's self-confidence was remarkable. He was still quite young, about thirty-one years old. But he had lived in the provinces of Peru from 1535, almost from the beginning of the settlement. Although he had remained mostly in the background, Noguerol felt that he knew the conditions in the colony sufficiently well to advise his sovereign on how the intricate situation should be handled.

"It seems to me that Your Majesty should order a person be provided, one who has much experience in the land, and personal valor because it is clear that these shameless people have so forgotten the service of Your Majesty that it is necessary to punish them severely. The principal, and even the entire cause that the men of that land are so impudent has been the little justice and little punishment that has been exercised there. Where justice is lacking, one is bound to have scandals and great evils. It pains me much that a land so important to Your Majesty should be lost."[6]

Noguerol complained that too many of the past officials had been inept and lacked understanding of the country and its problems. "Quick help is needed to save the realm. In the provision there should be no questions as to interpretation, as has been the case until now, because it would not only mean the perdition for all the Spaniards who are here, but also the natives will suffer total loss."

Francisco, who suspected that his property had been plundered as a result of the current upheaval, did not hesitate to point out the inequities in the distribution of wealth. "There are many men of quality in this land who have served Your Majesty, with their lives and their resources, who not only lack food, but are even tied up in owing great sums of money, and live facing excessive need. Then there are others who not only lack quality, but have never worked in the land, nor spent anything, but who are rich, and have very good Indians, from which neither God nor Your Majesty can be served. This alone has been the cause of a great part of the past scandals, as well as the present ones, because many good men coming experienced and poor have committed acts that they might not have, had they been paid for their services and labors. For this Your Majesty should order that the evil should be punished, because where there is no justice, there is neither rectitude nor tranquility, and the good should be rewarded."[7]

The eloquent refugee recommended that the king "give Indians to each according to his services and qualities, which has not been done before, on the contrary, it was as favors or presents." Further, the land was "filled with officials and other low types who, not only are not knowledgeable in the arts of war, but do not have any inclination for it, nor do they own the proper gear, the arms or horses; they are involved in civil activities, which is all contrary to what people of quality should be." Francisco's contempt for government bureaucrats was generally shared by the "people of quality," the Spaniards who considered themselves *hidalgos* and proudly displayed their attributes of warfare. Noguerol admonished the monarch, "look well, Your Majesty, what is ordered for this land this time. Let it be the final set of provisions and that which will root out all the confusions of this land, so that we will not be made to perish, and Your Majesty will not lose his land and vassals."[8]

Francisco had not, of course, written to Charles V solely to offer advice. The real purpose of the long missive was to ask the sovereign for a suitable reward for his loyal service to the Crown. Noguerol confided that he had made the present effort to inform His Majesty, leaving his estate and traveling to Panama, expecting to be despoiled in

Peru "because the men of Chile were ill disposed toward me." He had come to Panama to aid in the "pacification of the realm," but he was also much in debt. Francisco, ever confident of his quality and perhaps mindful of the king's promise following Mendo Noguerol's assassination, requested that His Majesty "have respect for my services and my great need, and grant me the office of the high constable of the land of Peru, vacated by the death of the Marqués Don Francisco Pizarro, and also some Indians that vacated by the death of a conquistador named Diego Rodríguez . . . with these *merceds* past expenses can be remedied, and present debts can be paid."[9]

Francisco was disappointed in his aspirations, for Charles V had already named Cristóval Vaca de Castro to fill the office Noguerol coveted. Although his hopes had been dashed, Noguerol returned to Peru and joined the new governor's army, made up largely of vengeful Pizarrists, which defeated the young Almagro at Chupas on 16 September 1542.[10]

IV

The Healthiest in Peru

The site and climate of this city is so good that
it is extolled as the healthiest in Peru, and
most pleasant to live in.—Pedro de Cieza de León

When Francisco Noguerol left Panama, he returned home, to Arequipa, a Spanish city flourishing since 1540 on the gentle slope at the base of the snow-covered volcanic cone of Misti. Francisco had figured among its founders, and like the other Spaniards who populated the settlement, he must have been pleased with the choice of terrain. The elevation was almost perfect, about 2,400 meters, high enough to avoid insect infestations yet not so high as to hinder crops or lead to altitude sickness, *soroche*, which afflicted many Europeans. Regular rainfall, from December to March, soaked the countryside. Furthermore, springs, melting snow, and glacial ice created streams and small rivers that provided water already used for irrigation by the natives scattered in a series of small hamlets. According to Pedro de Cieza de León, "the site and climate of this city is so good, that it is extolled as the healthiest in Peru, and most pleasant to live in."[1]

Francisco, as one of the original settlers, had been alloted land, where he had built his residence, amply furnished and filled with Indian servants and slaves. It was no secret that the young *encomendero* had left a wife in Spain, and many of Francisco's acquaintances were privy to his distaste for that marriage. It might have been at this time that Noguerol formally applied for annulment of his union with doña Beatriz de Villasur on the grounds of being related by the forbidden degree of consanguinity as well as having been forced to consent to the marriage. Regardless of Francisco's marital status, several women allegedly lived in his house.[2]

The *encomienda* of Los Ubinas, awarded Noguerol in 1540, provided him with a firm economic base, but it also created legal problems. Lucas Martínez Vegaso, another illustrious citizen of Arequipa, claimed that he had been given the same Indians by Juan Pizarro, to whom the power to grant *encomiendas* had been delegated by Francisco Pizarro. During an official inspection of the pueblos of Los Ubinas in 1540, a servant of Francisco Pizarro passed through the province and told the natives that they were no longer to serve Lucas Martínez. Martínez Vegaso was outraged and protested; the dispute over Los Ubinas continued for several years.[3]

Yet in spite of the pretentions of Lucas Martínez, Noguerol received the tribute due to him. Francisco's *encomienda* also contained lead and silver deposits, providing an additional source of income. On 26 January 1541, just as he was preparing the trip to Lima that led him all the way to Panama, Noguerol had entered into an agreement with Juan Vélez to hire Nicolás de Candía to build furnaces to extract metal from ore. Francisco promised to turn over to Candía one *fanega* of corn and one sheep per week, and to supply food for the miners and workers. Given the size of his *encomienda*, such provisions presented no difficulties; furthermore, tribute could be transferred directly to the miners.[4]

Arequipa, though still just a small settlement, functioned almost from the start as any city in the sixteenth century. It was governed by the city council, or *cabildo*. Most of the traditional events took place: the activities supervised by the Church, the religious observances and festivals, the rites associated with baptism, marriage and death; the exchange of goods and services in the marketplace; the distribution of land; the social relationships between *caballeros* and business partners; the drinking, banqueting, and carousing. Arequipa's citizens, a contentious and colorful conglomeration of colonists, were split into factions, usually linked by kinship or regional origin. Survival and success depended largely on skill and timing, and Francisco Noguerol was well endowed with both.

Local decisions were made by members of the city council. On the first day of January the town officials for the coming year were elected from among the *vecinos*. Important positions included that of the mayor or *alcalde mayor*, the town councilors or *regidores*, and the sheriff or *alguacil*. There were other, lesser officers, who were in charge of various functions, such as the overseer of weights and measures, and a surveyor. Francisco Noguerol regularly held municipal office in Arequipa, and in 1543 he was elected *alcalde*. Direct participation in city government allowed Francisco to supervise issues that influenced his well-being: the distribution of labor, land, and water, as well as the price of commodities in the public market. Noguerol knew that it was vital to keep abreast of local affairs, and to protect his economic interests.[5]

The position of an *encomendero* was truly enviable. There were only 500 in all of Peru. They enjoyed great privileges, and during the first years of the colonial regime they exercised almost unlimited powers. Although an *encomendero* did not actually own the land, the tribute extracted from the Indians, which included not only large quantities of goods but also various types of services, ensured a very comfortable life for these fortunate Spaniards. Until the worst abuses were curtailed by the Crown, the Indians were at the mercy of their often ingenious masters.

Francisco Noguerol must have savored his wealth and all the benefits due to him from his *encomienda*; however, there were a few obligations that had to be fulfilled. Francisco had to arrange for Christian indoctrination of his Indians. Although it was at times difficult to find religious men to assume the task, providing the religious instruction was not costly. It was the other obligation, the defense of the Crown, that proved a constant drain on his resources. The *encomenderos* were required to bear arms, to maintain men, horses, and equipment, to be prepared for any military emergency.

Francisco spent large sums maintaining a group of soldiers. At times, up to twenty-five men lived in his household, and Noguerol provided for all their necessities. It was expected of him, and Francisco, as an *hidalgo*, was glad to assist His Majesty. The crafty *encomendero* also realized that to further royal interests could result in future advantages. Noguerol was careful to keep the king and his representatives well informed of all his sacrifices, especially when he solicited favors.[6]

V

This City Is Traitorous

This city is traitorous, and the river is traitorous,
and the sun that shines on it is traitorous,
and the air that sustains it.—Francisco de Carvajal

Following a series of debates in the Council of the Indies in Spain, instigated by the vivid and persistent denunciations of the Dominican friar Bartolomé de Las Casas, the king had issued in 1542 a set of regulations devised to protect the native Americans from the recklessness and cruelty of their European masters. Simultaneously, the New Laws had formalized the administrative apparatus in the colonies, the viceroys and the royal courts of justice, the *audiencias*, which would impose royal authority over the increasingly disorderly populace. Blasco Núñez Vela, the first Peruvian viceroy, sailed from Spain in 1543, with four *oidores* (justices) who were to establish the first royal *audiencia* in Peru. Normally the viceroy would preside over the sessions of the *audiencia*, as it met to decide legal questions, and he would also act as captain-general, or chief military officer in the colony. The *audiencia* exercised administrative functions as well as judicial ones, and in case of the viceroy's death or disability, the *audiencia* would assume the chief executive power until the Crown named a replacement.[1] Blasco Núñez Vela and the *oidores* had entered a land in turmoil, as settlers discovered the true extent of the legislation that would severely limit their control over the Indians. Under such conditions, cooperation between the viceroy and the *audiencia* was essential. Unfortunately, Blasco Núñez Vela, an inflexible and overbearing administrator, proved to be a poor choice for such a delicate task. He haughtily disregarded the advice of the *oidores*, who had counseled the viceroy to proceed with prudence. Núñez Vela insisted on rigidly enforcing the provisions and maintained that he did not come to quibble over the validity of the laws, only to see them applied.

The arrogance of the viceroy was matched by the arrogance of the Peruvian *encomenderos*, who over the years had grown unruly and independent. The conquistadores had seen the arrival of other crown officials with strict orders, men who bent when it became evident that local conditions required review of ordinances that did not make sense in the New World environment. But Blasco Núñez Vela did not appear to be malleable. From the moment that the viceroy with his large retinue reached Panama in January of 1544, there were signs of future trouble, as he gathered and freed some three hundred Indians who had been brought from Peru to Panama and shipped them back to their native land. Blasco Núñez Vela had been duly greeted by a group of Peruvians welcoming their new governor, but his first official act did not endear him to his visitors. The king's representative arrived in Lima on the fifteenth of May, but his reputation had preceded him, filling the Spanish settlers with resentment and discontent.[2]

Opposition to the new legislation and the viceroy was almost immediate; it centered on the figure of Gonzalo Pizarro, half-brother of the assassinated *marqués*. The royal governor, Vaca de Castro, whom Núñez Vela had come to replace, had effectively neutralized Gonzalo by exiling him to his mines and Indians in the south, in Charcas and La Plata. Gonzalo Pizarro patiently waited in the highlands as the course of events unfolded in the capital. He knew that the viceroy had imprisoned Vaca de Castro, and he was well informed of Blasco Núñez's actions, including the brutal killing, in a fit of anger, of the royal *factor* Illán Suárez de Carvajal. Dissatisfaction with the viceroy had been growing daily but reached a fever pitch following the cold-blooded murder. Gonzalo Pizarro began to move slowly in the direction of Lima.

Relations between the self-assured viceroy and the *oidores* of the *audiencia* also deteriorated. Blasco Núñez Vela never concealed his contempt for the four crown officials. He had ignored and insulted them. He publicly stated that the king had given him four *oidores*, one of whom was still a boy (Diego Vázquez de Cepeda), another a fool (Pedro Ortiz de Zárate), one an idiot (Juan Alvarez), and the last a dunce (Doctor Juan Lisón de Tejada).[3] It was hardly surprising that the men who were sent to help the viceroy pacify Peru in the end turned against him.

Licentiate Cepeda, Doctor Tejada, and the other *oidores* determined that the viceroy was harming the cause of the Crown and that it was necessary to intervene. They established *audiencia* rule and imprisoned Blasco Núñez Vela on 18 September 1544, promising to send him to Spain for trial. Furthermore, the *oidores* suspended the New Laws pending a thorough revision of the offending legislation. Government by the *audiencia*, however, was doomed from its birth. Spurred on by supporters, especially his aide Francisco de Carvajal, Gonzalo Pizarro camped not far outside Lima. Pressure on the *oidores* mounted. When Carvajal executed three enemies of the Pizarros, it was clear who held the power. The *oidores* had little choice but to allow the troops to occupy the city. On 28 October of 1544, amidst popular rejoicing, the *audiencia* officially proclaimed Gonzalo Pizarro governor and captain-general.

Shortly before the Pizarrists entered Lima, the imprisoned viceroy had been put on board a ship that was to transport him to Spain. But the crafty Blasco Núñez prevailed upon the captain of the vessel to allow him to disembark near Tumbez, on the north Peruvian coast, where in the name of His Majesty he began to collect men and arms to fight the rebels. When the Pizarrists learned that the captive escaped and was amassing an army, it became plain that the obstreperous viceroy would have to be dealt with firmly. Gonzalo Pizarro had gone too far to compromise now. But first, someone had to be sent to Spain to defend the actions taken against the viceroy, someone who could be trusted to convey to His Majesty that it was the sheer incompetence and tyranny of Blasco Núñez that led to his incarceration and not a rebellion against the Crown. The new governor and his accomplices concluded that an *oidor* could best present the cause of the rebels and chose Doctor Lisón de Tejada to sail to Spain to explain the Peruvian turmoil. Tejada was accompanied by Francisco Maldonado, one of Pizarro's aides.[4]

Doctor Tejada left behind, in the house of his good friend Cristóbal de Burgos, his wife, doña Catalina de Vergara, the woman who was to play a prominent role in the life of Francisco Noguerol de Ulloa. Doña Catalina's beauty and grace were such that it was rumored that Gonzalo Pizarro himself was in love with her and sent Doctor Tejada as his emissary in order to rid himself of a cumbersome husband. Doña Catalina de Vergara remained in Peru as a hostage to ensure her husband's loyalty, and if Pizarro had hoped to gain her favors in the meantime, he must have been rather disappointed, as doña Catalina's good looks were matched by her respectability and virtue.[5] Gonzalo Pizarro further secured Doctor Tejada's troth by simple bribery: he promised him a rich *encomienda*. Tejada must have been chosen also because of his family connections at the Council of the Indies and his deep dislike of the viceroy, rooted not only in the derogatory treatment he himself had received but also in the disrespectful advances Blasco Núñez Vela made toward doña Catalina de Vergara. Unfortunately for Pizarro, Doctor Tejada became ill in Panama and died at sea shortly thereafter, in April 1545.[6]

Gonzalo Pizarro in the meantime had left Lima in March of 1545 and proceeded along the coast toward Tumbez to engage Blasco Núñez

Vela. The viceroy, militarily weaker, began a retreat northward, first to Quito, and finally as far north as Pasto in modern Colombia. He aimed to link forces with an old Pizarro antagonist, Sebastián de Benalcázar, then to face and defeat the Peruvian insurgents. The linkage did take place but did not have the desired consequence. The armies of Gonzalo Pizarro and Blasco Núñez Vela fought a bloody battle at Añaquito near Quito on 18 January 1546, and the deposed viceroy was killed. Pizarro seemed victorious in the whole Andean region.

The footsteps of Francisco Noguerol de Ulloa, as indeed those of many other men, are very difficult to follow during these months. Those who did survive into the post-Pizarro era found it necessary to erase all vestiges of participation in the rebellion. Noguerol insisted invariably that he had been always a loyal vassal of His Majesty, and numerous witnesses testified to that effect. Yet evidence exists that Francisco, his privileges threatened by the New Laws, had actively participated in Gonzalo Pizarro's uprising against Blasco Núñez Vela and the royal legislation the viceroy had so vigorously enforced.[7]

The Licentiate Pedro de la Gasca, appointed by Charles V president of the Audiencia of Lima, set sail to pacify the troubled provinces of Peru at the end of May 1546. He came without military support, but with something perhaps more important: blank papers signed by the monarch, and the power to pardon and to grant favors. Employing skillful diplomacy, exploiting dissension within the camp of the Pizarrists, and profiting from the natural loyalty of the Spaniards toward the Crown, Gasca had set out to win back for the king what Blasco Núñez Vela had almost lost. From Panama he had established contact with Gonzalo Pizarro and some of his key supporters, hoping to win them over. Gonzalo Pizarro showed no interest in submitting, but Gasca swayed Pedro de Hinojosa, commander of Pizarro's fleet, and other leading officers to shift to the Crown in November 1546.

The rebel cause suffered further setbacks. Pizarro's captain in Quito was assassinated. In the south near Arequipa the royalist captain, Diego de Centeno, who a year before had been driven into hiding by Francisco de Carvajal, emerged from El Desaguadero in May 1547. Centeno mobilized supporters of the Crown, and some Pizarro partisans such as Francisco Noguerol de Ulloa made the timely switch and joined the royal banner. For Francisco, as for many of the other Pizarro deserters, royal appeasement and guarantees promised by Pedro de la Gasca constituted sufficient attraction to pull back into the king's orbit. Centeno and his newly formed army marched on Cuzco and recaptured the important highland city for His Majesty. After the successful campaign in Cuzco, Centeno moved southward on Charcas, where he allied himself with other foes of Gonzalo Pizarro.

Earlier, in February of 1547, part of Gasca's fleet, under Lorenzo de Aldana, another former Pizarrist, had sailed from Panama for Lima. When the flotilla had halted at Trujillo, the citizens cheered. As the ships approached Lima, Pizarro abandoned the capital but camped nearby while Aldana, on 9 September 1547, in the name of the king entered the city. In spite of attempts to hold Lima's *vecinos* constant to the rebels, increasingly people were defecting to the Crown.

Pedro de la Gasca, meanwhile, had also sailed southward with the main fleet from Panama and had reached Tumbez on 13 June 1547. In August he marched on to Trujillo, then into the highlands to a base at Jauja, where he remained several months. Along the way men continued to enlist in Gasca's army.

After he had lost Lima, Gonzalo Pizarro turned toward Arequipa, expecting to reclaim the citizens there, but on the way almost half of his soldiers defected. Pizarro, facing such massive desertions, resolved to retreat to Chile, where he hoped to rebuild his army. He expected that the fickle Peruvians would shortly tire of restrictions imposed by the royal government and join him once more. In order to reach Chile, Pizarro would have to pass the forces of Diego de Centeno, concentrated near Lake Titicaca. Although negotiations failed to secure safe passage for Gonzalo, he nevertheless proceeded. Pizarro had attempted to conceal his true path, but Centeno's spies kept the captain well informed of the insurgents' whereabouts. It was near Huarina, a small village on the southeastern shore of Lake Titicaca, that the opposing forces clashed on an open level terrain on 26 October 1547.

The armies that met at Huarina were uneven in size. Centeno commanded nearly double the men that Gonzalo Pizarro led. Yet Centeno suffered significant shortage of *arcabuceros* as well as ammunition, about one hundred fifty men compared with Pizarro's three hundred and fifty.[8]

To the disadvantage of the Crown, Diego de Centeno fell ill and was forced to watch the events from a distance. The rebel *arcabuceros*, commanded by Francisco de Carvajal, ultimately proved decisive. Pizarro's men possessed superior firepower: each soldier had ready two to three loaded weapons, which had been collected during the earlier desertions. Francisco de Carvajal wanted to stand fast and provoke the king's forces to attack, so the firearms could be used to best advantage.

Initial skirmishes succeeded in doing just that. Carvajal held major fire until the enemy was within a close range; the discharge was devastating and was followed by an immediate second round, with a similar result.

The royalist cavalry, on the other hand, beat back Pizarro's horsemen in the first stage of the battle and succeeded in killing Gonzalo's own horse in the clash. Francisco Noguerol de Ulloa led the first cavalry charges against the rebels, but ultimately he did not fare well. He broke his lance in the attack, he was knocked from his horse, and an arquebus blast tore up his side. He was severely wounded but could not rest. Centeno's cavalry valiantly charged but confronted a solid wall of pikemen; behind these stalwarts the *arcabuceros* were firing. The royalists circled to attack Carvajal's rear, only to find the disciplined soldiers do a rapid reversing maneuver, so that once again they faced the immobile pikemen and the deadly hail of arquebus shots. In the end, Centeno's men broke ranks and fled for their lives.

The rebel *arcabuceros* proved effective against a superior cavalry and reduced the poorly disciplined royalist foot soldiers to a chaotic rabble. The battlefield, covered with corpses, echoed with pain of the hundreds of wounded. Some three hundred and fifty of Centeno's warriors perished during the melee; another hundred injured died that night. Pizarro's soldiers fared much better and revelled in their triumph. The vengeful Carvajal and others searched out enemy survivors that same night, looking especially for deserters, stripped them of their weapons and valuables, and unceremoniously dispatched them. The victors ransacked the royalist camp for silver.

Francisco Noguerol de Ulloa had cause to fear death if Pizarro's men spotted him, for indeed he was a turncoat. He might have recalled a letter he had sent from Arequipa to Gonzalo Pizarro only seven months before Huarina. How ironic the reversal of allegiance had been! It was Diego de Centeno, his current commander, that he had complained about to his present adversary. Noguerol had proposed to Pizarro that the "servants of your excellency, who are defending the pueblo," be compensated by simply taking property from Centeno and his followers. Indeed, Francisco had been outraged at the pillaging in and around Arequipa and expected Gonzalo Pizarro to aid the city that rose against the king with him, urging him to find and capture Diego de Centeno, who was then still in hiding. "The men of Centeno go about without shame, they commit crimes, they stir up the Indians and the land . . . you need quickly to clear this place of those rogues, and punish them . . . and look, your excellency, a small spark [*centenella*, perhaps a play on words referring to Centeno] can ignite a great fire."[9] Yes,

Noguerol had been committed to the rebels. And he had paid for it too! Centeno's men had stolen his horse; they had killed his slave; and Francisco, though he had tried to recover the kidnapped animal with the help of the *alcalde* Alonso de Avila and two others, had been unable to catch up.

Noguerol had been deeply implicated in the rebellion. There were witnesses to his deeds and several compromising letters. A fellow *encomendero*, Alonso Rodríguez Picado, had written to Gonzalo Pizarro from Arequipa on 15 March 1547, relating to him the death of a scout sent by the royal treasurer Manuel de Espinal. "Carrión was encountered about half a league outside [the city]. He had his sword in hand, and said 'Viva el Rey' and Noguerol came up to him and stabbed him in the head and cut his horse as well, and he fell, and Francisco de León gave him lance thrusts until Carrión the scout died."[10]

Noguerol himself had described the incident to Gonzalo Pizarro. "Wednesday night at midnight, the little treasurer Manuel de Espinal wanted to assault this city and kill us and rob us. . . . We knew of his intentions, and armed ourselves, and took the plaza before he entered. The *alcaldes* chose me to take eight [men] on horseback to find him. . . . One league away I came upon them . . . two of them came forward with swords drawn and shouted 'Long live the king and tip the hat.' We were taken by surprise and could not set up our lances. I drew my sword and attacked one of them named Carrión, and I shouted out for you, and with this, and three or four jabs at the face that I gave him, he died, and of the rest there did not remain one real man. In this way we liberated the pueblo of something, that had it gone their way, would have done very much damage. We took four of them. One was hanged, the other quartered, and the other two were left for certain reasons." In closing, Francisco Noguerol had advised Gonzalo Pizarro to "supply this town with some *arcabuceros* and pikes, because it is a small and unarmed pueblo." He had promised to notify Pizarro "of all that happens or occurs" and reminded him, "your excellency owes this city much, and it is necessary that you reward it."[11]

Gonzalo Pizarro had many supporters in Arequipa, but like Noguerol, in the end they deserted him. Francisco de Carvajal had cautioned Pizarro about the fickle population two months before Huarina: "Here the people are very confused, they want to return to you, but your excellency must believe that this city is traitorous, and the river is traitorous, and the sun that shines on it is traitorous, and the air that sustains it."[12] And Francisco Noguerol de Ulloa was traitorous.

Why did Noguerol abandon Gonzalo Pizarro and return to His

Majesty? The war was costing him too much. Pedro de la Gasca's assurances provided the opportunity to relinquish the precarious existence of a rebel, and recant. If the king could forgive his transgression and at the same time guarantee Francisco property and certain privileges, then Noguerol would have been foolish not to renounce the doomed pretentions of Gonzalo Pizarro. The future, at least before the battle of Huarina, had appeared more secure and lucrative with the Crown. Following the devastation at Huarina, many of the royalist survivors, including Noguerol, set out to find Gasca's camp, to join his growing army, and to escape capture by the rebels.

VI

This Is the Head

This is the head of the traitor Gonzalo Pizarro
who received justice in the valley of Jaquijahuana.
—Pedro de la Gasca

The defeat at Huarina, though a setback to the royal cause, did not weaken the determination of Pedro de la Gasca to crush the insurgents and establish order in Peru. He and his armed force had left Jauja in late December 1547, marched through Huamanga (now Ayacucho), and continued to Andahuaylas; the number of recruits, many of whom had deserted Pizarro's standard, had been swelling along the way. Furthermore, Diego de Centeno and the veterans of Huarina also joined the licentiate's ranks. The strong and disciplined army, under the command of Pedro de Hinojosa, set forth from Andahuaylas in March 1548. The troops, numbering almost two thousand, were bound for Cuzco. But they were delayed at the canyon of the Abancay River. Pizarro's men had cut the swinging bridge and it had to be repaired. At this forced stop, Francisco Noguerol, his painful wounds bandaged, finally caught up with Pedro de la Gasca and joined his cavalry. Once the river could be crossed, the royalists, without any further obstacles, headed toward the city that harbored the rebels. Gonzalo Pizarro, deaf to advice to retreat, remained in Cuzco to face the enemy. Some of his men urged him to negotiate with Pedro de la Gasca, but to no avail. The haughty Extremaduran, emboldened by his victory at Huarina, was resolved to meet the crown representative on the battlefield.

The two armies came together on 9 April 1548 in the valley of Jaquijahuana, west of Cuzco. Pizarro's soldiers were heavily outnumbered and demoralized. As the troops positioned themselves, Licentiate Cepeda, who led a detachment of Pizarro's cavalry, suddenly galloped off in full view of both sides and joined the royalists. This act of perfidy spurred on other defections. Pizarro's men were deserting so rapidly that Gasca, pondering the spectacle, ordered his men to pause. Gonzalo Pizarro, after a pitiful altercation, saw that any further resistance was useless and surrendered to Gasca. Francisco de Carvajal was captured fleeing from the battlefield.[1]

Both rebel leaders were executed the following day. Pedro de la Gasca ordered that Pizarro's severed head be sent to Lima and nailed on a post with the inscription: "This is the head of the traitor Gonzalo Pizarro who received justice in the valley of Jaquijahuana." The gruesome reminder of the price for treason was not to be removed under the penalty of death.[2]

The execution of the recalcitrant commanders not only ended a protracted strife among the Peruvian colonists that cost thousands of lives but also brought to a close the era of the Pizarros. The survivors of the Civil War, those who aided Pedro de la Gasca, found themselves richly rewarded. To the chagrin of the malcontents, the Spaniards who switched their allegiance from Gonzalo Pizarro back to the king fared better than those whose loyalty to the Crown had been constant. There was one segment of colonial society, people who suffered the consequences of warfare, whose daily activities were disrupted and whose villages were pillaged; they were never compensated, but rather became the prize. The Indians lost lives and possessions in a conflict that was not theirs, and they could only hope for accord among their masters.

VII

Such Little Penitence

I ask your excellency, where does it suffer to pay
so well for such little penitence?—Alonso de Medina

Five months after the defeat of Gonzalo Pizarro, Pedro de la Gasca, in Cuzco, on 10 September 1548, granted Francisco Noguerol de Ulloa, in recognition of his devoted service to the Crown and his active participation in pacifying the land, the *encomienda* of Los Collaguas. Francisco must have been satisfied with such generous compensation for his losses and deprivation. Los Collaguas was one of the largest and most lucrative *repartimientos* in Peru, and furthermore, its previous holder was Gonzalo Pizarro himself.

Provided that no new conflict broke out, Noguerol could look forward to a comfortable life. The *repartimiento* itself, situated in a breathtaking Andean valley about 120 kilometers northwest of Arequipa, was administered by a majordomo who would manage the *encomienda* and oversee the collection of tribute, thus freeing Francisco to pursue his other interests. Shortly after he awarded Los Collaguas to Noguerol, Gasca dispatched inspectors into the valley to assess the kind of tribute as well as the amount of each product that the Indians annually owed their *encomendero*.

The inspectors counted 1,100 men capable of contributing, although the Indians themselves, attempting to lessen their burden, claimed there were only 250 tributaries. In reality, Noguerol controlled several thousand Indians, who cultivated wheat, corn, oca, potatoes, and other foodstuff to satisfy their obligation. The *repartimiento* was rich in sheep, alpacas, and llamas that found abundant pasture on the highland grasslands. Noguerol received a large part of the tribute in the form of wool cloth, manufactured primarily by the women of the villages and then carried to Arequipa along with the other products, which included grain, vegetables, fresh bacon as well as salt, candlewax, saddles, even shoes. Every year the Indians had to give to Francisco a specific number of livestock: 123 sheep; 27 lambs; 120 llamas and alpacas with their leads and transport bags; 15 pigs, and lacking pigs, then sheep to replace them, at a rate of one pair of sheep per three pigs. The valley teemed with wild fowl and so did Noguerol's table, for every year he received 288 partridges. Furthermore, the Indians delivered to him 150 domestic birds, half of them female to assure a constant supply of eggs.

The Indians worked hard to satisfy the demands of their master, who collected the fruits of their incessant toil in his house in Arequipa. The journey on foot from the valley of the Colca River took days. The Indians carried much on their backs, while the llamas were loaded with as many bags as they could support. The caravan of men and beasts had to cross the high and forbidding puna before descending into the Arequipa valley. Twenty-five men and women from the *repartimiento* would remain in the city to serve in Noguerol's household. Some tended the fields Francisco owned in Arequipa; others cared for his livestock. Several Indians attended to Francisco's domestic needs, waiting upon him and ensuring that his guests were generously received with plenty of food and drink.[1]

Noguerol's wealth generated not only friends, always disposed to partake of his hospitality, but also envious enemies. Why should a turncoat be rewarded for his treason? A scoundrel who had supported the tyrant Gonzalo Pizarro went about unpunished, flaunting his riches! Alonso de Medina, an outspoken grumbler, did not hide his disgust at Noguerol's luck: "Look Arequipa, populated by men and widows, traitors by day, and traitors by night. Where can Divine Justice be found, when the president, Pedro Gasca sells the natives publicly for money?"[2] The outraged Alonso de Medina bitterly complained to Pedro de la Gasca himself: "Noguerol, instead of going to aid the king, when called on, went to serve in the path of Gonzalo Pizarro . . . he went to Quito with Gonzalo Pizarro, he returned with Carvajal . . . for penance the señor president gave him Los Collaguas. I ask your excellency, where does it suffer to pay so well for such little penitence?"[3]

Alonso de Medina attacked not only Noguerol but many other prominent citizens of Arequipa. The unscrupulous and rough settlers did not relish the spread of venomous statements about their conduct. The colorful author of the vilifying letters, fearing reprisals, was forced to take refuge in the Dominican monastery of the city, where he continued to expose the undercurrents of the community. Francisco Noguerol detested the rancorous meddler, and Medina was aware of his wrath: "Noguerol de Ulloa says that if anyone hangs me, he will give the money for it."[4]

In spite of such annoyances, the end of the civil war and the return to a more routine daily life allowed Noguerol to turn his attention to some personal matters. It is unclear exactly when his sisters' letters announcing his wife's death had reached Francisco, but given the turmoil of these years, it is doubtful that he would have had a chance to ponder the ramifications of doña Beatriz's demise until after his arrival in Arequipa following Gonzalo Pizarro's defeat. To officially declare the passing of a spouse, it was necessary to publicly display a written, certified proof of death. Noguerol took the two letters written by doña Ynés and doña Francisca, nuns in the convent of San Pedro de las Dueñas, and circulated them as evidence among his compatriots. Because the sources of the communication were highly respectable religious women, doña Beatriz de Villasur's death became generally accepted as fact. Doña Ynés and doña Francisca had also urged their brother to return to Spain, to please his mother who longed to see him before she died. Did Noguerol contemplate a trip to his homeland? He might have, but it is unclear whether he had planned a permanent return or simply a visit. For the moment, however, Francisco was reaping the reward for his services to His Majesty. The wealth generated from the *encomienda* of Los Collaguas and his other assets, combined with his status as a widower, had made Francisco one of the most eligible bachelors in the land, an excellent match, and an object of enterprising marriage brokers. Furthermore, Charles V had issued a decree that all *encomenderos* had to marry within a certain time, and if they had left their wives behind, they were required to bring them to the Indies. News of this royal order might have given Noguerol the final incentive to consider taking a new wife.[5]

VIII

Kissed Her on the Cheek

He kissed her on the cheek.—Gerónimo de Villegas
and Gonzalo Díaz de Pinera

Doña Catalina de Vergara had come to Peru with her husband, Doctor Juan Lisón de Tejada, one of the four *oidores* named by Charles V to assist the Viceroy Blasco Núñez Vela in the difficult task of governing the unstable colony. The fleet of fifty ships had set sail from Sanlúcar de Barrameda on 3 November 1543.

Doña Catalina de Vergara must have been apprehensive as she lost sight of land after the well-crafted galleon *San Medel y Celedón* she was traveling on left Sanlúcar. She had grown up in Villaflores, a small village near Salamanca, far from the sea. She had been accustomed to seeing the wind ruffle the ripe wheat as it swept across the vast fields. Watching the waves swelling around her as the boat left the protected coast must have provoked a new sensation. We can only guess what doña Catalina had felt. Surely her thoughts returned repeatedly to her young children, left behind in their paternal grandmother's care. It was not easy to exchange the comforts of a home and familiar surroundings for the tumultuous and rough life in the Indies. On the other hand, as the wife of a prominent official, doña Catalina might have expected to settle down in Lima, the thriving capital of the viceroyalty, to a life of relative ease and high status. Furthermore, before Doctor Tejada's appointment to accompany Blasco Núñez Vela, the couple had resided in Valladolid, the frequent seat of the migratory royal court and government as well as the headquarters of the Council of the Indies. Doña Catalina could not have been ignorant of the tidings from the New World, the descriptions of the lands and the customs of the natives who had become part of the vast Spanish empire. Also, she had family in Peru. Thus coupled with sadness and anxiety, the voyage to the Indies must have also kindled curiosity and thrill in this spirited woman.[1]

After crossing the Atlantic, the passengers had come ashore at Nombre de Dios to begin the cumbersome trek across the isthmus toward the Pacific coast. When the convoy was ready to leave Panama, the viceroy, weary of his officious companions, had refused to take the *oidores* on board and had left them stranded in the port. It had cost considerable effort and a large sum to hire a ship to take the abandoned advisors and their families to their final destination, yet they were able to depart three days after Blasco Núñez Vela. As the exasperated company disembarked in Tumbez, the *oidores* had learned to their further vexation that their heedless superior had not waited for them but had proceeded to the capital of Lima.[2]

Once they had reached the capital, Doctor Tejada and his wife took up residence in the house of Cristóbal de Burgos, an alderman of Lima.[3] We do not know much about doña Catalina's activities during the turbulent months that followed the viceroy's arrival in Peru. There was one incident, however, that involved Blasco Núñez Vela and doña Catalina that was recorded. Gerónimo de Villegas and Gonzalo Díaz de Pinera had written to Gonzalo Pizarro, assuring him that "Tejada is of true color," because the imprisoned viceroy had offended the *oidor* by kissing his wife; "and he [Tejada], having seen that he kissed her on the cheek, was filled with rancor, and because of this he was the enemy of Blasco Núñez." For a married woman, honor was synonymous with fidelity, and to be kissed by another man was to risk staining her reputation. The deposed and humiliated viceroy aimed to insult Doctor Tejada and his wife, and this episode seems to have deepened the *oidor*'s hatred of the man who showed nothing but ridicule and disrespect for him throughout their association. And doña Catalina, too, must have resented this public display of intimacy injurious to her honor.[4]

Gonzalo Pizarro had trusted Doctor Tejada sufficiently to send him as one of his emissaries to justify the overthrow of Blasco Núñez Vela before the Council of the Indies and the king. Doña Catalina de Vergara had not been allowed to accompany her husband and had remained behind as a hostage to ensure that Doctor Tejada carried out his mission without, in the safety of the court, betraying the impertinent colonists.

Tejada's trip northward was rapid. There was little to delay the champions of the insurgents as they followed on the heels of the agents who had been sent by Spaniards loyal to the Crown to give evidence prejudicial to Gonzalo Pizarro's interests. As the group trudged across the hot, humid, and mosquito-infested Isthmus of Panama to Nombre de Dios, Doctor Tejada had become ill. Many travelers fell victim to the disease-bearing sting of merciless insects, and this narrow strip of land had the reputation as one of the unhealthiest spots in the Indies.

Throughout his journey Doctor Tejada did find the time to write letters to his wife, mostly advising her on financial matters. Before setting sail from Nombre de Dios, the *oidor* had dispatched another missive to his spouse. He had omitted to mention any illness but reminded her of Gonzalo Pizarro's promises to cover doña Catalina's expenses during her husband's absence and to grant Tejada an *encomienda* in Cuzco. According to the messenger who had delivered the letter, "it was very well received," but it proved to be the last words he directed to her.[5] After a brief stop in Havana, the ships had continued onward. Having passed the Bahamas and shortly before the fleet reached Bermuda, Doctor Tejada's condition suddenly deteriorated, and the ailing *oidor* died during the night of 25 April 1545. His body was stripped of the black garb he habitually wore, and an attendant slipped a gold ring with a colored stone off his finger, all in the presence of the ship's scribe, who made a careful inventory of the dead man's possessions. The corpse was wrapped in a canvas sailcloth, and following the appropriate prayers, a Pater Noster and Ave Maria, the remains of Doctor Tejada were eased overboard.[6]

Doña Catalina de Vergara was left a widow. Verification of the *oidor's* demise was sent from Spain, but there had been earlier notices. Pedro de la Gasca had learned quickly of the decease of Pizarro's envoy. In a letter posted from Panama to the Licentiate Zárate in Lima, on 16 August 1546, Gasca referred to Tejada's death at sea.[7] Important confirmation came from Gonzalo Pizarro's emissary and from Tejada's fellow passenger, Francisco Maldonado, who the day after he had arrived in Seville wrote to Gonzalo Pizarro: "Our Lord has been served to take Doctor Tejada, whom we buried at sea off Bermuda. The inventory of his estate will come with this. May your excellency give his wife what is hers. Although he was not such a great friend of mine as they think here, I have wanted to send it because it concerns the señora doña Catalina."[8]

In her bereavement doña Catalina had sought out the company and protection of a close relative, possibly a cousin or perhaps a niece, doña Francisca de Vergara and her husband, Gómez de León, who had been living in Arequipa.[9] Doctor Tejada's widow moved to Arequipa and had remained in seclusion during the customary mourning period. As the long months went by, she must have often thought of her children, Elena and Antonio, who had been living in Logroño with her husband's family. Most of Doctor Tejada's property, including vineyards, was located in that city and the Rioja region. The church of San Bartolomé in Logroño had been endowed by the *oidor*, who had wished to be buried there along with his wife. Doctor Tejada's death at sea had foiled the plans last spelled out in a will prepared in Lima shortly before he left for Spain. The large estate in Logroño had passed to the couple's son. Doña Catalina de Vergara had received the Peruvian holdings and regained the money and lands she had brought into the marriage as dowry. It was expected that the widow of substance would in good time take a new spouse to help her administer the property.[10]

Doña Catalina was admired by those who knew her. She combined all the essential virtues of a Spanish woman. She came from a respected Castilian family, had shown courage, and at the same time had carried herself with humility; she had been educated as was conventional in women of her social standing; she had been taught to read, to write, and to count and probably could play a musical instrument. Furthermore, she was endowed with physical beauty and material possessions. Doña Catalina de Vergara, following her period of mourning and seclusion, was approached by many desirous bachelors or their intermediaries who had hoped to marry a woman of such obvious qualities. Yet they were all frustrated in their attempts to win the wealthy widow. Doña Catalina steadfastly refused to marry anyone who could not assure her that he would take her back to Spain. She was determined to return to her homeland and her children.[11]

IX

The Crown Jewel

The crown jewel of all the women of those parts.
—Francisco de Tapia

It is impossible to say when Francisco Noguerol de Ulloa first seriously considered marrying doña Catalina de Vergara. No doubt, Noguerol and doña Catalina had known each other for some time, although there is no evidence of a courtship. The circumstance that they were both widowed led others to broach the subject: arranged marriages were common, and it was up to the matchmakers to point out the merits of a given union and to convince each party of the benefits of such wedlock. The personal history of each protagonist was well known not only in Arequipa but also in Lima. People of their rank could have had few secrets, for neither of the two cities was large. Doña Catalina, "the crown jewel of all the women of those parts," was an enticing match for any man. She was "very honored and secluded, and of great fame," and she attracted various suitors.[1]

Shortly after Francisco Noguerol had publicly displayed the letters from his sisters attesting to the death of his wife, doña Beatriz de Villasur, it rapidly became "public and common knowledge that he was a widower." Noguerol, as one of the most prominent citizens of Arequipa, was also a good match, and some local gossips had later hinted that he could have wed a daughter of any conquistador.[2]

Doña Catalina de Vergara had agreed to marry Francisco Noguerol with the condition that he would take her back to Spain and even extracted an oath to that effect from her suitor. On the fifth day of October of 1549, the groom signed a receipt for all the goods doña Catalina was bringing as dowry, worth some 3,105,000 maravedis. This was an important document, because in the event of the husband's death or any unforeseen complication, the wife was entitled by law to receive back her dowry or the equivalent thereof plus one-half of any joint earnings.[3]

Francisco Noguerol de Ulloa and doña Catalina de Vergara were married in the cathedral of Arequipa shortly after the dowry agreement was completed. The wedding was an important social event, and many "knights and people of much authority and quality,"[4] including the president of the *audiencia*, Pedro de la Gasca, had attended the ceremony.

It is apparent why doña Catalina de Vergara had insisted so fervently on leaving Peru. She yearned to be reunited with her children and to once again behold the familiar countryside of her native Villaflores. But why did Noguerol agree to such a stipulation? Everything that he had fought for so hard, he had finally achieved. He possessed a large *encomienda* of Indians and other properties, and he wielded considerable influence in municipal affairs of the city of Arequipa. Why, then, was he willing to give it all up and return to Spain? Was it love for doña Catalina and a desire to win the hand of the unwavering widow at any price? Or did the mature conquistador become weary of frontier living and the constant threat of violence and deprivation? Perhaps Francisco missed his native Castile and his family. His sisters had begged him to come back, and his mother, aging and ill, longed to have him at her side. Life in Peru was unstable, and Noguerol had gained and lost his possessions several times during the turbulent years of the early colony. He had many friends but also many enemies in the New World. Why not then collect the booty and settle down in Spain and enjoy his wealth in tranquility? He would not be the first nor the last man who after a profitable sojourn in the Indies had returned home to retire. Noguerol, true to his promise, began selling off his properties in late 1549.[5]

X

They Would Kill Me

If I did not support them, they would kill me and cut me up into little pieces.—Francisco Noguerol de Ulloa

Several obstacles stood in the way of the recently wed couple before the journey home. Francisco knew that to retain the benefits from his *repartimiento* of Los Collaguas, he must remain in Arequipa. Yet he had attempted to get around the burdensome regulation by soliciting a leave of absence in order to plead before the Royal Audiencia of Lima as well as in the Council of the Indies in Spain the perpetuity of the *encomienda*, not only on his behalf, but as a representative of the *cabildo* of Arequipa. The Peruvian *encomenderos* had repeatedly, but without success, pressed the Crown to assent to the passing of a grant to heirs, not just for one or two generations, but in perpetuity. The king and his advisors were reluctant to allow the vast territories of the

Indies, conquered in the name of the Spanish monarchy, to slip away permanently from royal control into private possession and thus permit the establishment of a landed aristocracy in the colonies. The Crown preferred to reserve its prerogative to grant vacated *repartimientos* to men known to be loyal to His Majesty. Moreover, crown officials realized the financial benefit of incorporating vacated *encomiendas* into royal patrimony. For example, the revenues from the *repartimiento* of Los Collaguas could provide adequate annual stipends for six government officials or pensioners.[1]

Noguerol had learned that his trusted friend, the *factor* Lope de Mendieta, was planning to sail to Seville. Francisco was not yet sure when he would be able to depart with doña Catalina but felt that it would be wise to ship some of his silver away from the volatile Indies. He approached Mendieta, who readily agreed to the request. The fleet was scheduled to leave in May 1551, and Noguerol needed to travel to Lima with his bullion and deposit it in his friend's care. A total of sixty-five silver bars marked with Noguerol's insignia were carried from his lodgings in the capital to Mendieta's residence. Francisco, before he returned to Arequipa, empowered the *factor* to act for him and gave detailed instructions on how the fortune should be invested in Spain.[2]

Noguerol, in spite of his anticipated return to Spain, continued to be active in the government of Arequipa. In August 1551 he was sent by the city, along with Manuel de Carvajal, to welcome the new viceroy, don Antonio de Mendoza. In 1552 Noguerol acted as *alcalde ordinario*, and the following year he became a *regidor*. On 8 April 1553 Francisco was named *alférez general*, on 20 April *procurador general*, and in October the superintendent of the city's hospital. Doña Catalina must have become impatient with her husband, who happily occupied himself with municipal affairs and seemed to have neglected his prenuptial promise to leave the Indies with her. Francisco, a man of his word, would not listen to any more reproaches that he might be reneging on his oath, and on 10 November 1553 he notified the *cabildo* that he definitely planned to leave for Spain, under license from the king.[3]

But at this critical juncture a fresh obstacle to the couple's departure had surfaced, as Francisco Hernández Girón spearheaded an uprising against the Crown in Cuzco in November 1553. The latest insurgency, supported by many *vecinos* in Huamanga and Arequipa, was aimed against new tribute assessments, conducted under the Licentiate Santillán and the Dominican friar Domingo de Santo Tomás, that were favorable to the natives.

Francisco Noguerol, perhaps to ingratiate himself with the Crown, was loudly and vigorously defending the king in heated debates with dissatisfied citizens of Arequipa. "I reproached them many times, and told them to be firm in their service to His Majesty, but they concerted to kill me." Following a morning Mass at the Arequipa cathedral one day, Noguerol was on his way home when an angry mob "armed with firearms, lances, halberds" attacked him "with many stabs and lance thrusts."[4]

Francisco Hernández Girón had sent several dispatches to Arequipa, attempting to convince the city to name him captain general and chief justice. The new *corregidor* of Arequipa, Gerónimo de Villegas, once a supporter of Gonzalo Pizarro, was again openly siding with a rebel. Noguerol lamented: "The *corregidor* called me many times to join in the *cabildo*, but I knew they were planning to accept Francisco Hernández, so I pretended to be ill." But Noguerol's ploy was unsuccessful, and armed soldiers escorted him to the house of Gerónimo de Villegas, the headquarters of the hot-headed citizens defying the latest infringements on their privileges. Francisco considered escaping to Lima but abandoned the idea when he realized that he was heavily guarded. The following morning, as a *regidor*, he was summoned before the *corregidor* in the *cabildo*. "As I entered the house I saw that there were many *arcabuceros*, which led me to conclude that their evil plan and undertaking was that if I did not support them, they would kill me and cut me up into little pieces."[5]

The shrewd *encomendero* promised the *corregidor* to convene a meeting of the aldermen, but as soon as he left the building, he sprang into the saddle and "without entering my house nor stopping anywhere, I left, fleeing from the city." Noguerol sped toward Lima, where he joined the royalist army. But as Girón drew nearer to Arequipa, Francisco requested permission to return to the city he so hastily abandoned. Noguerol bravely parried in various skirmishes, but finally the royalists were forced out by Girón's master of camp, Juan de Piedrahita. Notwithstanding Francisco's repeated arguments, Arequipa acclaimed the rebel.[6]

The whereabouts of Noguerol's wife, doña Catalina de Vergara, remain a mystery. Did she risk retribution by Noguerol's infuriated enemies in Arequipa, or had she also fled to safety in Lima? Noguerol himself only bemoaned large material losses but never any injury to his wife. Doña Catalina could have taken refuge in Arequipa with her relative, Francisca de Vergara, who after the death of her first husband at the battle of Huarina married in 1549 Marcos de Retamoso, an *encomendero* whose Indians neighbored Noguerol's *encomienda* of Los Collaguas in the Colca Valley. Francisco's loyalty to the Crown had proved costly, as he vividly emphasized to His Majesty: "Piedrahita ordered my houses to be burned, and they were turned into ashes, and they burned and robbed everything that I had in them, including a great quantity of money because it all happened so quickly that I could save nothing; arms, horses, it was all worth more than 20,000 pesos, for the houses were the best of the realm."[7]

The upheaval created by Francisco Hernández Girón had lasted barely a year; the rebel was defeated by the army of the Royal Audiencia of Lima at a battle fought on the altiplano at Pucará near Lake Titicaca on 8 October 1554. Yet the conflict had erupted at the most inopportune time, precisely when Noguerol was preparing for the voyage to Spain. The untimely rebellion turned a good portion of Noguerol's estate into ashes and delayed the departure. If one of the reasons for Francisco's decision to return to Spain had been the insecurity to his life and possessions, he now must have quenched any doubts that still might have lingered. The repeatedly despoiled man must have become thoroughly convinced that in order to live in tranquility he must leave the Indies and settle down in Castile. But 20,000 pesos could not just be forgotten, and Francisco strove to win compensation from the Royal Audiencia. He had other business to attend to before the governing body in Lima: the perpetuity of Los Collaguas.[8]

Such delicate matters would have been difficult to negotiate long distance, so Noguerol and doña Catalina de Vergara took up residence in the capital. Probably in late 1554 the couple transported the household articles that were left after the assault on their home, and naturally they brought with them their servants. Noguerol had attended the Arequipa *cabildo* session of 3 November yet was able to present his laudatory service records at the *audiencia* in Lima on 18 January 1555. Noguerol did not want to risk losing his *encomienda*, and he needed to obtain authorization from the *audiencia* to leave Peru. This task proved to be more trying than Francisco had envisioned.

It was expensive to make the colonial bureaucratic system function smoothly. Francisco, in spite of the losses in Arequipa, was a wealthy man, and silver had often served as a useful lubricant for the slow-moving gears of the empire. Noguerol, well versed in the practice, had given shortly after he arrived in the capital a heavy silver platter worth about five and one-half pesos to Alonso de Galleguillos, his major-domo. Galleguillos passed the platter on to Juan de Padilla, an official of the secretary of the *audiencia*, Pedro de Avendaño. The secretary, a man with a large family, was an individual whose patronage was worth gaining. Pedro de Avendaño, charged with keeping all the records of the Indian grants in order, also supplied official certified copies of these documents, precisely what Noguerol needed. Furthermore, Secretary Avendaño controlled the *audiencia*'s busy schedule. This was not the first time that Noguerol had bought favors. Earlier, while he acted as *procurador* of the city of Arequipa, he was engaged in a suit with the Royal Audiencia. At that point Francisco had baited the justice, Doctor Cuenca, with "a silver platter and two silver candelabras."[9]

The *audiencia*, in spite of Noguerol's skillful maneuvers, did not seem inclined to grant him permission to leave Peru. To allow an *encomendero* to reside away from the closest city to his *encomienda*, to in fact give him license to return to Spain and still collect tribute, was not only impractical but would also set an unwanted precedent. Francisco, however, had never been easily discouraged, and his bribes, connections, and perseverance in the end resulted in a compromise solution: the *encomendero* of Los Collaguas obtained a temporary leave of absence from his official residence.[10]

Francisco and his wife, doña Catalina, did not delay further the long-sought journey. As soon as they were able, they embarked in Callao, accompanied by their servants and slaves, who loaded their masters' numerous trunks on board. The couple sailed for Tierra Firme, then on to Seville.[11]

XI

Silver Common As Copper

*Silver was there as common amongst the vulgar sort,
as copper money in other places.* —Mateo Alemán

The city of Seville had undergone many changes since Francisco Noguerol sailed from it twenty years earlier. Seville, as a result of the connection with the New World, had become a flourishing port of departure and entry for passenger and commercial vessels, and had grown both in size and population. To contemporaries it seemed that "silver was there as common amongst the vulgar sort, as copper money in other places."[1]

The skyline of Seville was dominated by the elegant Moslem tower that had not yet been crowned by the large weathervane that gave it its present name, the Giralda. The Christian cathedral that had been erected at its side was an enormous edifice, yet from a distance it was the old minaret, not the church, that attracted the attention of the traveler approaching up the Guadalquivir River from the south. To the southeast of the cathedral lay the royal Alcázar, a sumptuous and intricately decorated Moorish palace, which had undergone various modifications by successive Christian sovereigns. The lifeline of Seville was the Guadalquivir River, navigable to the Atlantic about forty-five kilometers downstream. Dozens, sometimes hundreds, of great ships lined the quay, as goods and passengers were loaded and unloaded for the Indies, for Genoa and Naples and points in the eastern Mediterranean, as well as for the Low Countries and the Hanse cities in northern Europe. A pontoon bridge connected Seville with Triana, the sailors' barrio on the west bank and the seat of the fearsome Inquisition. Seville, as many other cities, was fortified with a massive protective wall interrupted by occasional entry gates.

Most of the commercial activities in the city, before the construction of the Lonja (the Exchange) at the end of the century, were conducted on the north side of the cathedral, on the stone steps as well as in the Courtyard of the Oranges. Numerous bankers, merchants, and insurers surrounded the house of worship and, to the disgust of the pious, shamelessly carried out their transactions right at the doorstep of the temple, and during bad weather they even ventured inside. Shortly after the trade with the Indies had begun, the Casa de Contratación (House of Trade) was founded in 1503 to regulate and supervise the flow of goods and people between the colonies and the mainland. It was here that doña Catalina and Francisco, along with all the other passengers, were registered after they disembarked, just as they had been noted down before they set sail for the New World. Here too, in the Casa de Contratación, the silver that Noguerol had sent back to Spain, via Lope de Mendieta, was recorded.[2]

Francisco must have been especially relieved to stand on solid land following weeks of nausea below deck. Doña Catalina's thoughts probably centered on her children, Antonio and Elena, who since she last saw them had grown into young adults. Noguerol, too, must have been anxious to see his family. Another matter, however, occupied Francisco's mind and must have filled him with apprehension, a quandary that could, if not properly and swiftly resolved, shatter his life completely. He could lose everything, all that he had fought and suffered for in the Indies: his wealth, his prestige and position in society. Francisco Noguerol de Ulloa returned to Spain a prosperous and influential man, yet his money and his power were once again threatened. This time the threat did not stem from war or allegiance to the wrong faction, but rather from one woman. Doña Beatriz de Villasur, his first wife that he had believed dead, was alive; and while Francisco and doña Catalina de Vergara were making arrangements to leave Peru, doña Beatriz was preparing to file a suit in the Council of the Indies, demanding justice.[3]

XII

On the First Ship

Beatriz de Villasur asks, in the name of justice, . . .
that the said Noguerol de Ulloa be sent back to the kingdoms
of Spain along with all his properties on the first ship,
to begin married life.
—Sebastián Rodríguez

"Royal and Supreme Council of the Indies, Valladolid.

"Very Powerful Señores:

"On this day, the 30th of July of the year of Our Lord 1554. I, Sebastián Rodríguez, in the name of doña Beatriz de Villasur, resident of Saldaña, do hereby state that my client was married [*desposada*] by words,[1] entering into matrimony with Francisco Noguerol de Ulloa, the son of Mendo Noguerol, past *alcaide* of Simancas, and doña Costanza de Espinosa. . . . During that time the said Francisco received a dowry in confirmation of the relationship, of a large sum of maravedis. With the said money he was able to, twenty-two years ago, journey to the Indies, to the provinces of Peru, where he has resided ever since. In the Indies the said Noguerol de Ulloa has made a great deal of money; he had not even enough to travel there until he received the dowry of doña Beatriz.

"Further, the said Noguerol de Ulloa has been sending secretly large quantities of maravedis to Spain. He has sent with Lope de Mendieta, now deceased, more than 20,000 castellanos. With that money he has purchased from the Duke of Medina Sidonia 3,000 crowns of *censo*[2] each year. Of that, 1,000 ducats in *censo* are to be paid annually to Francisco Noguerol, certainly a large sum. Further, the said Noguerol de Ulloa has transported here gold and silver. Yet he remains in the

Indies and does not want to return to Spain to begin marital relations [*vida maridable*] and to be with my client as he is obligated.

"We now know that the said Noguerol de Ulloa has married in the Indies. Since he used her dowry to go to the Indies and acquire property, the said doña Beatriz de Villasur asks, in the name of justice, that a letter and royal provision be sent to the president and the *oidores* of the Royal Audiencia in Lima, ordering that the said Noguerol de Ulloa be sent back to the kingdoms of Spain along with all his properties on the first ship, to begin married life with the said doña Beatriz his wife. Further, in Spain the *censo* that Lope de Mendieta said belonged to Francisco Noguerol de Ulloa should be transferred to my party, along with any gold and silver that was sent by the said Noguerol de Ulloa to Spain.

"I present this petition on behalf of my client and request that you will act speedily, providing the justice that my aggrieved party so deserves."[3]

The Council of the Indies received this petition in Valladolid on 1 August 1554.

XIII

I Promise You

I promise you by the faith I owe God, that as quickly as I can I will come to where God willing we can rest from past tribulations.—Francisco Noguerol de Ulloa

Doña Beatriz de Villasur had initiated the lawsuit against Francisco Noguerol de Ulloa approximately two years before the *encomendero* and doña Catalina de Vergara arrived in Seville, and about five years after they were married. It is not clear why she had waited such a long time before she filed charges against her husband, for she had learned of his wedding about a year after it took place. Initial disbelief and difficulties in transatlantic communication in order to confirm Noguerol's second marriage must have contributed to the delayed action. Doña Beatriz, throughout the prolonged separation, had been kept informed as to Francisco's wealth and position by mutual friends. Furthermore, Saldaña, a small town in the province of León, generated enough commerce to provide contact with the wider world. Merchants traveling to the fairs at Medina del Campo or Villalón de Campos would, along with the profits, bring back the news and the latest gossip.

For nearly twenty years Beatriz de Villasur had lived quietly in the house of her father while her husband was away in the Indies. Was she aware that before Noguerol had learned of her alleged death, he had initiated annulment proceedings in Lima? She never said, although it seems likely that she had known. Nevertheless, to have a marital union declared invalid involved a long and complicated process, and should the Church find in Francisco's favor, doña Beatriz would have been assured the return of her dowry. On the other hand, Noguerol's open marriage to another woman while he was still bound to her was shocking, and doña Beatriz could not allow her honor as well as her family's honor to be stained. Bigamy was illegal, immoral, and sinful in the eyes of the Church. Furthermore, there was the money that her father had paid as dowry, money that had helped Francisco to set forth and establish himself in the Indies.[1]

Numerous documents were presented on behalf of doña Beatriz de Villasur along with the petition. One, a power of attorney, dated 2 June 1554, authorized her brother, Antonio de Villasur, along with four other men to put her cause before the Royal Chancellery. There was at first a question as to where the case would be heard. Since the marriage had been contracted in Spain, the Court of the Chancellery could have ruled in the litigation, but because Noguerol was a resident of Peru and some of the charges involved relations between Spain and her colonies, the Council of the Indies would arbitrate.

Doña Beatriz produced various legally binding papers from the time of her marriage to Noguerol. One of them, a letter of donation dated 7 May 1530, established that the young man and woman were about to enter into matrimony and that the parties had reached an understanding regarding the dowry.

"I, doña Costanza de Espinosa, wife of the *alcaide* of the fortress of Simancas Mendo Noguerol, now deceased, *vecina* of the *Villa* of Grajal at this wonderful hour of concord between señor Cristóval de Santander *vecino* of the *Villa* of Saldaña, and me, the said doña Costanza, of a marriage between my son Francisco Noguerol and Beatriz de Villasur, daughter of Cristóval de Santander. I am pleased that the marriage is to take place . . . and at this time make a donation and *mejoría* to Francisco and Beatriz of 15,000 maravedis each year, as long as I shall live."[2]

It was customary for the groom's family to bestow a gift on the newlyweds, which doña Costanza swore she bequeathed freely and irrevocably, although a clause was added to protect the donor. Noguerol was obligated to care for his mother. An annual income of 15,000 maravedis was adequate to support someone of modest requirements in the 1530s, but not nearly enough to satisfy Francisco's ambitions.

Doña Beatriz de Villasur might not have been the ideal woman in the eyes of the groom, but she had met the requirements of his family. The dowry she was bringing had delighted doña Costanza to such a degree that she showed no compassion for her son's dejection at the impending nuptials. On 9 May 1530 the bride's father had a letter of obligation drawn up: "I, Cristóval de Santander, *vecino* of the *Villa* of Saldaña, agree to pay Francisco Noguerol of the *Villa* of Grajal, 300,000 maravedis, of the money currently in circulation, with two *blancas* equalling one maravedi. I am making the said payment because Francisco Noguerol betroths [*desposeis*, the subjunctive] and weds [*caseis*] by true marriage, made in the eyes of the Mother Church, Beatriz de Villasur, my daughter."[3]

The marriage between Francisco and Beatriz had been arranged by their families. It was a business transaction between a wealthy merchant and less affluent gentry, where personal wishes of the young people about to be linked were not considered relevant. Doña Costanza, a widow of only four years, settled a modest annuity on the young couple, but her son's allure lay in his status. The Noguerols descended from a notable family in Galicia and could clearly be categorized as *hidalgos*. Cristóval de Santander was a merchant who could afford to endow his daughter with an enticing sum in order to attract a husband with a higher social standing. The parents had negotiated a mutually satisfying deal, and their children could only dutifully accept the terms. Francisco had protested; Beatriz had remained silent. They were betrothed, and the reluctant groom sweetened his fate with the delectable dowry.

On 21 December 1530 Francisco Noguerol de Ulloa, who must have been about twenty years old, acknowledged to have received from "Cristóval de Santander my father-in-law" 30,000 maravedis "for the dowry and marriage that you have promised me, and that you have agreed to give with doña Beatriz de Villasur, your daughter and my spouse."[4]

On 29 January 1532 Francisco accepted another "1,000 reales of silver that are worth 34,000 maravedis, that I receive as partial payment of the dowry." Two years had transpired since the original agreement, and Cristóval de Santander, apprehensive regarding the true intentions of his son-in-law, cautiously insisted that Noguerol sign the following statement appended to the receipt: "I am obligated, if I do not consummate the marriage, or I do not marry the said doña Beatriz de Villasur my wife, under the law and benediction of the Church, for whatever impediment or cause, then I will return to my father-in-law the said 34,000 that I just received. For security, I give as guarantor my señora and mother, doña Costanza de Espinosa, who is now present."[5] Cristóval de Santander's foresight proved valuable to his daughter's case years later, and indeed Noguerol's signed promise became one of the key documents her attorneys set forth as evidence.

Doña Beatriz de Villasur delivered to the court a detailed inventory of goods that had been sold to furnish part of the dowry. "The merchandise that I, Francisco Noguerol have received from Cristóval de Grajal until today, Tuesday the 17th of June of the year 1532, for the account and payment of earnings of the 300 ducats that Cristóval de Santander *vecino* of Saldaña has in the store of you, Cristóval de Grajal." The long list of textiles that Francisco "took in the August Fair of 1531" included quantities of grenadine cloth, black fustian, tawny frieze, double taffeta from Granada, and other fabrics that amounted to 15,213 maravedis.[6]

A few months later, in October of 1532, Francisco was given by Cristóval de Grajal, a merchant of Villalón de Campos who acted as agent for Cristóval de Santander, 50 ducats of gold valued at 18,750 maravedis. The young groom pledged, "if I do not consummate the matrimony or fail to marry the said doña Beatriz de Villasur, for whatever reason or impediment . . . in such case I will return to you the said Cristóval de Santander my father-in-law, or your agent, the said 50 ducats worth 18,750 maravedis and all else I have received from him."[7]

On the sixth of November a somewhat embittered Cristóval de Santander wrote to his merchant friend in Villalón. "Señor. Now we can well say that the case is that Noguerol has associated with the Count of Benavente, and in order to complete his outfit has need of buying a mule." (Was Francisco really buying a horse that Santander was sarcastically calling a mule?) "Lacking the money for such, please do me the distinguished favor and beyond the 50 ducats that a few days ago I wrote you about, give him now from my funds another 13,000 maravedis." In closing, Beatriz's father, who had been plagued for money by his insatiable son-in-law, expressed his "hope that there will be nothing else." Three days later Francisco came to Villalón, a town whose fair was promoted by the Count of Benavente, and presumably purchased the much-desired steed.[8]

The 13,000 maravedis dissipated rapidly, and the squandering *caballero* came back two months later for a further installment of Beatriz's dowry. Cristóval de Santander did not hide his embarrassment as he wrote to his agent in Villalón. "Señor, the needs of señor Noguerol are so great that it is difficult not to irritate you, and because of this I ask for the favor of pardoning me for this request. In addition to the 50 ducats that you gave him by my letter, and the 13,000 maravedis by another, I now authorize you to give him a further 20 ducats worth 7,500 maravedis, that he needs to finish outfitting himself for his position. I promise not to bother you again, and that at the fair, if it pleases the Lord, we shall sharpen our account."[9]

Francisco Noguerol had read the letter in Villalón a day later, on 9 January 1533, and signed it in recognition of payment. He must have been annoyed to read the cryptic comments regarding his "needs," but he had swallowed the humiliation and concentrated on his ultimate goal, which might or might not have been known to his wife and family. It had become apparent, however, that Cristóval de Santander was losing patience and that in the future it would be more prudent to turn to Beatriz for help.

Doña Beatriz de Villasur kept some correspondence from her vagrant husband, and two letters were included as evidence against him twenty years later. The first epistle, written from Valladolid sometime after January 1533 and before Noguerol's departure for the Indies in 1534, seems genuinely solicitous of doña Beatriz and her parents following the death of her sister. Yet, at the same time, the headstrong would-be conquistador did not shrink from asking the bereaved woman, "for the love of him," for more money. Francisco was in trouble and had a bond placed on him which he was unable to pay.[10]

"Señora, when the Frenchman came here he gave me some news that has greatly altered my state, and I was near to losing my mind, and he told me that you felt ill disposed, and that our sister was then approaching death. Later they told me that you were well, and because of this and the business that is occupying me here in Valladolid, I have not gone to you. They also related to me the death of our sister, from which I have suffered much, and I swear by the Faith that I have, that other than the death of my father I have not felt anything so deeply.

"I beg you to console Cristóval de Santander my señor and my señora Ana de Villasur, as I believe they need it very much, having lost such a daughter. I give many thanks to God for having granted you health and if it had not been for that I would have been lost myself.

"I am not going to you because of a certain denoted demand that they have placed against me here for a bond, and lacking the money at present to continue the case I ask you in any event, because I am very much immeshed in it, that you search out for me a loan of 15 or 20 ducats, and ask Herrera for them, or another secret person. Say that I will repay them the most rapidly that I can. This I ask that you do for love of me, and send them to me soon; the money I can very well guarantee.

"Regarding your health let me know everything, because I have a great desire to know of it." At the very end, Francisco reiterated his need for money and expressed his preoccupation with the potential response of his father-in-law, should this new tactic be discovered. "This of the money, I ask you that the señor Cristóval de Santander does not find out, because I will pay it as quickly as I can."[11]

The other letter that doña Beatriz de Villasur presented contained the strongest evidence in her favor. It had been sent from Panama in 1534 shortly before Noguerol had embarked for Peru.

"To my señora, my wife doña Beatriz de Villasur in Saldaña. Señora, along with other letters that I have written to señor Cristóval de Santander I have written to you, and I am certain that they must not have reached you, because if they had, I am sure that although he would not write to me, you would not fail to do so, considering your greetings brought to me by Juan Quixada and other *caballeros* who came from there. You must not cease acting as the daughter of such a father and of the most honorable mother that ever a woman had, and thus I beg you to always hold her before your eyes and do not neglect doing so in all.

"The reason why I have not gone for you, have been the strange things that have happened in this land since I have been here and continue happening at present, which have caused us not to be able to get a real [at the time, one-eighth of a peso]. But believe me, that if God is willing to pacify the land, then with whatever I might have I would go, because the time of 10,000 or 15,000 pesos is over. And I promise you that if I could get three or four thousand ducats, I would retire as soon as I could.

"God willing, with whatever I bring and what we had there we can get by. If God disposes of my mother, make sure to remind señor Cristóval de Santander your father to collect that property, after all he has the contract that was made when we betrothed [*desposamos*]. You live in comfort that I promise you by the Faith I owe God, that as quickly as I can I will come to where God willing we can rest from past tribulations.

"I kiss the hands of all dependents of this house and remember me to the servants and all my friends. There is not another thing, other than to beg our Lord to protect me and to enjoy with you many years in His Holy service. From this city of Panama, ready to leave for Peru, today Sunday 12 of December [1534]. Your servant who likewise loves you. Noguerol."12

Francisco's ostensibly affectionate letter to his wife before his departure for Peru unveils a different facet of their relationship, but at the same time casts doubt on his sincerity. Was the young man really planning to return to Saldaña as soon as he saved the necessary sum? Noguerol's earnest assurances contradicted every assertion made by him, numerous other people, and implied by his sisters: that he had gone to the Indies to escape from wedlock. The witnesses who testified for Francisco could easily have altered the truth in order to paint a picture that would benefit their friend. But the nuns' allusions, long before the second marriage and the court case, to an embarrassment regarding doña Beatriz and to there being no more obstacles to their brother's return because she was dead, suggest that Noguerol indeed left Spain, in part, to be far away from his wife. It is possible that, knowing all the dangers and considering that he might have to return in failure, Francisco might not have wanted to completely sever his relationship with doña Beatriz. On the other hand, Noguerol's lawyers dismissed the letter as false, and although the issue was not pursued any further, a forgery might explain the discrepancies between the tenor and content of the epistle and all the other evidence.

XIV

Relieve My Conscience

This I declare to relieve my conscience.—Lope de Mendieta

The organization of a successful suit required time and patience. The Spanish legal system was very different from the Anglo-Saxon, with its trial by jury and the cross-examination of witnesses. In Spain a judge, or judges, took testimony, reviewed the evidence, and finally issued a decision. The judges were appointed by the king; they served at his will, and their term could last a decade or more, even a lifetime. Most judges boasted university degrees; the licentiate was common, while the doctorate was not unusual. Wages though adequate were not lavish, and the magistrates often found it difficult to lead the life they preferred solely on their salary. The judges' position of authority left them susceptible to offers of gifts from friends, associates, and at times from parties whose cases were under review. Yet justice was not necessarily purchased by the highest bidder. Regular reviews (*residencias*) of officials who completed their tenure were conducted as checks on flagrant violations of ethical standards. Unannounced and often secret inspections (*visitas*) provided an added curb to abuses. A notorious judge who regularly accepted bribes could be fined, lose his position, and even be jailed for his transgressions. A litigation could continue indefinitely, as the court decisions could be, and frequently were, appealed. Spanish justice in the sixteenth century may not have been the best, but neither was it the worst.[1]

One of the first steps in setting up a case was to consult with and hire a lawyer. The counsel tended to be a relative or a friend or someone from the same village or region, as trust and compatibility were important. Usually the client was represented by a principal attorney, *procurador*, as well as several others who could proceed when he was unavailable.[2]

Doña Beatriz de Villasur had met her *procurador* in Saldaña in the late spring of 1554. It had not been a precipitous decision, but one that she and her family had contemplated for some time. The accusations against Noguerol were serious, and doña Beatriz needed verification before she could file formal charges in the court. Given the distance and the slow communications between Spain and the Indies, it had taken several years before all the necessary proof was procured.[3]

The key points of the preliminary report, or brief, that the lawyer drew up for his client to be presented in court were straightforward. Doña Beatriz de Villasur had been living as the wife of Francisco Noguerol. Their betrothal (*desposorio*) had been celebrated in the presence of many knights and honorable guests from Saldaña, Sahagún, and Grajal. The groom had received a dowry of 300,000 maravedis from the bride's father, and concurrently, Francisco's mother had given her son one-third of her estate and would pay the couple 15,000 maravedis yearly until her death. Following the ceremony Francisco Noguerol had stayed in the house of Cristóval de Santander as the spouse of doña Beatriz, and the two treated each other as *desposados*. Francisco had received 118,463 maravedis from his father-in-law before he left for the Indies, where, using doña Beatriz's dowry, he had earned a large sum of money. The relationship had continued in spite of the distance, for Francisco had written to his wife from the Indies and had told her that if his mother died while he was away, Beatriz could take possession "of all the goods that remained."⁴ Further, four years ago Francisco Noguerol de Ulloa had entrusted Lope de Mendieta with sixty-five bars of silver. The agent had brought the bullion to Seville and invested it for Francisco in 1,000 escudos of annual income.

The attorneys contended that the charges were simple and thus could be easily demonstrated. As corroboration of doña Beatriz's allegations, her lawyers had included sworn affidavits provided by credible though flagrantly biased witnesses. The *interrogatorio* was a common device used in the courts, and in the course of a litigation both parties would present several detailed questionnaires always favorable to their particular position. The *interrogatorio* prepared in Saldaña in July of 1554 on behalf of doña Beatriz de Villasur contained twelve questions based on the preliminary brief. There was no need for a large number of *testigos*; it would only require a few people, if they were trustworthy, to convince the court to consider further the issues raised by the attorneys.

The first deponent, Francisco de Herrera, aged forty-eight, was a longtime servant of Cristóval de Santander. He had often traveled to Grajal, sent by his master, and took altogether about 30,000 maravedis to Francisco Noguerol de Ulloa. Herrera affirmed all the points raised regarding the relationship between doña Beatriz and her husband, and scoffed that Noguerol could not touch his mother's money during her lifetime.

Carlos Enríquez de Cisneros, aged forty-five, was a distant kinsman of the Santanders, but he had assured the lawyers that this tie would not prevent him from telling the truth. He remembered well the honorable guests who had come for the festivities of the union between Francisco and doña Beatriz. He claimed that in the old days he had been a good friend of Noguerol and had often asked people returning from the Indies how Francisco fared. He had learned that "he was *alcalde* in Arequipa, that lies in the provinces of Peru." He also heard that Noguerol "had earned and acquired, twenty-five or thirty thousand castellanos."⁵

Francisco de Barcena, another *vecino* of Saldaña, had a son who lived in Cuzco and regularly wrote to his father. In one letter he had said that Noguerol "is a great, and affluent man who has over 40,000 gold pesos" (15 million maravedis).⁶ These figures, though based on hearsay, were precisely what the attorneys hoped for. The image that was emerging of Noguerol as a wealthy and influential man served the case well.

Hernán Gallo, aged forty, a relative who lived in the house of doña

Beatriz, claimed he "set up the agreement for the original *desposorio*" and later saw Francisco and Beatriz living together under the same roof, treating each other as customary with *desposados*.[7]

Thirty-eight-year-old Francisco de Estrada often traveled to Seville on business, and during one such trip he had seen Lope de Mendieta's will. Thus he had learned that Francisco Noguerol de Ulloa had sent to Spain sixty-five silver bars. Estrada must have shared his knowledge with doña Beatriz de Villasur and her family, who had used the information in the charge that Noguerol was secretly transferring large sums of money from the Indies to the peninsula.

Doña Beatriz's attorney had acquired a copy of Lope de Mendieta's testament, and he included it in the documentation presented to the court. Mendieta had died not long after he had arrived in Spain. On 15 July 1553 the ailing man had given in Seville a power of attorney to his father-in-law, the treasury official Diego de Zárate, his nephew Lope de Mendieta, as well as Friar Agustín de Barroya and Constantino de la Puente, masters in sacred theology. In his will Mendieta had affirmed, "I transported in my power, belonging to Francisco Noguerol de Ulloa, 65 bars of silver," which were deposited in a separate account pending investment. "In accordance with an agreement that I have made, it was ordered and declared that from the sum of these 65 bars, I buy from the señor Duke of Medina Sidonia 3,000 ducats in annuities [*rentas*], at a rate of 18 per thousand, and I state that he gave me another 1,000 for which I bought for the said Noguerol de Ulloa 1,000 ducats of them, and that from this time forth the interest and principal of the 18,000 ducats are his, and this I declare to relieve my conscience."[8]

XV

Used Force

They had instilled in him many fears and used force in order to bring him into the said matrimony.
—Alonso de San Juan

Notice of the stir in Saldaña had reached doña Costanza de Espinosa, Francisco's mother, soon enough to enable her to appear in Valladolid the same day that the charges against her son were filed, 30 July 1554. She demanded copies of all material that had been presented on behalf of doña Beatriz de Villasur. Noguerol was absent and could not have known of the crisis that he was the protagonist of, and it fell to his nearest relatives to take the initial steps for his legal protection. Doña Costanza, apparently not as frail as her daughters had indicated, hired, after she returned to Grajal de Campos, Alonso de San Juan to represent her and her son Francisco.[1]

Alonso de San Juan responded rapidly to doña Beatriz's accusations. The rebuttal covered all possible angles that would be used in the defense. Attorney San Juan first complained that the petition had not been filed in the required order and format. More important, "the said Francisco Noguerol was never married [casado] nor veiled [velado refers to the act performed after the nuptial benediction whereby a piece of white gauze is thrown over the married couple] to the contrary party." Further, the documents produced "are not public, nor authentic, nor signed by public notaries." San Juan contended that the letters exhibited by the plaintiff "were never written by my party. They are not in his handwriting nor signature, they are false and must be regarded as such."[2]

Perhaps even more significant was the argument that Francisco had not freely consented to the marriage, because "he had been much terrorized, and they [Francisco's mother and relatives] had instilled in him many fears and used force in order to bring him into the said matrimony, and they were such that they would have succeeded in any constant young man, even older than my party, and at that time he was a boy of tender age."[3]

In addition, there was a notorious impediment that would have made it impossible to marry: Francisco and Beatriz were related by "consanguinity and affinity." The "loans" that had been extended by Cristóval de Santander had been repaid; hence Noguerol owed nothing more to the Santander family. The key argument was the fait accompli: Francisco Noguerol de Ulloa had married some six years before, in Peru. The marriage had taken place in the Church, and the relationship with doña Catalina de Vergara had been consummated. The couple now lived together as husband and wife.

The defense attorney also announced that a demanda (petition) had been put before the archbishop of Lima, and the case was pending there.[4]

In conclusion, Alonso de San Juan argued that the assertions of doña Beatriz's representatives were groundless, and he urged that their ambiguous claims should be rejected by the court. Francisco Noguerol was plainly innocent and none of his goods should be embargoed.

Noguerol's defense was complicated by erratic communications. Any missive directed to Peru would first make the slow overland journey southward to Seville. There was no regular, continuous service between Spain and the New World. Correspondence was held in Seville for weeks or months until the next fleet sailed. Nor was the voyage itself rapid. There was generally a layover of a few days on the Canary Islands, off the African coast, in order to take on fresh water and last-minute provisions, as well as to allow for any necessary repairs. Following a trip of three to eight weeks, or more, the ships might stop for several days on the island of Hispaniola (Santo Domingo). Here the fleet divided. Half headed for Veracruz and New Spain; the remainder sailed for Tierra Firme, the mainland of South America. The vessel carrying the mail destined for Peru would land at Nombre de Dios on the Gulf shore of Panama. Passengers disembarked, and all goods were unloaded and transported across the isthmus by mule train. In Panama the mail was placed on board a new ship and sent southward toward Callao, the port of Lima. The distance from Panama to Lima was not great, but the voyage was generally slow. It could take weeks, as ships struggled with the strong northward-flowing Humboldt Current and almost continuous breezes from the southwest, before they could lower anchor in Callao. Often, exasperated passengers, when they had reached Paita on the north Peruvian coast, preferred to proceed to the capital on foot. If the correspondence was addressed to a *vecino* of Arequipa, several days were added before the expectant recipient opened the letter. Under very favorable conditions the mail could reach the addressee in four months, but more often it would require seven months to a year. Furthermore, many letters never arrived. The journey was dangerous; fires, shipwrecks, attacks by foreign corsairs, all took their toll of correspondence.[5]

The *procurador* engaged by doña Costanza to represent her son found himself in a difficult position. In his rebuttal to the numerous charges he had carefully covered as many issues as possible. Alonso de San Juan was drawing out the procedure in an effort to contact his client and with his help develop a solid defense, a task that could take over a year. Alonso de San Juan needed a signed authorization by Noguerol de Ulloa to defend him. The most recent power granted by Noguerol was given to Lope de Mendieta before his departure for Spain and was dated 29 January 1551. The document had specified Francisco Gómez de Vergara, secretary in the King's Royal Council, or in his absence the merchant Lope de Mendieta, to act on Noguerol's behalf. Lope de Mendieta was dead. It was therefore Francisco Gómez de Vergara who on 4 August 1554 displayed Noguerol's power of attorney in order to answer for the absent defendant along with Alonso de San Juan, a lawyer hired by the mother of the accused.

Francisco Gómez de Vergara had stepped forward not only as the representative of Francisco Noguerol but also of his sister, doña Catalina de Vergara, whose interests were closely linked to the suit. He vehemently rejected the allegations of doña Beatriz de Villasur and proceeded to deliver a punctilious discourse upholding the legality of Noguerol's marriage to his sister doña Catalina. Gómez de Vergara argued the couple was wed according to the law of the Church, and with its benediction. Furthermore, "they had married in the presence of the bishop of Palencia [Pedro de la Gasca], president at the time of the provinces of Peru, and of the archbishop of Lima, and the most principal people of the realm." Francisco and Catalina had been living together as a married couple for six years. Doña Catalina's brother contended that any challenge to that union should have been lodged in the ecclesiastical courts and ruled upon by Church authorities. He further insisted that doña Catalina had married Francisco Noguerol de Ulloa "as a free person, not subject to the said matrimony," and it was so announced during the banns in Peru. Gómez de Vergara affirmed that Noguerol was a "good Christian, a man of God, a servant of His Majesty."[6] As a final argument, Francisco's brother-in-law reiterated the contention voiced earlier by Alonso de San Juan. There was a case pending before the archbishop of Lima in Peru concerned with the grave impediments of consanguinity and affinity to the alleged wedlock between Noguerol and doña Beatriz de Villasur. It follows that only the ecclesiastical courts could pronounce judgment in the present litigation.

There were, however, also economic issues to be considered, and Francisco Gómez de Vergara watched over his sister's estate. Doña Catalina "was first wed to the Doctor Tejada, and when she married the said Francisco Noguerol she carried into the matrimony a dowry of more than 30,000 castellanos, and part of this sum was sent to these realms in the form of silver that Lope de Mendieta brought" and later invested in 1,000 ducats of rental income. Francisco Gómez de Vergara insisted that these funds, being rightfully hers, should be immediately released into her possession. Francisco Gómez de Vergara faced problems similar to those facing Alonso de San Juan. He defended Noguerol and doña Catalina with sincere conviction, yet he, too, lacked direct consultation with the couple. Although as a close relative he was privy to certain information, he was forced to resort to words unsubstantiated by material evidence. Moreover, the secretary was not an attorney and was thus disallowed to argue before the court of the Council of the Indies. Hence, Vergara empowered Gerónimo Vélez de Portillo and Antonio de Avalia to proceed in his stead. In a curious turn, Antonio de Avalia transferred this power to Alonso de San Juan, *solicitador de causas* of the council, the man originally hired by doña Costanza de Espinosa.[7]

The multifaceted case presented before them must have intrigued the members of the Council of the Indies. The issue of the marriage, or lack of it, between Francisco Noguerol and doña Beatriz de Villasur, and the legality of the bond with doña Catalina de Vergara, could have been reviewed more appropriately in Church courts. But there was the denunciation that Francisco had illegally shipped treasure back to Spain. The claim that Noguerol had become one of the richest men in the Indies must have pricked their interest. On 22 August 1554 the council agreed to arbitrate the litigation. The contenders were given fifty days to prepare their arguments.[8]

In August of 1554 Francisco Noguerol de Ulloa was in Peru, waging war against the rebel Francisco Hernández Girón, offering his life in the service of the Crown. As Noguerol watched his houses in Arequipa burn after a thorough looting by the insurgents, he was ignorant of the well-documented accusations voiced by his resurrected spouse. His marriages, his escapades in Spain and the Indies were discussed, his wealth assessed, his conduct judged, yet it would be many months before the key figure would be apprized of the legal clamor in Spain.

XVI

Justice Will Not Be Lost

Thus justice will not be lost, although delayed.
—Alonso de San Juan

The accusations against Francisco Noguerol de Ulloa were grave and involved offenses against the Crown; therefore, an official known as the *fiscal* (prosecutor) entered the litigation. The *fiscal*, a lawyer by training, took part in criminal suits in order to safeguard the king's interests and to ensure that anyone challenging or disobeying the law was punished. The *fiscales* were representatives of the monarch in the courts and did play a significant role in procuring a penalty for the guilty party.[1]

On 27 August 1554, almost one month after Sebastián Rodríguez had initiated legal action against Noguerol on behalf of Beatriz de Villasur, the Fiscal Licentiate Martín Ruiz de Agreda addressed the Council of the Indies, grimly reiterating the charges already outlined by doña Beatriz's attorney.[2] Agreda, however, did not stop there and condemned the heirs of Lope de Mendieta as well. He contended that the estate of the deceased *factor* should be levied a fine.

The prosecutor stated Noguerol's guilt simply but uncompromisingly. The defendant had defrauded the Crown by illegally shipping silver to Spain, and moreover he was a bigamist. He should forfeit all his property, "be imprisoned, and brought before this court." The case against the illustrious *encomendero* of Los Collaguas and distinguished citizen of Arequipa was becoming very serious. At the same time that he was defending His Majesty's interests in Peru, Noguerol had been declared a criminal in Spain by an agent of the king.

There was no time to lose. Four days later Alonso de San Juan responded in two separate briefs to the indictment. In the first he rejected doña Beatriz's claims point by point and concluded that she lacked rights to Noguerol's property and that nothing should be sequestered. In the second brief San Juan responded to the accusations of the Fiscal Agreda. He emphasized that at this juncture it was impossible to communicate directly with Francisco, who was in Peru providing important service to the *oidores* of the Royal Audiencia and the Crown in the uprising of Francisco Hernández Girón. It would not be just to proceed against him at this time as demanded by Agreda. Alonso de San Juan petitioned for an extension to elaborate a proper defense, "thus justice will not be lost, although delayed."[3]

On 7 September 1554 the members of the court of the Council of the Indies reviewed the materials and rendered two separate decisions. First, the judges asked the *fiscal* to furnish more concrete proof against Noguerol de Ulloa. Second, Alonso de San Juan's party was given twenty days to put up a bond or security for the absent Noguerol to cover the denunciation by doña Beatriz de Villasur.

The intrepid *fiscal* knew where to find the necessary evidence. He asked the council to grant him permission to examine the records of the ships and cargoes that were returning from the Indies. The court complied and Martín Ruiz de Agreda, confident that he would expose the fraud, hastened to Seville. The registers were kept at the Casa de Contratación, and the prosecutor wasted no time. Before long he was peering in the books containing the entries of goods and money imported from Peru.

On 23 September Alonso de San Juan presented the *fianzas* (bonds) for his client Francisco Noguerol and at the same time requested another extension. He pleaded that he could not prepare an adequate case in the alloted number of days because of the slowness of communications, and he asked for three years "because in any other way it would be impossible to discover the truth, and justice for my party would be lost." The financing of the bonds was provided by doña Catalina de Vergara's brother, Secretary Francisco Gómez de Vegara, and by Noguerol's mother, doña Costanza de Espinosa, who had surreptitiously remarked that Beatriz de Villasur "had pretended to have contracted a certain *desposorio* with the said Francisco Noguerol de Ulloa my son."[4]

Noguerol's mother had changed her attitude. After all, it was she who had coerced the reluctant Francisco into matrimony with Beatriz, an act that had distanced mother and son not only physically but spiritually as well. Two decades later she virtually denied any alliance between her son and the plaintiff. It is unlikely that her memory failed her; rather, doña Costanza, perhaps to atone for her past conduct, determined to help her son as best she could. She was well aware that Noguerol and the family would lose a large fortune if he were found guilty. Doña Costanza had longed for Francisco's return.[5] They had parted in discord, and it pained her not to have him at her side as she was growing old. She had heard about his exploits in Chile and Peru, and must have been proud of his achievements, just as his father would have been. There was one stain on his honor that doña Costanza could not ignore. Francisco had married in the Indies a woman who by all accounts was respectable and came from a distinguished family. He did well for himself and should not suffer for the mistakes of his youth. His mother was willing to perjure herself to deliver her son from the clutches of the courts.

In the coming weeks Alonso de San Juan repeatedly petitioned for an extension to prepare the case, while Sebastián Rodríguez argued vehemently against any delays. There was nothing to be proven in the Indies; the proof existed right there in Spain. Doña Beatriz de Villasur had waited long enough. She needed the dowry back, plus one-half the earnings, to pay for her food of today, as well as her sustenance of the past twenty years. Moreover, Rodríguez insisted, the bond posted for Noguerol was inadequate, and his goods should be embargoed and sequestered at once.[6]

On 23 November 1554 the council denied the three-year term requested on Noguerol's behalf. Furthermore, the judges wanted, within twenty days, more specific information concerning the value of the bonds. Two days later Alonso de San Juan, boiling with indignation, protested that the refusal to grant ample time to present testimony from the Indies was "very unjust and is a grievance against my parties, and should be revoked." The evidence, contrary to what Sebastián Rodríguez charged, was to be found in Peru; the case could not be proven in Spain. Further, doña Catalina de Vergara would have to make a declaration (*probanza*) regarding the money she had sent through Lope de Mendieta. In refusing, the members of the council "remove from my parties their defense, which is contrary to right." Also, notice of the ransacking of Noguerol's property at the hands of Girón's supporters had just reached the lawyer, and he did not omit to extol his client's faithful service to the Crown and to deplore Francisco's ruin.[7]

In the meantime the Fiscal Agreda had found the entry he had been searching for in the Casa de Contratación in Seville. Anxious to return to Valladolid, he urged the *contador* Diego de Zárate to provide him with a copy of the material as quickly as possible. The document detailing Lope de Mendieta's cargo was faithfully transcribed, and the *fiscal* set forth on his return journey. He had time to ponder the information before reappearing in the Council of the Indies. Mendieta had set sail from Peru in 1551 on a ship named the *Santa Catalina*. He had carried personally on board 200 bars of silver. The second ship of the fleet was the *Concepción*, piloted by Alonso Meléndez. "On 15 May 1551 . . . the said master registered and took into his power, and received from Lope de Mendieta, resident in this city [Lima] 65 bars of silver that he carries for Noguerol de Ulloa, that weigh 3,500 marks and are worth in gold 15,000 pesos, more or less, to be given in Seville to the said Lope de Mendieta or to the *contador* Diego de Zárate. They travel at the risk of the said Lope de Mendieta, because they are his, and I sign my name, master Meléndez." When the fleet had reached Seville, Mendieta claimed the silver, scribbling in the margin, "the 12th of September of 1551 I received what is included in this entry."[8]

Alonso de San Juan had not been idle either. While periodically petitioning for extension, pointing out the unfairness of the court's rigidness, he had been arranging the *fianzas* for his faraway client. As a precaution against his opponents' outcries about insufficient guarantees, the harangued attorney had obtained sworn statements concerning the assets of the bondsmen.

On 2 January 1555 witnesses, in and around Grajal de Campos, testified to the wealth of doña Costanza de Espinosa. Her estate was evaluated in the presence of Pedro de Sobera, the governor and *justicia mayor* of the town. Francisco's mother owned houses, lands, vineyards, mills, and *censos*, which along with furniture were worth some 18,000 ducats (6,750,000 maravedis). She had "many *censos*, and in her house there were wine caves with more than 1,500 *cántaros* [the *cántaro* was a measure of wine, the equivalent of about 32 pints], . . . and much wheat in storage." Doña Costanza also possessed many "pieces of silver." She was a woman "famed in the town who had much money in secret" and was universally seen as "very rich." Another witness stated that doña Costanza had two mills on the riverbank, and between 1,600 to 2,000 *cántaros* of wine.[9]

The most complete and probably most accurate testimony came from doña Costanza's majordomo of twenty-two years, Juan de Mahudes el Viejo. According to the longtime employee, his mistress had *censos* not only in Grajal but in Perdigón, south of Zamora, as well. Doña Costanza received an annual income of 56,000 maravedis from two *censos* in Perdigón, a possible compensation drawn from the estate of Antonio de Acuña, the bishop of Zamora, her husband's assassin. In addition to the houses, mills, vineyards, farmland, money, and furniture already detailed by the other witnesses, he also mentioned a "vegetable plot with a pigeon house, and an orchard that was large and of good quality."[10] In spite of minor discrepancies in the assessments, the picture was clear. Doña Costanza de Espinosa was undoubtedly a woman of substantial wealth, independent and capable of controlling her own estates.

Francisco Gómez de Vergara was a resident of Villaflores in the jurisdiction of Salamanca, and it was there that on the twelfth of January testimony on his possessions was taken down in the presence of Francisco de la Vegua, *alcalde ordinario* of the village. Vergara had several houses in Villaflores, the principal one, opulently furnished, fronted on the plaza. There were also garden plots, pasturelands, plus extensive farmlands near the village. These holdings alone were valued at some 6,000 ducats (2,250,000 maravedis).[11] Doña Catalina's brother also received income from properties in and around Medina del Campo. In the town of Cantalapiedra his land yielding wheat and barley was assessed at 2,000 ducats (750,000 maravedis). Furthermore, he collected 58,000 to 60,000 maravedis each year in interest from *censos* in that village. In Navos, in the jurisdiction of Medina del Campo, Francisco de Vergara possessed more farmland, which according to the renters in Medina del Campo was worth 1,000 ducats

(375,000 maravedis). Medina del Campo, especially during the fairs, attracted masses of merchants from all over Spain and other countries. The secretary Vergara owned an inn and houses in the city and through his agent, Benito de Fresneda, collected 12,000 maravedis yearly from the innkeeper Martín Beltrán.[12]

Alonso de San Juan must have smiled with satisfaction as he studied the depositions. The combined assets of Francisco Noguerol's mother and brother-in-law should be sufficient to guarantee the bonds for his client, and to silence the foes.

XVII

She Should Receive

She should receive from Francisco Noguerol de Ulloa
100,000 maravedis each year.—Council of the Indies

On 1 April 1555 the Council of the Indies revoked its decision denying Noguerol's extension but at the same time urged the parties involved in the litigation to avoid long delay. Although the judges, satisfied with the bonds and the quality of the guarantors, had finally yielded to Alonso de San Juan's persuasive arguments and allowed more time to collect evidence, they did not wish to prolong the proceedings unnecessarily.

Sebastián Rodríguez willingly complied and immediately filed a series of petitions on behalf of doña Beatriz, in which he asked for the estate of Noguerol to provide maintenance payments for his client. The lawyer, however, had no new evidence to present, and his demands paralleled those voiced on earlier occasions. Rodríguez, unmoved by the collateral mustered by Noguerol's relatives, repeated that the bonds were not sufficiently high.

Alonso de San Juan, in turn, disputed the legality of forcing Francisco to feed doña Beatriz even if he had been married by words (*desposado por palabras*). Further, even if he had received a dowry, it was not a complete one, and there was no cause to ask for half the resulting increment. San Juan emphasized that the marriage had never been consummated. Francisco had never led doña Beatriz into his home, "there had never been copulation," and they did not lead a married life (*vida maridable*) together. Noguerol's *procurador* scornfully maintained that the bond was more than adequate and it was unreasonable to insist on his client's return to Spain, for only the ecclesiastical judge in Lima was competent to rule in this case.

Undaunted, Sebastián Rodríguez began to press for a judgment on the matter, stating that his side had proved its case well and the evidence was strong enough for "victory in this cause. . . . The other side had proven nothing."[1]

For the next two months the opposing attorneys engaged in a bitter contest, each rebutting the other and reiterating the main points of their respective arguments. Rodríguez was pushing for a verdict while San Juan was pleading for extensions, because "it is notorious, that for many days neither an armada nor men have come from Peru, because of the uprising and altercation caused by the rebellion of Francisco Hernández [Girón]."[2]

Alonso de San Juan, in spite of his perseverance and skill, failed in his defense, which from the start had been handicapped by the distance. Although Noguerol's lawyer did not lack in eloquence, he was unable to match the persuasive documentation piled up by Sebastián Rodríguez. Noguerol was many leagues away, and his attorney could only appeal for time. He had failed to produce any testimony upholding Francisco's position and did not even possess direct power from his client to act on his behalf. His effectiveness was limited, and the judges, not surprisingly, inclined toward the banished wife. Before the reforms of the Council of Trent (1563) a marriage simply involved a verbal agreement between two freely consenting parties. A clergyman was normally present, but the bond did not have to be solemnized in a church ceremony. Consummation bestowed the final sacrament of marriage, and if either of the partners were too young, this could occur later when they reached the appropriate age. Doña Beatriz presented sufficient evidence that her marriage to Francisco Noguerol was valid even though consummation might not have taken place.[3]

The court of the Council of the Indies handed down a decision on 6 June 1555. The judges ordered Francisco Noguerol de Ulloa to return to Spain with all his goods and begin married life with doña Beatriz de Villasur. (Francisco and doña Catalina de Vergara were at this time making preparations for their voyage). The council authorized doña Beatriz, in a somewhat vague motion, to continue her search for justice in the case she had undertaken. The claims made by doña Beatriz on the estate of Lope de Mendieta were negated. But with regard to her request for support, the Council of the Indies "finds in her favor and decrees that a royal provision be issued for all justices in the realm," to the effect that during the "said suit she should receive from Francisco Noguerol de Ulloa 100,000 maravedis each year" to provide for her maintenance and to pay her legal fees.[4]

Almost a year had passed since doña Beatriz de Villasur first presented her case in the Council of the Indies to the day a formal judgment was handed down. When did Francisco Noguerol de Ulloa first hear that doña Beatriz filed a suit against him, and did he know she was alive when he married his second wife, doña Catalina de Vergara? A year was sufficient for the tidings from Valladolid to find him, even given the possibility of shipwrecks and the instability in Peru due to the uprising of Francisco Hernández Girón. Noguerol, who had been in Lima several months before his departure for Europe, knew when he left Peru that there was a legal action against him. It is unlikely that only one letter was sent to him regarding this development; there had to have been several. Aside from the official summons, various people, such as his mother, Alonso de San Juan, doña Catalina's brother, and probably a few others, had to have written to Francisco warning him of the charges brought against him. There is, however, no evidence that Noguerol had known on his wedding day that doña Beatriz was alive.[5]

XVIII

No Case Is So Expensive

No case in the Indies is so expensive.
—*Alonso de San Juan*

Following the ruling by the Council of the Indies, both sides were allowed three days in which they could file their response. The respective attorneys made their appearance in the court on 9 June 1555, predictably with different opinions of the judgment.

Sebastián Rodríguez acknowledged that "the decision was just and rightly given," but he disputed the notion of further pursuit of justice in the courts. Francisco Noguerol and doña Beatriz were already married: "Why should we have to go from court to court in the Indies in search of justice?" Rodríguez was also dissatisfied with the stipend awarded to his client. She should be paid a larger sum; after all, Noguerol could readily sell and hide assets from his client.[1]

Alonso de San Juan had nothing but reproach for the judges, as he decried the unfairness of the verdict. It was unjust to force a defendant to bear the expense of a suit against himself. Francisco Noguerol and doña Beatriz de Villasur should never have married, given the impediments to the union. "If there had been words exchanged, there was never copulation, nor transferral to the house; one cannot say that there was an act of possession in the said marriage. Therefore, my client owes nothing for support." In addition, the 100,000 maravedis that the council awarded was excessive. "No case in the Indies is so expensive. My costs for the year totalled only 6,000 maravedis."[2] He urged the court to review the evidence and reverse the ruling.

In a separate response, on behalf of doña Catalina de Vergara, San Juan stressed that the *censo* that had been purchased in Seville was bought with funds from her dowry and did not therefore belong to Francisco Noguerol de Ulloa. Doña Beatriz de Villasur had no right to any part of doña Catalina's dowry, money that had come from her prior marriage to Doctor Tejada.

Sebastián Rodríguez could not leave Alonso de San Juan's assertions without a due objection. He returned on the eleventh of June to again denounce the miserly sum awarded to his client, who could not meet her expenses on such a pitiful annuity. If Francisco Noguerol should persist in evading his conjugal obligations, then the scoundrel should compensate doña Beatriz materially. Francisco had, after all, received half the dowry. The other half was used by doña Beatriz to live on and to defray the costs of the suit. Rodríguez scornfully added that to ask for a review, without new evidence, was an act of "maliciousness and with the intention of delaying justice." Repeatedly, throughout the month of June, the lawyer plagued the council with petitions to declare the case closed.[3]

There was another matter of contention between the two attorneys. Alonso de San Juan had obtained documents from the court regarding Noguerol's case. Sebastián Rodríguez resented his opponent's being in possession of this material, now that the case had been decided in doña Beatriz's favor, and he was trying to have it concluded. The unrelenting *procurador* pressed the council to subpoena the papers from Alonso de San Juan; if necessary, an "*alguacil* should take them from his control." The court acquiesced and threatened Alonso de San Juan with a two-ducat fine should he procrastinate. Two days later, on 21 June, Sebastián Rodríguez again complained that the documents were still in San Juan's grip, and the council was obliged to issue another ultimatum to the refractory solicitor. Alonso de San Juan proved to be obdurate, for on 24 June, Sebastián Rodríguez, along with his demand to have the case closed, still charged that his opponent "has the records and will not return them." As there were no further complaints on a later date regarding this matter, we can assume that the ensconced exhibits were finally surrendered. Alonso de San Juan's delay cost him the opportunity to obtain court papers in the future. When the lawyer asked permission on 19 August to remove certain records from the case files in order to study them for two days, the council flatly refused to grant it. To antagonize the court was not advisable and hardly helpful to Noguerol's cause.[4]

The Council of the Indies heard the contrary arguments of the two *procuradores* regarding the verdict. The judges remained unmoved by Alonso de San Juan's pleas and on 23 August 1555 confirmed the award of 100,000 maravedis, "that are 400 ducats," to Beatriz de Villasur. Following Sebastián Rodríguez's request for clarification as to when the payment was to commence, the council issued on 12 September a declaration that the 150,000 [*sic*] maravedis were to be paid from the day that doña Beatriz had presented the petition to the council, that is, from 26 March 1555. Payments were to be made at regular intervals until a satisfactory conclusion of the litigation.[5]

The twelfth of September 1555 was an inauspicious day for Noguerol. After the court ordered Francisco to provide for doña Beatriz, it also ruled in the case that had been presented by the *fiscal*, Licentiate Agreda. "A decree and royal provision should be issued to all the justices of the realm, and especially the Royal Audiencia of Peru, to sequester and put in the power of appropriate authorities half of all the goods and income, gold and silver, royalties and shares, that in any form belong to the said Francisco Noguerol de Ulloa."[6]

Five days later a subdued Alonso de San Juan, in two separate statements, appealed the decision of the council, taking a strong exception to the sum of 150,000 maravedis. Licentiate Agreda, on the other hand, was gloating and came to the court on 19 September to voice his approval. Confiscating half the goods of Noguerol de Ulloa was well founded in such an unscrupulous individual who committed so odious a crime as bigamy and did not shrink from illegally sending money to Spain. And it was right to sequester the 1,000 ducats of income from the *censo* of the Duke of Medina Sidonia.

One week later, on 28 September 1555, the Royal and Supreme Council of the Indies rigidly upheld their decision.[7] But where was the condemned transgressor? Francisco Noguerol was still in Peru, although he would soon learn of the castigation facing him. We do not know the exact date when the couple and their servants left Lima or when they reached Seville. But we do know that Noguerol, once in Spain, lost no time and promptly traveled north to find out the details of the lawsuit and to collect evidence for an appeal.

XIX

In Truthful Ignorance

We did so in good faith and in truthful ignorance.
—*Francisco Noguerol de Ulloa*

More than a year after the Council of the Indies had issued its ruling, a public hearing was held in the patio of the cathedral of León, on 22 December 1556. Francisco Noguerol de Ulloa, as resident of Grajal in the jurisdiction of the diocese of León, had come to the city to humbly petition the diocesan court to release him from any marital bond with doña Beatriz de Villasur. He addressed the *provisores*, Juan Quadrado and García de la Bandera, with all due reverence.

Francisco related the circumstances of his first marriage. "I was a young man of tender age. My father, Mendo Noguerol, had died, and I lived in the house of my mother, doña Costanza de Espinosa, and under her power and authority. There it was decided that I should marry [*desposase*] Beatriz de Villasur." Noguerol conceded that he had espoused doña Beatriz but insisted it was "against my will, and without giving my consent. . . . I did it out of fear and other reasons." Francisco emphatically denied "carnal copulation having taken place" and argued that without it the marriage never became a reality. He told the judges that shortly after the betrothal he had left Saldaña and lived in various parts of Spain until he had gone to Peru. "I spent 23 years there, sixteen of them without a spouse, nor did I become betrothed to anyone, not because I had scruples about the said betrothal being valid, it was not for that, but it was because I am obedient to the commandments of the Holy Mother Church, and wait until Your Excellency, or a competent judge rules and sentences over the nullity of the said *desposorio*."[1]

Francisco then proceeded to explain the reasons for remarrying. "It could have been some eight years ago, more or less, that I was in the said provinces of Peru with no intention of marrying or modifying my status until there should be a judgment and decision regarding the nullity and invalidation of the said *desposorio*. At that point I had letters from many friends and relatives resident in the homeland and near the *Villa* of Saldaña who confirmed to me that doña Beatriz de Villasur had died . . . and thusly knowing positively with certified letters that the said Beatriz de Villasur was dead, I was motivated to marry doña Catalina de Vergara. We did so in good faith and in truthful ignorance and began married life. . . . I later learned that she [Beatriz de Villasur] was really alive." Noguerol concluded the account of his misfortunes by impressing upon his listeners that as soon as he had found out that doña Beatriz de Villasur was still alive, he had "moved on the question of the invalidation and annulment of the *desposorio*," and with all speed came "personally before the *provisores* of the diocese of León."[2]

Francisco Noguerol de Ulloa was back in Spain. He had consulted his defense attorneys, his mother, and his family. He knew he had been condemned by the Council of the Indies and fully realized the gravity of the sentence and the stigma attached to his person. Francisco's salvation depended on a swift maneuver to cleanse himself of the shameful spot on his honor. He went to León to throw himself at the mercy of the ecclesiastical courts. It was crucial to convince the Church authorities of his innocence and good faith at the time of the second marriage: he had believed that doña Beatriz was dead when he contracted matrimony with doña Catalina. More important, Noguerol had to obtain an annulment of his first union and thus be completely cleared of any charges of bigamy. Only then could Francisco hope to successfully appeal the decision handed down by the civil court.[3]

The diocesan authorities in León acted immediately, and without pity. The ecclesiastical judges ordered that forthwith Noguerol not "cohabit nor lead *vida maridable* with the said doña Catalina de Vergara, nor be with her in any place" until the delicate issue was settled. The *provisores* warned Noguerol that a violation of the ban was subject to a fine of 1,000 ducats that would be applied to pious works (*obras pías*) of the Church.[4]

THE TRIAL

XX

He Should Be Jailed

He should be jailed and brought before this court.
—*Licentiate Agreda*

A new year came and a new phase of the litigation was initiated. Francisco had dutifully put his marital plight before Church authorities, yet the judgment handed down in his absence by the Council of the Indies could not be ignored. Noguerol traveled to Valladolid in January 1557 with the object of augmenting his defense counsel before launching an appeal in the council. Once there, he hired Juan de Oribe and Yñigo López de Mondragón, *provisores* of the Royal Council, and also the solicitor Antonio de Avalia, who were to represent the interests of doña Catalina de Vergara as well.

Yñigo López de Mondragón presented himself in the court on 20 January with the power of attorney just signed by his client and requested copies of the two verdicts issued against Noguerol: the first, regarding the sequestering of half the properties; and the second, concerning the payment of 400 ducats to Beatriz de Villasur. The next round of the litigation began.

Two days later, on 22 January 1557, Juan de Oribe petitioned the court of the Council of the Indies on behalf of Francisco Noguerol de Ulloa. Oribe argued that his client was innocent and without blame, and he asked for copies of all previous material regarding the case. The following day the Fiscal Martín Ruiz de Agreda, loath to see his prey escape, sternly reminded the judges that Noguerol was a criminal, that all his goods should be confiscated, and that "he should be jailed and brought before this court."[1]

The economic interests of doña Catalina de Vergara were closely tied to the fate of Francisco Noguerol. Substantial part of the goods under the threat of embargo was legally hers. On 9 February Yñigo López de Mondragón presented a petition on behalf of doña Catalina in the Council of the Indies. The lawyer stressed that his client had married Francisco "ignorantly, and in good faith, as a man who was free." When they had wed she brought a "dowry of 9,000 ducats and more," and together the couple had acquired 24,000 ducats; 6,000 of these were in the Casa de Contratación in Seville, and the other 18,000 had been used to purchase *censos* from the Duke of Medina Sidonia. The annual interest earned from these investments amounted to 1,000 ducats. Consequently, and in conformity with the Laws of Toro, doña Catalina was entitled to one-half the joint earnings.[2] Mondragón insisted that before any payment could be made to any other party, his client should be given back the 9,000 ducats of her dowry as well as one-half of the gains that were partly in the Casa de Contratación and partly held by the Duke of Medina Sidonia.

Three days later the Fiscal Agreda, unimpressed, declared that Catalina de Vergara "did not carry the dowry she said into the power of the said Francisco Noguerol de Ulloa, not in the said quantity, nor in reality." The prosecutor also rejected her equity in any gains "since in reality, the truth of the matter is that in the marriage the property of the said Noguerol de Ulloa constitutes capital goods, because he had all the possessions when they married." In conclusion Agreda urged the judges to "negate what the opposition asks, and of it put perpetual silence." The *fiscal*'s position was seconded by Sebastián Rodríguez in the name of Beatriz de Villasur.[3]

The *provisor* Mondragón, not intimidated by the unbending *fiscal*, reaffirmed on 22 February of 1557 that doña Catalina had indeed given her groom a dowry of 9,000 ducats. The property (*bienes*) in question were not "*bienes capitales*" of Noguerol, but "*bienes multiplicados*" (jointly earned assets), and his client had every right to one-half of them.

To the annoyance of Yñigo López de Mondragón, the counsel for doña Beatriz de Villasur had repeatedly refused to enter the dispute over doña Catalina's assets. Sebastián Rodríguez received regular briefing on all pertinent developments in Valladolid but insisted that his client was not a party in the present case. Mondragón saw it otherwise. Doña Beatriz had been a litigant against Noguerol, coveting a large portion of his possessions, half of which legally belonged to doña Catalina. Mondragón, impatient and determined to force Sebastián Rodríguez to act on behalf of doña Beatriz, threatened to charge him with intentional dilatoriness. The solicitor, however, disdainfully maintained that the prior suit was over and a decision had been rendered. Moreover, he lacked power to represent doña Beatriz in this particular case. Mondragón, infuriated, demanded that Rodríguez be fined if he did not exhibit the original grant of power issued by his client. He wanted to prove that Rodríguez did indeed have the authority to represent doña Beatriz on the issue, and thus avoid further delay.[4]

XXI

In Search of the Fugitive

*They did not know his exact whereabouts, but said he was
in León, so I went to that city in search of the fugitive.*
—García De Torres

King Philip II had been informed of the misdeeds of the *encomendero* of Los Collaguas, whose offenses against the Crown and one of the sacraments were contemptible. The king concurred with the *fiscal*'s call for incarceration of the culprit, and on 13 February 1557 he issued a warrant for Noguerol's arrest. He entrusted the constable (*alguacil*) of his palace and court, García de Torres, with apprehending the criminal: "It is now known that Francisco Noguerol de Ulloa has recently arrived in Spain from Peru. You are commanded to travel to Grajal, or wherever else it is necessary to go to seize the said Noguerol de Ulloa. He is to be placed under your custody and brought to the jail of the royal court. Bring him in and turn him over to the *alcalde*. Further, his properties are to be sequestered. You have a commission of twelve days to complete the orders, with a salary of 500 maravedis per day."[1]

García de Torres arrived in Grajal de Campos on the first of March and roused the *teniente de gobernador* of the village, Bartolomé de Villaverde, asking him to call together various people to help arrest Francisco Noguerol. The group then set out for the house of doña Costanza de Espinosa. Noguerol was not there. Someone suggested to the snooping *alguacil* that Francisco might have gone to visit his sisters at the nearby convent of San Pedro de las Dueñas. The search party trudged over to the Benedictine convent, expecting to take the reprobate into custody. Instead, "in the house and monastery of the place in a chamber we discovered in bed one Gaspar Noguerol, brother of the said Francisco Noguerol." The disappointed García de Torres nevertheless looked "with great diligence and care for the said Francisco Noguerol, or his properties," but his efforts were in vain. The exasperated constable pressed Gaspar Noguerol "to reveal under oath where he [Francisco] was, and when he had left from the said monastery." Gaspar, ostensibly helpful, conceded that "his brother had been there some days, but that he had left to go to the city of León, however, that he did not know if he was there, or indeed his current whereabouts." Gaspar claimed ignorance with regard to his brother's possessions and emphatically denied any were to be found in the monastery.[2]

Realizing the futility of further stay in San Pedro de las Dueñas, García de Torres returned to Grajal and with great resolve demanded to be admitted again into the house of doña Costanza. The *alguacil* was not to be fooled. It was apparent that Noguerol was deliberately evading imprisonment, and García de Torres intended to force the reticent family to divulge his hiding place. He insisted that Francisco's mother and everyone else in the household swear to their obstinate assertions of not knowing where the fugitive was. The family and servants clung to their original story and vowed that when they last saw him, Francisco was headed to visit his sisters in the convent. The king's bailiff saw his labor undermined and in frustration read again the Royal Provision, impressing upon his listeners the consequences of concealing evidence from His Majesty the king. Gaspar Noguerol then mentioned that his brother would probably return that same day. The *alguacil* waited, but Francisco never materialized. Finally, fuming and empty-handed, the duped official left.[3]

The Fiscal Agreda, upon learning of Noguerol's escape, thundered against him all the more vigorously and succeeded in having the phantom defendant declared "*en rebeldía*," for failing to appear in court when summoned. In addition, the prosecutor urged the judges to conclude the case. Francisco Noguerol had been found guilty in the council, and the king had ordered his arrest and confiscation of his properties. By hiding from justice, Noguerol clearly confirmed his guilt.[4]

García de Torres pursued Noguerol for days, following various leads and traveling extensively, yet without success. Francisco seemed to have vanished, and the weary *alguacil* ultimately abandoned his mission. It was customary for the fugitive or his family to defray the expenses incurred by the hunter, and Noguerol's pursuer curiously came to the door of doña Catalina de Vergara, whose marriage to Francisco had been invalidated by the Council of the Indies, to collect his pay.

Doña Catalina, however, was not a woman to rashly accede to demands, nor was she particularly impressed by the *alguacil*'s performance. She promptly appealed to the Council of the Indies. Doña Catalina questioned the eleven days García de Torres claimed to have spent tracking Noguerol. He could not have engaged in his chase for more than six days, and it was preposterous to request a salary of 6,000 maravedis when he was barely entitled to half that amount. Doña Catalina "consented to taking out, for security, a silver pitcher with some fancywork, and a silver bowl with handles" and paid García de Torres the 3,000 maravedis she felt he deserved. "If he wants more salary, he had better report to Your Excellency about the actual number of days."[5]

García de Torres was sent for by the Council of the Indies. Licentiate Gómez, who presided the hearing, asked the constable to detail his exploits. Torres insisted that he "spent eleven days in going from and returning to this court." He had gone to Medina de Ríoseco and other places whose names he "did not remember." He hid himself for two and a half days to discover the location of Francisco Noguerol. He finally learned that Noguerol might be in the convent of San Pedro de las Dueñas and so went there with a search party of twelve men. But Francisco was not to be found at San Pedro. There he discovered and took an oath of Gaspar Noguerol, the criminal's brother, and from others. "They did not know his exact whereabouts, but said he was in León, so I went to that city in search of the fugitive." He employed spies and learned Noguerol was in Sahagún, or a place near Saldaña whose name he could not remember. He hurried there, only to be disappointed. Again he returned to Grajal. There the innkeeper told Torres that he thought that Francisco was in Villaflores. Before proceeding with his search, he rode to Valladolid. When he arrived, he was informed that Francisco Noguerol de Ulloa was actually secreting himself in Valladolid, and "for that reason I did not continue on my quest."[6]

Doña Catalina's complaints were of no avail. After a careful review of García de Torres's convincing account of his exertions to locate the criminal, the judges of the Royal Council decided that the official indeed deserved to be paid for eleven days of work, albeit fruitless.

The *alguacil* had zealously crisscrossed the countryside looking for Francisco Noguerol. Yet Noguerol always had stayed ahead of him and in the end chose to turn himself in. The warrant for his arrest had been issued on 13 February; García de Torres had arrived in Grajal on 1 March; and Noguerol presented himself in the Council of the Indies on 30 March.[7] A month and a half had elapsed since the king ordered his incarceration. Why did Francisco evade his imprisonment? His flight was regarded as an admission of guilt and was used against him. He must have known he could not hide indefinitely and that eventually the king's agents would capture him.

A plausible explanation manifests itself in the list of places that Noguerol had allegedly visited, including a town close to Saldaña, the residence of doña Beatriz de Villasur and her family. It is unlikely that doña Beatriz would have offered him a refuge, and it is equally unthinkable that Francisco would have asked her for sanctuary. Noguerol, however, had a purpose in getting as close to Saldaña as he safely could, as well as visiting anybody who could supply information helpful for his defense. Francisco Noguerol had never shied away from taking risks if he felt he could profit from it. He had been absent for twenty years, and before he would surrender himself, he needed to collect pertinent facts regarding doña Beatriz and her life during the time he was in the Indies. He could have left it up to his lawyers, but there were too many questions that had to be asked, including questions of his sisters at the convent of San Pedro de las Dueñas.

XXII

I Have Presented Myself

I have presented myself before Your Excellency . . .
so that I may be able to defend myself and receive justice.
—*Francisco Noguerol de Ulloa*

Valladolid, 30 March 1557, in the Council of the Indies.

"I, Noguerol de Ulloa, say that it has come to my notice that certain petitions have been placed against me here, by Licentiate Agreda, your *fiscal*, as well as doña Beatriz de Villasur. Because I am without blame, and because Your Excellency will do me justice, I have presented myself before Your Excellency. I ask and supplicate that as I have come before you of my own accord, that you will order that a copy be made of all charges that have been made against me, so that I may be able to defend myself and receive justice.

"Further, it being the case that Your Excellency has ordered that I be imprisoned, and because I have a very large head wound and other wounds that I have received in the service of His Majesty in the kingdoms of Peru, where I have provided many and very distinguished services, as can be seen in the report that I present to you, I supplicate Your Honor that you will be served to order that the confinement not be in the public jail, but that I be given a house in conformity to the quality of my person. I am ready to tender bonds in whatever amount is necessary."[1]

The council acted swiftly. Now that they had the fugitive in their power, the grim-faced judges were not kindly disposed toward him. Notwithstanding Francisco's petition for house arrest, he was mercilessly led to the royal jail of the Council of the Indies and left there to

await his fate. That same day, the court's *relator* (reporter), the Licentiate Santander, escorted by the notary and scribe Francisco de Gálvez,
visited and interrogated Noguerol in his cell.[2]

Noguerol, in spite of his quandary, must have felt some hope as he
answered the questions put to him. Before surrendering, he had accomplished what he had set out to do. He had visited his friends and
relatives. He had talked to his mother, his brother, and his sisters. He
had initiated a case against doña Beatriz de Villasur before ecclesiastical authorities in the city of León and conferred with his attorneys
about the full extent of the charges against him. He was now at the
mercy of the court but possessed of a better knowledge of the case.

XXIII

Are You Married?

Are you married?—Licentiate Santander

Francisco de Gálvez faithfully recorded the interrogation of Francisco
Noguerol de Ulloa, careful not to omit any relevant details. The prisoner was attentive and responded courteously, attempting to unravel
his complex situation, always mindful to point out his integrity and
faultlessness. After several preliminary questions, Licentiate Santander
queried Noguerol about his activities in the Indies. Francisco briefly
related his adventures in Chile and Peru, embellishing his selfless participation "in all the wars against the tyrants who in those realms rose
up against the service of His Majesty."[1]

Next, the licentiate asked, "Are you married?" Noguerol proceeded
to somberly elucidate his marital status. "Some 26 or 27 years ago I was
under the charge of doña Costanza de Espinosa, my mother, because of
the death of my father Mendo Noguerol, the *alcaide* of the lieutenancy
of the fort of the *Villa* of Simancas. My mother on many and diverse
occasions insisted that I marry [*desposase*] doña Beatriz de Villasur,
and having seen personally several times the said doña Beatriz I refused,
many and diverse times. Nevertheless, the said my mother told me that
I would be cursed if I did not do it, and in order to obey the command of
the said my mother I went with Alvaro Vázquez Noguerol, the paymaster general of His Majesty at that period, who was my uncle, and with
other knights. I was conducted to the *Villa* of Saldaña and there saw the

said doña Beatriz de Villasur, and wished that the *desposorio* would never take place. But as a man at that age who did not understand well what he was doing, and of shame, and out of fear of those present, and in order to obey the command of my mother, I in reality married by words the said doña Beatriz de Villasur, in front of all the aforesaid and many learned people who were found present, and by the hand of a clergyman, although I was not consenting of my free will, but out of respect and fear of what I have said before."[2]

Could Francisco, a young man of twenty or twenty-one years of age, have been pressured into such onerous bond? Perhaps, but coercion and lack of free consent were important determinants in an invalidation of a marriage, and it served Francisco's case to claim that he married doña Beatriz only because he was forced to.[3]

Francisco avowed, "I have never had, to this day, access to nor have I copulated with the said doña Beatriz de Villasur." He acknowledged that after the marriage he "returned two or three times to the said *Villa* of Saldaña, but not with the intention of visiting the said doña Beatriz. On the contrary, for other business that offered itself to me at the time in the said *villa*. Some of these times that I went to the said *villa* I resided in the house of the father of doña Beatriz." In all probability the business in question referred to the collection of the dowry payment from his father-in-law, Cristóval de Santander. Noguerol nevertheless insisted that he had embarked for Peru "without taking with me more than ten ducats."

The prisoner continued the account of his conjugal imbroglio. "After having resided in the said kingdoms of Peru thirteen years I received letters from my siblings, and reports from many other people that said and affirmed that the said doña Beatriz de Villasur was dead." Francisco declared that he was "in mourning for her three or four months" and did not remarry for more than two years. But to please his mother and to fulfill a royal provision "that ordered that the conquistadores and *encomenderos* of Indians marry, because of the said reasons I, in good faith and without any fraud, married of my own will and consent doña Catalina de Vergara, with whom, and under the said good faith, I cohabited without the slightest knowledge nor understanding that the said doña Beatriz might be alive."

Francisco Noguerol persistently affirmed under oath that he had no knowledge that his first wife was living when he married doña Catalina de Vergara. When, then, did he first become aware that doña Beatriz was not dead?

"As I arrived in Tierra Firme, in the city of Panama, a man told me that he had heard it said here in Spain that the said doña Beatriz was alive." Francisco, however, was skeptical because his informant "did not have the face of an honest man. That being the case, I could not give credit to something I never knew." Even if he did believe the rumor, he could not have left doña Catalina "in the power of sailors and pilots before putting her in her land and country."

This declaration was a lie. It was advantageous to profess ignorance regarding his first wife, and to make a pretext of his duty as a gentleman to safely see doña Catalina reach Spain. Letters regarding doña Beatriz's legal action had reached him in Peru, and he must have consulted doña Catalina about his plight. He could not have kept it a secret for long. After all, doña Catalina's brother had been in possession of Noguerol's power of attorney and did play a role in defending him shortly after the lawsuit was first filed in the courts. Doña Catalina de Vergara would not recoil from adversity and would fight alongside her husband for the validity of their marriage. They would together, in Spain, confront doña Beatriz de Villasur.

Francisco continued his story. After he had arrived in Spain, he sent another brother-in-law, Juan de Guzmán, "to find out, and to see with his own eyes if the said doña Beatriz was alive." When Juan de Guzmán confirmed that he had seen her, Noguerol "did what was necessary under the circumstances. I came to the city of León and presented myself before the *provisores* of the diocese. I also separated myself from the said doña Catalina de Vergara for the present, until the matrimonial suit is decided. I also took the steps that I have in order to put the question to the señores of the Council of the Indies of His Majesty."

The licentiate inquired whether Noguerol had ever brought doña Beatriz any jewels or if he had received any gifts from her. Francisco denied giving or accepting anything, "although I did hear that my mother, doña Costanza, had sent certain clothing to doña Beatriz."[4]

When asked if he had any proof concerning doña Beatriz's demise, Noguerol replied that after his sisters had written that doña Beatriz had died "I saw three or four people from the kingdoms of Spain" who concurred, but he could not remember their names. Two years later, before remarrying, "I turned to inquire from other people that had come from these kingdoms, regarding the death of the said doña Beatriz, and I gave credit to the said death. It seemed to me that sending to Spain for proof or getting a full report on the said death, to be unnecessary. Having had it for very certain, I did not take any more diligences than I have already mentioned."

Licentiate Santander then turned to the accusations regarding the shipment of treasure from Peru. Noguerol nostalgically recalled Lope de Mendieta as a "very great friend" and readily admitted that since he had planned to travel to Spain with doña Catalina, he had asked Mendieta to transport a certain number of silver bars, worth about 15,000 pesos. That bullion had been registered by Lope de Mendieta and had arrived "assayed taxed [*quintado*], and marked in conformity with the ordinances."

Licentiate Santander queried in whose name did Noguerol instruct to record the shipment. Francisco remembered that he had asked "to enter them in the name of Lope de Mendieta, or me, or of either of the two; the said silver came at the risk of this confesser as my own and it was clearly seen as mine by the inscriptions that the same bars of silver carried."[5]

The interrogation of Francisco Noguerol de Ulloa ended. He read and signed the deposition and the two court officials left. The prisoner was alone in the unhospitable cell, allowed to contemplate his past and his future. He might have also wondered whether his apparent candor served to establish his clear conscience. Francisco had tried to imprint on the mind of his interrogator that he had remarried only because he felt certain that doña Beatriz had died, and that his silver was sent to Spain legally and openly. In his melancholy he might have pondered his fate should he be acquitted. Would all his property be restored to him; and perhaps more worrisome, who would he be restored to, doña Beatriz or doña Catalina? Many anxious thoughts must have whirled through Noguerol's aching head as he lay prostrated on an uncomfortable cot, bothered by his old wounds.

XXIV

This Claim

*This claim of being in the Indies, or Peru, has
always been used against the interests of His Majesty.*
—Licentiate Agreda

Aghast at how much he had lost, Francisco Noguerol asked a few days later to be heard by the Council of the Indies. He demanded that the court nullify all decisions handed down in his absence. "I say that the action that has been taken against me in this process is void, and it should be pronounced as such. The power I had given to my lawyer was insufficient, nor was I called or examined, as they should have done in such a serious case."

Noguerol complained, "The report against me is false; I reject it." Furthermore, many of the documents that were presented were "private, and as such are not necessarily the truth." The *fiscal*'s charges against him could best be answered by Lope de Mendieta, were he alive. "Whatever he may not have registered of the monies does not prove anything," advanced Noguerol, "because all that I brought from the said provinces of Peru was registered and taxed, and the bars came in my name, and on each one of them there was a mark put in my own name, done that way because I told the said Mendieta to register and manifest my estate as personal property." The heated *encomendero* sneered: "The *fiscal* proved nothing against me, nor am I to be blamed."

Francisco, furious regarding the charges of bigamy, indignantly rejected any future cohabitation with doña Beatriz. "There is no place in the law to make me do what the *fiscal* asks." He insisted that there had been no positive proof presented in the case regarding the alleged marriage, only hearsay evidence, which should have been inadmissible in the court. Noguerol tirelessly repeated that when he had married doña Catalina de Vergara in Peru, he was certain that doña Beatriz de Villasur was dead. He admitted that the laws required that "one has to substantiate the death of the first wife by a *nuncio cierto* that the spouse was indeed dead. In any other fashion one could incur penalties. But when the husband is in places so far away, as in the said provinces of Peru, where I was, which are more than 3,000 leagues from where the said doña Beatriz resided, there should be cause for excusing the penalties."[1]

Not only was doña Beatriz's demise public knowledge in Peru, but there were letters "which my sisters had written to me more than two years before I married the said doña Catalina de Vergara." Francisco, with a dramatic gesture, gave the crucial missives to the judges to examine, swearing "to God and on the sign of this Cross" that the letters were authentic. Noguerol pointed out that "the said my sisters were at the time that they wrote me, and are now, professed nuns of very good life, and great Christians, and of much faith, and are such as to whom with just cause I give credit."[2]

The accused lamented, "I am ignorant in the law, and a knight," and Peru, in a state of continuous war, had "only a few *letrados*," or men with university degrees. Given the widespread acceptance of his status as a widower, he had to endure countless propositions by fervent matchmakers, and even then he did not remarry immediately. Noguerol reminded the stern tribunal to consider the nature of his first union, undertaken under duress; his second marriage was of his choice, and the wedding was attended by the current bishop of Palencia, Pedro de la Gasca, and many "knights and people of much authority and quality."

Francisco insisted, "I have always been a very good Christian, fearful of God and the commandments of His Holy Mother Church, and as such it is certain that I would not, unless the said death had been certified, have married the said doña Catalina de Vergara, nor would it have even passed through my mind." He decried the denunciations against him as unjustified, "being as I am a knight and *hidalgo*, zealous of my conscience and honor," who unceasingly defended the interests of His Majesty with "estate and life and blood."

The eloquent defendant had not finished; he had more to add. Francisco declared that had he known Beatriz de Villasur was still alive, he would not have returned to Spain with doña Catalina. Certainly, if he had, it would have been in bad faith, and he would have deserved punishment at the hands of doña Beatriz and her relatives, and she had many. "Nor should one believe that a person of my quality would have to come to these kingdoms to receive affront, and shame." Noguerol scorned at the *fiscal*'s defamatory statements, because "such a thing is so repugnant in all right, and so alien to people of my profession and quality."

Yet Noguerol must have realized that his return to Spain was inevitable, either on his own accord or following his arrest in Peru. Much of the case dealt with people and issues involving Spain, and he would have been sent there for trial. Since he did arrive in the company of doña Catalina, however, he did need a plausible explanation. To refer to the code of honor of a knight and to stress that an *hidalgo*, a person of his quality, could never stoop as low as he was being accused of, was a clever as well as a valid argument of the period.

The court sent copies of Noguerol's petition to all interested parties. The Fiscal Agreda, unmoved by the adroit gentleman and his professions of sincere ignorance, retorted, "This claim of being in the Indies, or Peru, has always been used against the interests of His Majesty."[3]

XXV

Foul Odors and Vapors

*I have suffered because of the noise of the prison
and the foul odors and vapors coming from it.*
—Francisco Noguerol de Ulloa

∋●∈

Several days had gone by since Francisco had surrendered to the authorities. His request for house arrest had been ignored, and he was still locked up in the royal jail. Noguerol was miserable, uncomfortable, and outraged that a person of his quality was treated with such disrespect. He begged to be delivered from the noxious hovel, "as I am wounded in the head, and many other parts of my body are very split from the works and wounds that I have received in the service of His Majesty, I have suffered because of the noise of the prison and the foul odors and vapors coming from it."[1]

Similar complaints were heard from many other prisoners, but Noguerol's position in society, his offer of bonds "to secure the imprisonment," and the standing of his relatives meant that his plea would be considered. The council sent Licentiate Gálvez, "physician of His Majesty and of the court of the General Inquisition," to evaluate the condition of the prisoner and his surroundings.[2]

The doctor found Francisco "in bed with a slight fever, and with some cough," complaining "of a headache and faintness." He had been unable to sleep because of the clamor "until two after midnight" by prisoners going to bed; and to add to the torment, they rose with equal clatter in early morning hours. Noguerol lamented that the forced insomnia exacerbated the chronic pain in his head. To prove his point, Francisco displayed his war trophies, "a large sign of a wound that he had on the face above the left eyebrow. He also showed to me other scars: from the left armpit to the lower ribs he has wounds from arquebus balls."

The physician later reported to the council: "It seems that the head problem is aggravated by the said noise, and the sleeplessness will cause him very much harm, as will the fever, and if it rises there is danger also, and especially in this weather."[3]

Those sleepless nights, the noise, the stench, the intermittent fever, and the tossing about—Francisco Noguerol de Ulloa, the man who had attained both power and wealth in the Indies, was reduced to a pitiful state. One adversary after another in the past had been met, and overcome. Was Noguerol finally losing his propensity to vanquish misfortune? Was he to be left to rot in this wretched prison? He, who had achieved so much, was he to sink into anonymity and poverty? Even the bravest soldiers can suffer from depression in similar confinement. And Francisco, approaching his fiftieth year, had much to contemplate and worry about. His past was filled with adventure and his future was quite uncertain.

There was a little relief afforded the fallen conquistador. The Licentiate Gálvez did recommend: "It will be very beneficial for both the remedy of the present as well as for the preservation of his future health if he might be moved to lodgings where the said inconveniences would not be present, and that is the truth of what I say."[4] Shortly thereafter, and following the posting of a 2,000-ducat bond, Francisco Noguerol was tranferred to more comfortable quarters, the house of Alguacil Santiago. He was to remain in his new confinement for several months, while the litigation was in progress in the Council of the Indies.

XXVI

I Consent

Regarding the dowry that the said doña Catalina asks for,
I consent and give and hand over to her that which
she carried in dowry at the time we married.
—Francisco Noguerol de Ulloa

Sebastián Rodríguez had left Valladolid about the same time that Francisco had surrendered. Rodríguez, who had been harassed by Yñigo López de Mondragón to speak up for doña Beatriz de Villasur, had petitioned to be allowed to go to Saldaña to confer with his client. To Mondragón's dismay, the council had granted the request and accorded the protracting adversary twenty days' leave.

Over a month had elapsed, and Sebastián Rodríguez had not returned. Yñigo López de Mondragón, incensed by the effrontery, denounced the breach on 26 April 1557. He reminded the judges that Rodríguez had been given twenty days to chat with doña Beatriz, yet thirty-six days, almost double the allotted time, had transpired and the attorney had not reappeared. Mondragón demanded that the case regarding doña Catalina's dowry be closed and justice be dispensed "according to and as my party has asked."

The Council of the Indies immediately notified Sebastián Rodríguez of the motion. Two days later Alonso de San Juan, on behalf of Francisco Noguerol, concurred with Mondragón that the case be declared concluded. More days had gone by and Saldaña remained silent and aloof; Mondragón continued to prod the council to rule in his client's favor, as it was evident that doña Beatriz had defaulted.

Doña Catalina de Vergara, in order to safeguard her assets and separate her goods from her husband's property, made a formal demand for the return of her dowry. Along with the petition, doña Catalina presented a receipt, signed by Noguerol in Arequipa on 5 October 1549, listing all the items she had brought into the marriage.

On that day Francisco had acknowledged that he "took into his power and received the following: 1,400 pesos of gold, at the time we marry, to be collected by the agent Juan de Salas of Cuzco, for the sale of horses and slaves; another 1,400 pesos of gold from Alonso de Mesa, a *vecino* of Cuzco, before the marriage; 750 pesos of gold from the properties of don Alonso de Montemayor when he went to Mexico on the ship *San Pedryllo*; 2,000 pesos of her own from debts owed her by Diego de Centeno, for the sale of certain mares and colts she sold him while he was in El Desaguadero in the camp of His Majesty; 100 marks of silver, her own, received as debts from Captain Diego Centeno; further, worked silver and pieces of gold, and a silver coffer all worth 1,350 pesos of gold."[1] The total value of the dowry added up to a sizable sum of 6,900 pesos of gold at 450 maravedis (3,105,000 maravedis), plus 100 marks of silver and gold.

The list of doña Catalina's personal property provides a glimpse of her activities during the revolt of Gonzalo Pizarro. The widow of the Oidor Tejada, the man who had left for Spain on a mission to sway the king to look favorably on the rebellion, was involved in the conflict as well. The sale of her horses to Diego Centeno put her clearly in the royalist camp. Had she always been loyal to the king, or had she oscillated between sympathizing with Pizarro's cause and the Crown, as both her husbands had done? It was not surprising that doña Catalina had not been paid at the time of her marriage; it was too soon after the upheaval. But when was she finally reimbursed?

Francisco was in complete agreement with doña Catalina and communicated to the court his consent to "give and hand over to her that which she carried in dowry at the time we married." Noguerol was equally compliant in turning over "the half of earnings that she asks for."

As generous as Noguerol's gesture might appear, it was only right according to the law. A woman was legally entitled to the restitution of her dowry, should the marriage terminate. For example, if the husband died, the value of the original dowry was set aside for the widow, before the estate was divided by the heirs. Furthermore, it was equally common for the wife to receive one-half the *bienes gananciales*. That was precisely what doña Beatriz de Villasur was asking for as well: the return of her dowry and one-half of Noguerol's earnings.

The Fiscal Agreda, not as acquiescent as Noguerol, stiffly rejected the sworn statement as just a simple receipt that was of no value in the courts.

On 7 May 1557, regardless of Agreda's disapproval, the Council of the Indies ruled in favor of doña Catalina de Vergara. She was granted all that Noguerol had endorsed and the issue was declared as concluded. This was a propitious development, not only for doña Catalina but for Francisco Noguerol as well. As a result of the decision, Noguerol's potential losses to the Crown and to Beatriz de Villasur were halved.

Following this minor victory, Yñigo López de Mondragón was also anxious to settle the matter with Beatriz de Villasur regarding the portion of doña Catalina's dowry used to purchase a *censo* from the Duke of Medina Sidonia. The attorney had been repeatedly trying to elicit from the court a ruling favorable to doña Catalina on the basis of truancy and persistent silence by Sebastián Rodríguez and his client.

Rodríguez, however, had been regularly informed of every minute maneuver employed by his adversary, and he did not, in spite of his apparent apathy, plan to surrender. When he was ready, he stormed into court and began an exhausting tirade against Noguerol and doña Catalina. The suit had not been filed within the specified time nor did it follow the proper form, and most importantly, it was based on false arguments. Noguerol's confession was flagrantly inaccurate. Doña Catalina did not turn over to Francisco Noguerol the goods in question, and legally they could not have acquired any property together as a married couple. Lope de Mendieta brought the 20,000 ducats "before the said two joined as one." Rodríguez attacked doña Catalina, accusing her of entering matrimony "knowing that the said Francisco Noguerol was married with the said my party." The lawyer insisted that all of Noguerol's property constituted *bienes gananciales* with doña Beatriz, "because he has earned and acquired them during the marriage" with her; naturally, one-half of these assets should revert to his client. In conclusion Rodríguez thundered that doña Catalina's claims should be irrevocably negated.[2]

Yñigo López de Mondragón went before the council two days later, on 17 May. The attorney, unimpressed by the passionate attacks and rebuttal, simply pointed out that three terms had passed before Sebastián Rodríguez acted and reiterated his earlier call for conclusion of the case.

Sebastián Rodríguez had misjudged the mood of the Council of the Indies. He had waited too long and had failed to counter the impact of weeks of arguments by his opponent. The judges, not convinced by Rodríguez's tardy, albeit forceful, baiting of Francisco and Catalina, acquiesced to Mondragón's appeals. The issue was herewith concluded.

While the litigation between doña Catalina de Vergara and doña Beatriz de Villasur had been pending, Alonso de San Juan sustained the defense of Francisco Noguerol. He reminded the council that his client had presented to the court two letters, originals, written by Ynés and Francisca Noguerol. San Juan demanded that copies of these important documents be furnished to all involved parties and asked for the return of the originals; the judges authorized this request. San Juan also pressed that the extension of twenty days alloted his client earlier not begin until Noguerol had received the copies of the proceedings he had petitioned for. The council consented and ordered on 13 May 1557 that the twenty-day count begin from that day.[3]

Noguerol's defense was exultant, for it had gained one extra week to amass vindicating evidence. Francisco's legal counsel at this point consisted of Alonso de San Juan, Juan de Guzmán, and Benito de Fresneda. In early May the attorneys had composed an extensive, thirty-three item questionnaire and had drawn up a list of reputable witnesses who were expected to shed light on various aspects of the defendant's life. Some people could be queried in Valladolid; in many cases, however, it would be necessary to travel to distant towns and villages to obtain the information. It was a formidable and time-consuming task. Benito de Fresneda had filed the *interrogatorio* with the Council of the Indies on 17 May, and with this step completed, the legal team could set forth to collect and record the multifarious testimonies.

XXVII

No Hope of Survival

*It was alleged that she was to the point of death,
and physicians had given up on her cure,
and said that they had no hope of survival because of the
gravity of her illness?*
—Interrogatorio *prepared by Noguerol's attorneys*

The aim of the inquiry was to portray Francisco Noġuerol de Ulloa as a dutiful and distinguished gentleman, a victim of false tidings and malevolent denouncements. The answers were expected to fit into the scheme, proving the innocence of the prisoner.

Most of the questions were leading questions, yet such depositions were a common and an important tool of Spain's sixteenth-century legal profession. Precise questions would elicit the desired response from the carefully chosen witnesses. Although the opposing counsel could not cross-examine, the lawyers would furnish sworn depositions of their own, naturally favorable to their client. Thus in the end it was the skill with which the evidence was gathered and presented, the social standing and importance of the deponents, as well as the perseverence of the attorneys that would prove decisive in the contest for justice.[1]

The first part of the questionnaire on Noguerol's behalf covered the illegal transport of treasure. The defense counsel intended to show that the sixty-five bars of silver that Noguerol had sent to Spain in 1551 "were all completely registered, and taxed" according to law.

A more extensive set of questions dealt with the issue of bigamy. The witnesses would be asked to corroborate Noguerol's assertions. Was Noguerol influenced by his mother to marry doña Beatriz, and did he do so against his will? Did Noguerol three or four years later travel to Peru, where he had remained about thirteen years without remarrying? After thirteen years did he receive letters from his sisters certifying that doña Beatriz was dead? Are the signatures and letters authentic, and were they written by credible nuns? In Grajal, Sahagún, and San Pedro de las Dueñas was it generally believed that doña Beatriz had died? Was it known that just before the letters had been written doña Beatriz was "very much afflicted by chest pains, very great ones, and it was alleged that she was to the point of death, and physicians had given up on her cure, and said that they had no hope of survival because of the gravity of her illness?" Was Noguerol informed by others who came from Spain of the death of doña Beatriz?

The witnesses would also be asked if they knew that for many years Noguerol had been uninterested in marriage, although he was rich and could have had any wealthy and "principal" woman of Peru, because he was bound to doña Beatriz. After it had become common knowledge that doña Beatriz was dead, did many people try to convince Noguerol to remarry, preferably in Arequipa? Before he had married doña Catalina, had he "never had dealings [tratado] nor conversed [conversado], nor known [conocido] her?" This question implied not only verbal exchange but also carnal knowledge.[2]

The attorneys took care to demonstrate the difficult communications between the old and the new continent, drafting several questions to prove that point. Was the distance between Peru and Grajal, Sahagún, and the convent of San Pedro de las Dueñas more than 4,000 leagues, and was the road bad and dangerous? Did it sometimes take three and four years for news to pass from one to the other, "and are many times those who travel lost and shipwrecked?"

The last part of the interrogatorio concentrated on the marriage to doña Catalina de Vergara, the trip to Spain, and most important, the moral fabric of the defendant. Did Francisco and doña Catalina marry publicly, "being present many knights and people of great authority and scrupulousness and Christianity?" After the wedding did the couple plan to come to Spain "on business that they had with His Majesty and for the said Noguerol de Ulloa to see his mother and sisters?" While in Peru did Francisco and Catalina live together in good faith, believing that doña Beatriz was dead? Had they returned unaware that she was alive and knew nothing to the contrary until in Spain "they had certain notice of it?" Did the witness believe that if Noguerol had known Beatriz were alive, he would never have sent money back to Spain, nor would he have brought doña Catalina? Was Francisco a good Christian, fearful of God, a man of good conscience who had guarded the commandments and supported the authority of the Sacred Mother Church, and done good works and services? Was he a man of good reputation, an hidalgo? In the Indies had he been a loyal servant of His Majesty?[3]

Only few witnesses were competent to answer every point raised in the inquiry. Most would discuss events with which they were particularly familiar. Noguerol's friends from the Indies would attest to his life there, while local people might expound on his youth and pedigree.

XXVIII

Give Me the City

Give me the city and its outskirts as a jail.
—Francisco Noguerol de Ulloa

Francisco was restless. He had been in custody for almost two months, and though he was living in relative comfort, he longed to bring his forced repose to an end. The house of the Alguacil Santiago had become too oppressive and the monotony of the days too tiresome for a man accustomed to uninhibited activity and the bustle of a thriving city.

Before Philip II established Madrid as Spain's permanent capital in 1561, Valladolid had served as the favorite seat of government. It was the largest city in Castile, and it boasted a university, the court of the Royal Chancellery, and also a tribunal of the Holy Office of the Inquisition; it was the center of artistic endeavors as well as controversial debates and colorful festivals. The presence of the Council of the Indies attracted a wide variety of people to voice their opinions on the administration of the colonies and the treatment of the natives. Bartolomé de Las Casas, the most fervent champion of the Indians, was a frequent resident, and he wrote the still controversial *Destruction of the Indies* in Valladolid.[1]

It was Valladolid that the energetic *encomendero* yearned to move around in, to freely partake in the attractions of the metropolis, as well as to "solicit my business." Noguerol, though miserable, did not yield to despair. Instead, he boldly petitioned the council: "Give me the city and its outskirts as a jail,"[2] hinting at ample financing. The judges curtly advised him to continue his quest for justice but made no reference to lifting his confinement.

Undaunted, Noguerol repeated his request a few days later, on 31 May 1557. He argued he was of "little blame," since his offense was committed inadvertently. The court should not overlook his assiduous services to His Majesty. He pleaded, "It is already Easter," and if the judges granted his request, Francisco assured them they "would do great service to God, because the season is so appropriate." The answer remained the same: "The señores said that there was no place for what the said Noguerol de Ulloa had asked."

Two days earlier, on 29 May 1557, the council had issued a ruling directed at all the protagonists: Francisco, Fiscal Agreda, doña Beatriz, and doña Catalina. "Each of the said parties should receive and have at its disposition, the proof of what each had said and alleged," and they were given 120 days to review the documents. The disputants had potentially until the end of September of 1557 to prepare their charges and positions.[3]

<h1 style="text-align:center">XXIX</h1>

A Wise Man

I take him for both a Christian and a wise man.
—Friar Domingo de Santo Tomás

Noguerol's defense counsel could not afford to dally; *interrogatorio* in hand, the lawyers dispersed to accomplish the intricate mission. Some of the people were interviewed in Valladolid, but most of the evidence was to be found elsewhere. The sworn depositions were minutely recorded by a scribe in the presence of an authorized official, usually the *corregidor* or mayor of the town, as well as the defendant's attorney.

Cristóval de Aguilar, a fifty-year-old cleric who testified in Valladolid, in Pando, had known Francisco and Catalina well in Peru and had traveled with them from Arequipa to Lima, where the couple had remained while he continued immediately on to Spain. As a man of the cloth, Cristóval de Aguilar had needed a special ecclesiastical permission before he could respond to the questions drafted to benefit the accused *encomendero*, who, the cleric insisted, "was taken as a man who could marry and betroth" until he wed doña Catalina. Aguilar assured his questioners that he would certainly have known had it been otherwise, for he was "priest of the church of the said city of Arequipa."[1]

The cleric remembered that Francisco had shown him two letters from his sisters, "and it seemed they advised him that his wife was dead." But as the clergyman did not know the names or handwriting of the nuns, he could not confirm the authenticity of the notes. He could attest that after Noguerol had brought out the missives, "from here onwards it was believed and said in the said city of Arequipa that his wife was dead in the realm of Spain."

Francisco had become interested in doña Catalina as a widower should, long after the death of his spouse. "This *testigo* never believed, nor saw, nor heard it said, that the said Noguerol de Ulloa might have had conversation or carnal access to the said doña Catalina de Vergara until publicly he married her because the said doña Catalina de Vergara was a woman who was very honored, and secluded, and of great fame." The enthusiastic witness vouched that following their wedding, "I always saw them live and reside together within a single door, and make the married life."[2]

Gaspar Alonso de Castro, interviewed on the second of June in the *Villa* of Alixo, had known Noguerol since their joint voyage to the Indies more than twenty years before and would have returned with him and doña Catalina to Spain, had the couple not been detained in Lima. Nevertheless, he did sail with Francisco and his wife from Arequipa to the capital.

Gaspar Alonso de Castro's early years in the New World paralleled Noguerol's ventures. Both men were together during the disastrous campaign in Chile, later in Cuzco, as well as in Arequipa. The witness confirmed that Noguerol had fought in many battles, because he "was with him and saw him one time receive an arquebus blast in the ribs that brought him to the brink of death, and he was wounded other times in the service of His Majesty." Their shared experience resulted in a close friendship, and the fellow soldiers had spent many hours in conversation. Alonso de Castro affirmed it was well known that Francisco had been pressured to marry doña Beatriz de Villasur, and "that while she was alive he would not come to the kingdoms of Spain."[3] Gaspar Alonso de Castro remembered the letters announcing Beatriz's death and was convinced that Noguerol would never have remarried had there existed any doubt regarding her demise.

Another witness, Hernando de Silva, had shared quarters in Lima with Lope de Mendieta and had sailed with him on the same ship to Spain. Hernando had also visited Noguerol and had glimpsed some silver bars in the room. Hernando had watched as the silver arrived at the posada of Lope de Mendieta. Curious about the bullion, Hernando de Silva had questioned Mendieta, who told him: "I am sending this silver to the ship, and the bars that are marked are those of Noguerol de Ulloa," and he also told him that Noguerol was planning "to employ them in annuities."[4] Hernando insisted, "none of the bars that I saw there was unmarked." He added as a further proof that he as well as Mendieta had resided in the house of the royal accountant, Juan de Cáceres, who had entered Mendieta's room and had seen the silver bars: "From which it clearly appears that it would have been impossible for any unmarked ones to have come."[5]

Hernando de Silva was a valuable witness. Lope de Mendieta was dead, but his confidant was able to corroborate the assertions of No-guerol's defense. Furthermore, he was also Francisco's close friend, privy to many particulars of his life, and it was Hernando who had been instrumental in bringing about the union between Francisco and Catalina. Many important people had wanted Noguerol to marry their daughters, "he being such a principal person." In the matchmaking Hernando had acted "on the part of a señora with whom the said doña Catalina had much friendship and conversation." He insisted that there had been no contact between Francisco and Catalina before their wedding, "other than that he might have seen her sometime, because the said doña Catalina was so secluded and was so honored, that he could not have had communication nor dealings with her."[6]

It was important for the defense to establish the purity of the bride's character, and a lack of any relationship between Francisco and doña Catalina before their marriage. There could not be even a hint of a love affair between the *encomendero* and the widow of Oidor Tejada, for such eventuality might give rise to suspicions regarding "the truthful ignorance" that Noguerol insisted on.

Hernando de Silva testified that Noguerol had planned to leave Peru even before his marriage and had "sold the bulk of his properties in order to come to Spain." Hernando had been luring his friend into matrimony with doña Catalina de Vergara, but Francisco resisted: "Certainly, if I were not so close to the point of going to Spain, and with good purpose, I would do what you are telling me, because I am very pleased with this señora and her good reputation." The indefatigable matchmaker had countered, "this señora also wants to go to Spain." Hernando had told Noguerol that he "knew it for a fact, because they had tried to arrange marriages with the most principal men, knights, and the richest men of the realm." But doña Catalina had always responded, "I will not marry anyone, unless that person would go to Spain." It had been clear to Hernando that his friend Francisco was the ideal man for the determined widow, and he had used all his persuasive powers to bring about the marriage, one day pleading with doña Catalina, the next day coaxing Francisco: "Although you might have to go to Spain, who might you be able to marry there, who can compare with this señora, being such a principal person, and so honored, and who has also lived in this land?" How could Noguerol have resisted the qualities of such a woman? He had yielded, acknowledging, "You are right, and I say that I will do it with pleasure."[7]

Juan Vázquez, a *vecino* of Arévalo in his mid-thirties, had often conversed with doña Catalina de Vergara in Peru, and she had confessed to him on various occasions "that she had a great desire to return to Spain because she had her children there." The witness also recalled that after Noguerol and doña Catalina had married, they "put into plan their trip [to Spain] and traveled to the Ciudad de los Reyes [Lima] to take ship. But they were detained for awhile, and I heard it said, in fact it was public and notorious, that the delay had been because the *oidores* had told the said Noguerol de Ulloa that they would remove his Indians if he left."[8]

Juan Vázquez was certain that if doña Catalina had not insisted on returning to Spain, "she would have married someone with a larger estate than the said Noguerol de Ulloa." Vázquez, a rival of Hernando de Silva as a marriage broker, had failed to convince doña Catalina to take as a husband Captain Gabriel de Rojas, "a person of much quality, and of much greater wealth than the said Noguerol de Ulloa," and who had "great intentions of marrying doña Catalina de Vergara."[9]

Sixty-year-old Gonzalo de Bustillo, a resident of Cuéllar, attested that he had heard from the brother of Lope de Mendieta, Juan Ortiz de Zárate, that Noguerol had shipped much silver to Spain. The bars had come with the royal mark on one side, and the mark of the owner on the reverse. Ortiz de Zárate had confided to Bustillo that Noguerol had insisted that the silver be registered in his name.[10]

Gonzalo de Bustillo recalled that he had been in the mining center of Porco when the letters containing the report of Beatriz's demise had reached Arequipa, but her death had become common knowledge in Peru. While he lived in Peru, he always believed she was dead, "without hearing anything to the contrary," and when he had learned that she was alive, he "marvelled greatly at the news."[11]

As had other witnesses, Gonzalo de Bustillo praised the honor and character of doña Catalina. He knew her well, because he "went in her company from these kingdoms to the said provinces of Peru, and she always lived with much seclusion when she was married to Doctor Tejada, and even more when she became a widow." He had spoken often to both Francisco and Catalina, before and after their wedding, and believed Catalina had chosen Francisco because he, too, wanted to return to Spain. Bustillo insisted that when he had sailed from Peru a year and a half after Noguerol and his wife had left, doña Beatriz's death had been still undisputed. He therefore assumed that the couple had found out that Beatriz was alive when they had reached Seville. Bustillo was convinced that had Francisco known his first wife was alive, he would never have sent money to Spain, nor would he have left Peru, because it would have been "against all reason."[12]

Another *vecino* of Arévalo, Francisco de Tapia, in his mid-forties, called Noguerol one of the earliest conquistadores, "*conquistador antiguo*." He praised Francisco as "a very good Christian fearful of God and a man of conscience" and claimed to "have seen him do very good works for the Indians of his *repartimiento*." Tapia eulogized doña Catalina as "the crown jewel of all the women of those parts." He was certain that Noguerol could not have had any dealings with her, other than perhaps seeing her, before they were married. The flattering witness confirmed that after the marriage the couple had traveled to Lima, "to deal with President Gasca so that he might transfer the Indians to a relative of General Pedro de Hinojosa, but the said president did not wish to do it." Yet even such obstacle did not prevent the return to Europe. "The desire of doña Catalina was so great that she had to come to Spain," and, according to Tapia, "she had taken an oath of the said Noguerol de Ulloa for him to bring her to these kingdoms."[13]

Dominican friar Alonso Méndez had known Noguerol and doña Catalina about ten years and had returned to Spain on the same fleet as the couple. They traveled as man and wife, and he thought that they did not discover that doña Beatriz was alive until they reached Seville. The friar was surprised when he had heard that Francisco's first wife was not dead and remarked that, certainly, had the truth been known in Peru, "the archbishop and the Royal Audiencia would have punished him [Noguerol]."[14]

One of the key witnesses, from the standpoint of both credibility and his position of knowledge and authority in Peru, was the Dominican provincial, Friar Domingo de Santo Tomás. At the time of the inquest he was about forty-seven years old and already had an established reputation as a protector of the natives against the more negligent conquistadores. He had lived among the Indians teaching them the Christian doctrine, and had been compiling extensive dictionaries and grammars in the Indian languages.[15]

Domingo de Santo Tomás stated that he had known Noguerol and doña Catalina for almost fifteen years. He recalled that "it was public knowledge in Peru that Noguerol had been *desposado* in Spain; he did it with reluctance, and as a result of the disgrace of it, he had gone to Peru." The friar could not say with certainty who had written to Noguerol "that his wife was already dead." But the witness confirmed that "it was publicly believed and famous in the said provinces of Peru that he had received the said letters."[16] Friar Santo Tomás insisted that had anyone in Peru suspected anything contrary to the death of Beatriz de Villasur, Noguerol and doña Catalina would not have married.

The witness recalled that Noguerol was "at the least among the first that came after the conquest," although he could not be classified a conquistador of Peru in the sense of the original Pizarro expeditions. The friar considered doña Catalina a virtuous woman and doubted that any relationship with Francisco had existed before the marriage, because "the said doña Catalina would never have given to him the opportunity, because of her honesty and goodness; but if they had discussed the said marriage before or not I cannot say, because at that time I was in the Ciudad de los Reyes." He had been also in Lima when they married, but he had heard that all the elite of Arequipa had attended the wedding.[17]

Six years later the couple traveled from Arequipa to Lima "with their whole household in order to come to Spain." Domingo de Santo Tomás remembered that "it was during their residence in Lima that I entered into discussions with doña Catalina concerning her trip and about the harm that might come in leaving her Indians, and their indoctrination, and other matters of this nature, wanting to persuade her that for the good treatment and indoctrination of them, she should remain in the said Peru." Yet doña Catalina had remained unmoved and confided, "for a long time I have lived discontentedly feeling the absence of Spain."[18]

Francisco Noguerol de Ulloa was a good Christian in the eyes of Domingo de Santo Tomás. He had received the sacraments before setting sail, and the friar could not conceive that Francisco could have taken the sacraments had he not believed that he was legitimately married to doña Catalina. Santo Tomás concluded that if Noguerol had suspected that Beatriz de Villasur was alive, "he would not have ever done such an evil act as to marry, nor have been so ignorant as to come and to send his estate to Spain, because I take him for both a Christian and a wise man."[19]

The sheer bulk of testimony was enormous. There was much repetition; however, occasional pieces of new information did surface. All the witnesses had agreed that Noguerol was unaware that doña Beatriz was still alive when he had married doña Catalina, a woman of great esteem.

It is evident why doña Catalina had married Noguerol: she wanted to return home and he agreed to fulfill that desire. Why, however, would Noguerol want to marry a woman whom, according to the witnesses, he did not know, and who placed conditions on the marriage that could have potentially cost him his *encomienda*? Notwithstanding the affirmations of numerous witnesses to the contrary, Francisco and doña Catalina had been no strangers to each other prior to their marriage. The Spanish community in Peru in the early 1550s was small; most "people of quality" were well acquainted and thrived on gossip regarding their compatriots' private lives. Almost everything concerning an individual sooner or later became "*notorio y público*," as for example Noguerol's ill-fated first marriage and the alleged demise of doña Beatriz de Villasur. Arequipa was a small town, and even a secluded widow, as doña Catalina undoubtedly had been, would have had ample opportunity to hear about and to see Noguerol. Furthermore, their paths might have crossed while doña Catalina was still married to Doctor Tejada. It seems unlikely they had known each other intimately, yet they must have met in public, glimpsed one another in church, and perhaps even exchanged a few words. Doña Catalina was an active widow. She had conducted business with Diego de Centeno; she had inherited a small *encomienda* from Doctor Tejada and had been concerned with collection of tribute as well as indoctrination of the Indians.[20] By many accounts, doña Catalina de Vergara was beautiful as well as intelligent, and Noguerol had been sufficiently attracted by her and her wealth to wish to marry her and even to acquiesce to her stipulations. For the purposes of the lawsuit, however, the less contact acknowledged between them, the better it served the defense.

XXX

Shock and Great Sadness

*The said doña Beatriz was in a state of shock
and great sadness, because she had never known, until then,
of the marriage.*—Juan de Ortega

Noguerol's brother-in-law, Juan de Guzmán, in his capacity as attorney traveled to Grajal de Campos, the village where doña Costanza de Espinosa had resided since the death of Francisco's father. Juan de Guzmán arrived in Grajal on 5 June 1557 and presented the *interrogatorio* and papers from the Council of the Indies authorizing the inquest to the local authorities. Juan de Guzmán expected that many people would recall the betrothal between Francisco and doña Beatriz as well as the events leading up to it. Noguerol's defense also hoped to clarify the rumor regarding doña Beatriz's death.

The first deponent was Alonso Vélez, a sixty-year-old *vecino* of the Villilla de Guardo. He remembered that some ten or eleven years before he had seen doña Beatriz, and she "was very ill from the illness [*enfermedad*] . . . and people and physicians said she was very ill."[1]

Testimony of Juan de Mahudes el Viejo of Grajal was more explicit. "In the year 1546 this witness was in the *Villa* of Saldaña, and saw the said doña Beatriz very ill in bed with the illness. I heard as very public and notorious in this *Villa* of Grajal and in the locale of San Pedro de las Dueñas that the said doña Beatriz de Villasur was dead, and had died of the illness." Her condition had been described as hopeless by physicians and those who knew her, and "this witness thusly believed it, and took it for certain because he had left the said doña Beatriz de Villasur so ill."[2]

Fifty-two-year-old Miguel de Prado of Grajal told the inquirers he had gone to Saldaña about fifteen years before (1542) when doña Beatriz "was unwell and sick from the illness and very weakened."[3] He placed doña Beatriz's indisposition four years ahead of the time others had affirmed, probably just in error. Most witnesses described doña Beatriz's malady as *dolor de costado* (chest pain), a rather imprecise but widely used phrase that could refer to a variety of pulmonary or cardiovascular illnesses. She might have had pneumonia, or she could have contracted pneumonic plague, not an uncommon disease in Spain in the mid-1540s.[4]

The most complete deposition regarding the ailment of doña Beatriz came from fifty-year-old Gonzalo de la Mota of Grajal. Ten or eleven years earlier Gonzalo had traveled frequently between Grajal and Saldaña and knew the Santanders well. He had heard that doña Beatriz died and believed it, but later he learned that "she was not dead, but still very ill from the said malady." Gonzalo, baffled, had wanted to ascertain the actual state of doña Beatriz and went to see her. "She was still ailing and thin [*flaca*] from the sickness that she had had." The family told him that she had been "near the end of her life, and without memory, and that it was understood that she would not live." When Gonzalo had visited the patient, she complained about the severity of her own illness, which kept her "three days without memory and hallucinating," and she confided in her friend that during the worst hours "she prayed that God would carry her away, and bring death to end her suffering."[5]

The next deponent, a forty-four-year-old cleric and rector of Mosclares, Juan de Ortega, was the most informative of Noguerol's acquaintances. The loquacious priest conscientiously responded to every question with minute detail. He knew all the protagonists well; he had traveled extensively throughout the Indies, including Mexico and Guatemala; but eventually he had settled in Cuzco. From there he had often crossed the highlands to Arequipa, where Noguerol "had his seat and I went there to see and to speak to him, and we talked and discoursed." Ortega not only confirmed that Noguerol had received notice of his wife's death from his sisters and that the news spread through "Cuzco and Collao and its provinces," but when shown the two missives, he authenticated the signatures and writing of the nuns. Ortega had met the sisters when he returned to Spain about seven years before (1550) with the bishop of Palencia, Pedro de la Gasca. The cleric vowed he had seen them write and sign their names and knew them well, and "had received letters from them, from doña Francisca and doña Ynés." They were "very good *religiosas*" whose word could be taken seriously, and their dispatch believed. The cleric insisted that the death of doña Beatriz was well known in Peru, and "Francisco Noguerol de Ulloa had made a very good marriage with the said doña Catalina."[6]

Ortega was far from tongue-tied as he chattered about his friend Francisco. Noguerol had two *encomiendas*, first the Ubinas, and second, the Collaguas. In addition to the tribute the Indians were expected to pay, some served in their master's house as well. Francisco owned several black slaves and perhaps a few Indian slaves, possibly captured during the Chilean campaign. Juan de Ortega remarked that before Noguerol had married doña Catalina, he "gave and divided certain Indian women that he had in his house among certain of his Spanish friends." What had prompted such generosity, and who were these women? Francisco would not have lavished slaves on his friends; they were worth too much; nor would it have been easy to transfer directly *encomienda* Indians to other Spaniards, for that was prohibited by law. Noguerol's household probably had contained Indian dependents, called *yanakunas*, and he could have favored his friends with female *yanakunas*. Juan de Ortega did not divulge if the impulse had been inspired by Francisco's beneficence, or if the exit of the women was another prenuptial stipulation by doña Catalina de Vergara. Very little escaped public knowledge in Arequipa, and doña Catalina must have been aware of the purpose of some of Noguerol's servants. Propriety required that before she came to live with Noguerol, he would have been obliged to remove his concubines.[7]

Juan de Ortega hinted that Francisco did not marry doña Catalina for purely monetary gain, as he could have "found very good marriages with *doncellas* of good blood and rich, because the said Noguerol de Ulloa had great reputation as a knight and conqueror and lord [*señor de vasallos*]."[8] The ardent clergyman, in an attempt to extol the splendid qualities of his friend, exaggerated Noguerol's status. The *encomendero* was not the equivalent of the Old World landed aristocrat.

The scribe's quill, propelled by the cleric's interminable recount, was still far from a final dip in the inkwell. When Juan de Ortega disembarked in Seville, he had heard rumors about the resurrection of doña Beatriz. He was disturbed by the gossip and curious, and without much delay he hastened to Saldaña. There he had found doña Beatriz indeed alive, "and of it I was greatly surprised, given the fame in the said provinces of Peru that she was dead." Ortega must have called on doña Beatriz sometime in the fall of 1550 or early winter of 1551. Once the priest had overcome his astonishment, he "told her as the said Francisco Noguerol de Ulloa her husband, being certain, and certified that she was dead, he had married in the said Indies in the city of Arequipa." It was a cold day when doña Beatriz received her visitor, and his tidings had produced "a state of shock and great sadness, because she had never known, until then, of the marriage of the said Francisco Noguerol her husband." The kind churchman had tried to console the shaken doña Beatriz that "she should not marvel that the said Francisco Noguerol had married in the said Indies because he had it for certain that she was dead, because his sisters, nuns of San Pedro de las Dueñas had written it."[9]

The meeting between Juan de Ortega and doña Beatriz de Villasur was distressing for both. Ortega had left Noguerol shortly after his wedding to doña Catalina; and now he was facing Francisco's first wife, recovered from her illness. His friend was enmeshed in sacrilege, and Ortega, as a priest, had realized the implications. Did the conscientious cleric warn Noguerol that doña Beatriz de Villasur had not succumbed to her illness and that his marriage with doña Catalina de Vergara was illegal and sinful? No one ever said.

Juan de Ortega's well-intentioned revelation to doña Beatriz had come as a tremendous blow to the middle-aged woman, who had spent twenty years waiting for her husband's return. How bewildering and difficult to absorb such a painful disclosure. She had lived in Saldaña since her marriage and had been universally considered the wife of Francisco Noguerol, absent in the Indies. There was nothing unusual in her situation; other women in Spain were separated from their spouses who were exploring the unknown world across the ocean. Did she hope that one day Francisco would fulfill his pledge and return to her? She had been probably notified of the annulment proceedings initiated by Noguerol, but since they were not pursued further, she might have continued to believe that Francisco would come back. Such hope, if it still existed, had melted away as doña Beatriz, stupefied, listened to the merciless chatting of her guest.

The witness also elucidated, with his usual verbosity, the method to calculate the distance from Arequipa to Saldaña and Grajal. He stated it was "at least 4,000 and more leagues as the cosmographers and people who understand such things say and discourse, and who travel and steer the helm on the sea. They are people who know how to measure distances and longitude from some lands to others by the elevation and degrees that there are in the heavens to the earth, and they take the readings by the astrolabe when they take the height of the sun." And to wipe away any doubt as to his expertise, he added that he knew this because he had "traveled and navigated the said path on the *Mar del Norte* and the *Mar del Sur*, and Tierra Firme."[10]

The perils of the intercontinental voyage proved to be another topic that the cleric delved into with gusto. "Many persons that come from there are delayed for a long time, sailing from the said provinces of Peru to these kingdoms of Spain. I know that many times those who journey from the said Indies . . . are lost, and the vessels are sunk in the sea. During the time when this *testigo* traveled from the said Indies to Spain with the bishop of Palencia, don Pedro de la Gasca, we approached on the seas a lost ship and it remained there because there was no place to put on the gudgeon of the rudder in order to steer it, and beyond this, we were approaching the time of the calms and we might have lost all the men on board the said ship, from which I can say that the road is an uncertain one."[11]

Noguerol's valor during the battle of Huarina had impressed Ortega, who saw him riding in the lead during the initial charge against the forces of Gonzalo Pizarro. The cleric testified that Francisco had broken his lance and in the ensuing battle had received a "very bad wound."[12]

The talkative priest could not restrain himself from relating the latest gossip. He had heard a number of people say, "especially Casildo de Santander *vecino* of Saldaña and brother of the said doña Beatriz de Villasur, who told him that the said doña Catalina de Vergara had separated herself from the said Noguerol de Ulloa in Valladolid in a house, because she had learned that the said doña Beatriz de Villasur was alive, and the said Francisco Noguerol de Ulloa had set himself up in another house."[13]

The exhausted defense team, surely wishing for respite after such thorough witness, had to continue their quest for information, though they might have hoped for more taciturn deponents.

XXXI
Never Forgive the Nuns

I implore that God will never forgive the nuns that have written such a thing; it has been the cause of such great evil.—Doña Beatriz de Villasur

The key testimony in Grajal de Campos came from seventy-year-old Diego Quixada, a close friend of the family. Quixada's son, Juan, resided in Peru and regularly wrote to his father, and he had occasionally mentioned Noguerol's fortunes. Diego had also received letters from Francisco himself. He held the Noguerols in great esteem and praised Francisco, his father, and even his grandfather as good and honest men, "knights and principal figures, natives of Galicia." To emphasize their caste, he declared, "There exist in certain monasteries celebrated tombs of their ancestors. Thusly the said Noguerol de Ulloa seems and represents, and the said Mendo Noguerol seems and represents his nobility and good blood [*buena sangre*]."[1]

The elderly man's commentary on the character of Francisco's sisters was even more laudatory. The two nuns were "very good *religiosas*, and fearful of God and of good conscience and life and customs, and persons of much faith and credit," and anything they might have written "one should and can believe." Diego's daughter was also a nun in San Pedro de las Dueñas, and he had known doña Ynés and doña Francisca since they were novices. He visited his daughter often during the past twenty-four years and had the opportunity to converse at great length with Noguerol's sisters as well, and had "seen in them all the qualities that they possess." Diego Quixada was impressed by doña Ynés's performance as abbess. "She acted as a good prelate and faithful Christian was obligated to do, and afterward she had been elected other times and confirmed and reelected to the said dignity of abbess which she now has and governs with all Christianity and good example." Doña Francisca also "was a good Christian . . . of great merit and good example."[2]

Though much of Quixada's testimony reflected his admiration and respect for the Noguerols, his declarations were remarkably candid. Juan de Guzmán showed the witness the two crucial letters sent to Peru by the sisters and then read them to him. The old man confirmed that the virtually illegible scribble came from the "hand of the said doña Ynés and doña Francisca."[3] He was familiar with their script because he frequently saw them write and had received notes from them himself. Diego stated forthrightly that as a result of those letters that had certified the death of doña Beatriz, Francisco Noguerol remarried in Peru.

Sometime after Juan de Ortega had visited doña Beatriz, Diego Quixada called on the distressed woman, who had still not regained her composure following the cleric's news. Quixada had comforted her: "Señora, do not be surprised nor marvel that the señor Noguerol de Ulloa might have married in the Indies, because from here they wrote to him that you were dead." Futhermore, since the news came from such reputable sources, he "was obligated to give faith and credit."[4]

Doña Beatriz had not shared his respect for the nuns and angrily responded: "I implore that God will never forgive the nuns that have written such a thing; it has been the cause of such great evil."[5]

Diego Quixada, trying to console her, had hinted at the reason for the deception: "Señora, do not marvel that his sisters might have written him that you were dead. I have it for certain that they wrote to him with the end and proposition, that knowing that you were still living, he would never come to these parts."[6]

It is doubtful that doña Beatriz de Villasur was cheered by these comforting words. Had she ever suspected that she was one of the primary reasons of Noguerol's absence? Nevertheless, it must have been unpleasant to be told that her husband would never have returned to Spain as long as she was alive.

In spite of his ties to the Noguerols and his reverence for Francisco's sisters, Diego Quixada did not hesitate to reveal that the nuns deliberately lied. "If they wrote him it was for this effect, that he might return, because speaking to the said doña Ynés and doña Francisca Noguerol about the aforesaid, they told me that they had written to the said their brother, that the said doña Beatriz was dead, only with the end that he might come to these parts, and with no other end whatsoever, thinking that of it no one would receive damage, nor would they injure anyone."[7]

When Ynés and Francisca Noguerol had implored their remiss sibling to return, they did not foresee any complications. They had expected their brother to be swayed by their arguments and to hasten to the side of his ailing mother. They did not anticipate another marriage. Their small deception had backfired. Francisco was in deep trouble. Their lie had become public knowledge, and they had lost their brother forever. Francisco never forgave his sisters and had very little contact with his family till the day he died.

XXXII

He and She Knowing

The said Francisco Noguerol married a second time
with doña Catalina de Vergara . . . both he and she knowing
that the said doña Beatriz was alive.
—Cristóval de Santander

While Noguerol's defense lawyers were meticulously collecting answers for their client's *probanza*, a new and very indignant plaintiff burst forth on 10 June 1557 and presented an angry petition to the Council of the Indies.

"Very powerful Señor. Cristóval de Santander, *vecino* of the *Villa* de Saldaña and legitimate brother of doña Beatriz de Villasur, wife of Francisco Noguerol prisoner in this court, by me regarding that which concerns me, and in the name of the said doña Beatriz my sister." Santander recapitulated the story of the "true matrimony" between the unscrupulous Noguerol and his sister. They had been "publicly married and betrothed in the house of the father of doña Beatriz," and Francisco had received the greater part of the dowry that had been promised. Cristóval de Santander insisted that the couple had been united "in peace and according to the order of the Sacred Mother Church." About eight or nine years ago, "with little fear of Our Lord and in even less consideration of royal justice," Francisco Noguerol remarried and had been cohabiting with the other woman ever since, "both he and she knowing that the said doña Beatriz was alive." The fuming champion stated bluntly that doña Catalina de Vergara had been well aware from the start that Francisco was married.

In conclusion the petitioner stressed that "Francisco Noguerol committed a very atrocious and serious crime, and deserves a very great punishment and penalty." He demanded that Noguerol be condemned "in the greatest and most grave fines, and by right, privilege, laws and *pragmáticas* of these kingdoms . . . his person and goods should be sequestered."[1]

Two years had elapsed since the Council of the Indies had ruled in favor of doña Beatriz and encouraged her to continue to seek justice, presumably in ecclesiastical courts, with expenses paid by her protesting husband. The judges had also ordered Francisco to resume marital relations with his first wife. Yet Noguerol was in no position to fulfill the court's decree; he had been imprisoned and would remain in jail while the suit filed by the Fiscal Agreda was pending. Although officially doña Beatriz's case had been concluded in the secular court, her attorney and even her brother made appearances in the council to complain, and to remind the judges of Noguerol's dastardly behavior toward doña Beatriz in order to influence the subsequent ruling.

Only a few days after Cristóval de Santander's stormy performance, doña Beatriz's lawyer, Sebastián Rodríguez, registered a further aberration. "Your Excellency knows that although the properties of Francisco Noguerol de Ulloa were ordered sequestered, it has not been done. Our side has argued that the financing posted by the other party was insufficient, and not bonded. The guarantors were not bonded, and one, Francisco Gómez de Vergara, has died. Your Excellency should order Francisco Noguerol de Ulloa to provide adequate and bonded security."[2]

The unexpected death of Secretary Vergara complicated Noguerol's position, for he had relied on the influential man, but more than that, it was a hard blow to doña Catalina. Her brother's moral as well as practical support during these trying months of harassment in the court and separation from her husband had alleviated some of the strain.

The fervent attack by Cristóval de Santander was swiftly neutralized by Miguel de Villanueva. He pointed out that doña Beatriz's case had already been heard, and decided. More important, Santander did not have the authority to act in the court, and unless he could contract a *procurador*, he should pay a fine.

Doña Beatriz's brother hastily contacted Sebastián Rodríguez, who duly came to court and in the name of Cristóval de Santander demanded justice "in the injury received by the said doña Beatriz and her relatives."[3]

Unimpressed, Miguel de Villanueva that very day reiterated that the issue was closed. At the same time he reminded the tribunal that the Fiscal Agreda was tardy in his presentation of evidence against his client and asked the council to order publication of the proofs.

The solemn judges of the court reached a decision and announced it on 18 June 1557: "The señores of the council order this business, that is, the presentation of the evidence, to be seen as concluded." The learned men were ready to retire to peruse the charges and countercharges, the sworn testimonies in favor and against the prisoner, and on the basis of the piles of petitions and depositions they would rule.

Noguerol's defense team converged upon their client immediately following the council's pronouncement in order to obtain his signature to a document that would be included with the evidence. "I ratify and approve all the *autos* that in my name have been prepared, and presented, by Alonso de San Juan, *procurador* of the court, and by others in his name. I declare and recognize by this letter that I make and constitute as my certain, sufficient, and legitimate general *provisores*, you, Miguel de Villanueva, and Yñigo López de Mondragón, *provisores de causas* in the Royal Council of the Indies of His Majesty that resides in this Court and *Villa* of Valladolid."[4]

A few days later, on 25 June, Miguel de Villanueva returned to the Council of the Indies and delivered the exhaustive data with an eloquent speech on Noguerol's behalf. "Regarding the criminal accusation I say that you must see and examine the principal brief and depositions of the said suit. Your Excellency will see that my party has proved well and fully his intention, and all that proof should lead to victory and this with sworn statements and a large number of *testigos*." The attorney maintained "the contrary party has proven nothing, nor has it made a *probanza*, to which end I ask and supplicate Your Excellency to find as I have argued, and to negate what the opposition demands." The lawyer implored the court "to see the proofs of my party, and given that he is not to blame, order the imprisonment be lifted." As to the bail, the financing had been arranged, and "it is not enough to say that Francisco the *fiador* [Francisco Gómez de Vergara] is dead, because the bond of his properties remains."[5]

The Fiscal Martín Ruiz de Agreda did not find it necessary to engage in a long rebuttal of Miguel de Villanueva's address. As was customary with the laconic prosecutor, he limited his answer to a stringent observation. Agreda advised the court to read Noguerol's confession and "you can see and then sentence."[6]

XXXIII

Married Life Together

*They have to have a married life together
as they had done before.*
—*Yñigo López de Mondragón*

The twenty-fifth of June 1557 was an eventful day in Valladolid. The judges of the Council of the Indies were to hear from yet another protagonist in the drama, one who had remained in the background for the past few weeks. Doña Catalina de Vergara had been subjected to insults by doña Beatriz, her brother, and their attorney, who repeatedly accused her of willfully entering into matrimony with a man already married. She could not be silent in the face of such grave allegations. Doña Catalina could no longer confine herself to fiscal matters alone while being openly vilified. Nor would she passively stand by, watching her undeserving rival win Francisco. Doña Catalina had married a widower whose status was never questioned. She and Noguerol had been legally joined during a Church ceremony; they had consummated the marriage and had lived as man and wife for several years. Doña Beatriz could not equal such indispensable requisites of a true wedlock. Doña Catalina intended to resume conjugal relations with her husband, and Yñigo López de Mondragón was her voice in court.

On 25 June doña Catalina's attorney stepped before the bench to express his client's discontent. He stressed that she and Noguerol were legitimately married and had lived together "for more than eight years being both free, and as such have been taken and are commonly reputed." About six months ago, Noguerol "of his own authority and in fact" separated himself from his wife who since then had been deprived "of having him in her house and company and mutual cohabitation." The couple had been living apart, and doña Catalina unjustly found herself "separated from her *posesión*," that is, the intimacy and fellowship she was entitled to. "Your Excellency should order that she be restored and reintegrated above all things in her *posesión* because during the suit she should not be separated from her husband. They have to have a married life together as they had done before."[1]

Mondragón argued that with regard to the dowry of 9,000 ducats and more, a demand had been presented. Doña Catalina should receive one-half of the earnings accumulated during the marriage, "plus the pledge [*arras*] that he [Noguerol] promised, along with the jewels that he vowed when they were *desposados*." The lawyer flatly repudiated doña Beatriz de Villasur's rights to any profits "because she was never married nor veiled nor did she cohabit with the said Francisco Noguerol de Ulloa." He concluded passionately that, above all, doña Catalina de Vergara yearned to have "in her house and company and mutual cohabitation the said Francisco Noguerol de Ulloa, her husband, with whom she was married."[2]

XXXIV
Compel and Force

There is no ecclesiastical judge who can compel
and force him to return to her.
—Miguel de Villanueva

The Fiscal Agreda had worked relentlessly collecting evidence against the deceitful bigamist and delivered the damaging data to the Council of the Indies by 18 July 1557. The judges already had received Noguerol's *probanza*, so they now formally withdrew to study the proofs and deliberate the guilt or innocence of the unusual prisoner. Finally, in early August of 1557, almost five months after Noguerol had surrendered to the court, the Council of the Indies passed a sentence.

"We, Licentiates Tello de Sandoval, Virivesca, Juan Sarmiento, and Villagómez, in the court of the Council of the Indies, in the city of Valladolid on this the ninth day of August of the year of Our Lord 1557, find in the case of the *fiscal* of His Majesty, Licentiate Agreda, against Francisco Noguerol de Ulloa, the following.[1]

"The blame that results against the said Francisco Noguerol de Ulloa in the first charge, for having married twice, we must condemn and do condemn him to exile from this court for a distance of five leagues, and from the *Villas* of Grajal and Saldaña and their jurisdictions the same, for a time of three years. . . . If exile is broken the punishment will be a doubling of the distance, and he must leave to comply within three days of the notification of our sentence. And in like manner we condemn him to 2,000 ducats of gold to be applied in the following form and manner: a third part for the treasury of His Majesty; another part for the transport and provisions of the *doctrineros* that by his order travel to the said Indies, and the other third for the royal constables of this the said council to which effect the said Francisco Noguerol de Ulloa must pay to Ochoa de Luyando within twenty days. . . . And we order that the said Francisco Noguerol de Ulloa not meet in any secret place with the said doña Catalina de Vergara with whom he married the second time, without the penalties established by law.[2]

"With regard to the second article, over registration of the silver, we must absolve and we do absolve the said Francisco Noguerol de Ulloa of the demand and accusation that was put against him on the part of the said *fiscal*. We give him freedom and release him, and for this our sentence is definitive, with costs [the defendant does not have to pay court costs]."[3]

The decision seemed final, but the case or cases were far from over. Although Noguerol was found guilty for marrying twice, banished, and fined, such a verdict would hardly have satisfied doña Beatriz de Villasur. The sentence was mild. The exile of three years from Valladolid, Grajal, and Saldaña was insignificant, and the fine of 2,000 ducats was minimal. Moreover, Francisco Noguerol would once again be free, his property would remain in his possession, and with the exception of the three forbidden places, he would be able to roam uninhibited. The severest punishment was, of course, the interdict regarding any association with doña Catalina de Vergara. Yet, the council did not reiterate its ruling of two years earlier, ordering Noguerol to take up residence with doña Beatriz de Villasur and begin the long overdue marital relations. By exiling Noguerol from Saldaña for three years and also denying him the company of his second wife, the court left the issue of which woman was to have Francisco wide open. That question would have to be decided by an ecclesiastical court.

Miguel de Villanueva did not tarry in a reaction to the judgment, and not surprisingly, the response was twofold. With respect to the silver, Villanueva was delighted: "I say that the sentence given and pronounced by those of this your Royal Council inasmuch as my party was absolved and freed from the demand and accusation that was placed against him regarding the registration of the silver that Lope de Mendieta carried for him and in the remainder that is or can be in favor of my party is good and just, and for it I ask confirmation and a *carta executoria* [enforcement order]."[4]

On the other hand, Noguerol's attorney was thoroughly disgusted with the condemnation to exile and the exorbitant fine placed against his client. Miguel de Villanueva attacked, point by point, the harsh decision, using the original premise that Noguerol's first "marriage and *desposorio*" had been forced upon him and therefore was invalid.

Francisco's remarriage took place only because it had been widely believed, even in Saldaña, that doña Beatriz de Villasur was dead; not an astounding opinion, given the gravity of her illness and the doctors' observation that she would not recover. Furthermore, two highly respected and pious women wrote their brother of his wife's demise, "and they certified the said death as can be seen in the two original letters that he presented, which is enough to excuse him of any blame and guilt because one certified messenger is enough for the Church to give license to marry a second time. So much the better to have two certified letters from his two sisters, professed nuns, religious women, and of much truth and credit."[5]

Miguel de Villanueva argued that Noguerol was obviously a victim of misinformation, and "according to law a much lesser cause is enough to excuse the guilt of a person that marries a second time." And to Francisco's credit, as soon as he had realized that doña Beatriz de Villasur was alive, he separated himself from doña Catalina de Vergara, "and with this he complied with the disposition of canon law, and he was not, nor is he obligated to return to the said doña Beatriz de Villasur, considering that neither was there copulation nor carnal conversation between them, nor did she ever have possession of my party. There is no ecclesiastical judge who can compel and force him to return to her. They can only compel him to complete the original marriage [se vela] with her or enter the Church" [apparently to become a monk]. In conclusion, the eloquent attorney appealed the decision and called for nullification and revocation of the odious parts of the sentence.[6]

The Fiscal Agreda did not let the council wait for his reply. He was satisfied with the decision in favor of the king's treasury, though he objected to the amount to be paid. The fine should have been higher, as befitted the crime; Noguerol, after all, remarried without a legal certification of his first wife's death.

And what was Noguerol's and doña Catalina's reaction to the long-awaited sentence? Relief at the exculpation in the illegal shipment of silver was surely the first emotion of both. But what disappointment must have accompanied the rest of the verdict! The couple had been separated for several long and difficult months, and the rigid stipulation banning any future connection shattered their hopes for an immediate reunion. But dejection, if they felt any, was not an attitude either one of them harbored for long. Their relationship was solid. Love, though never explicitly mentioned, nevertheless emerges from the crumbling documents. Neither one would capitulate and accept their enforced separation. The decision could be, and indeed was, appealed.

XXXV
Leave the House

*I supplicate Your Excellency for permission to leave
the house only to attend Mass;
such would be of great service to God, Our Lord.*
—Francisco Noguerol de Ulloa

The verdict clearly stated that Noguerol was exiled from Valladolid
and should comply within three days. Yet while the appeal was pending, he remained in confinement, and though he petitioned that his
imprisonment be lifted precisely because of the sentence banishing him
from the city, the judges responded by moving him from one house
arrest to another, "on the Calle Nueva de Jerez, that is in the Plaza
Mayor, in the house of the Falcones Viuda." And they warned that he
was not "to break it or leave from it by foot or in any other way," or he
would forfeit the 2,000 ducats held as a bond.[1]

A few days later Francisco returned with a new petition, lamenting
that during the preceding five months he had been unable to go to
Mass. "I supplicate Your Excellency for permission to leave the house
only to attend Mass; such would be of great service to God, Our Lord."
The council could not easily deny such a plea and allowed Francisco to
hear Mass on religious days in the church of Santiago, since he resided
within that parish.[2]

On 23 August 1557, the Council of the Indies, acting on the defendant's appeal, reviewed the records of the litigation between Francisco
Noguerol and Licentiate Agreda. The judges requested more complete
proofs from Noguerol and accorded him twenty days to furnish the
documents. At the same time Francisco's defense was granted a *carta
recetoria*, a writ to take certified testimony. Four days later Miguel de
Villanueva solicited to present the two key letters written by Noguerol's sisters. The council obliged and ordered that a court reporter be
sent to collect the evidence.[3]

Time was running out, and as the twenty-day limit expired, Miguel
de Villanueva returned to the council to plead for an extension, asking
that the count not begin until the court recorder was named. The judges
benevolently conceded the appellant thirty days, beginning on 13 September, to supply the evidence.

XXXVI

Contrary to the Truth

*I have not been induced, nor suborned, nor terrorized
into saying anything contrary to the truth.*
—Doña Ynés Noguerol

Several men sped in mid-September 1557 from Valladolid to San Pedro de las Dueñas with one purpose: to quiz the hitherto silent nuns about the puzzling letters, the apparent cause of Noguerol's misfortunes. It was not easy to obtain testimony from cloistered nuns, but it had become crucial for Francisco's case to attempt an interview with the sisters. If the appeal was to succeed, the attorneys needed to establish the high credibility of the authors of the letters used by Noguerol as proof of his first wife's death. The lawyers stopped first in Sahagún, in the Benedictine monastery, to secure from the abbot, Francisco de Castellanos, a license allowing the nuns to testify.

The following day, fortified with the necessary documentation, Noguerol's brother-in-law Juan de Guzmán, his close associate Benito de Fresneda, as well as a court reporter and two witnesses from Sahagún, arrived in San Pedro de las Dueñas. The Benedictine convent was founded in the eleventh century, and by the middle of the sixteenth century it had flourished into one of the most renowned houses in the region. The abbess, doña Ynés Noguerol, was apprised of the visitors' business and arranged for the questioning. The cloistered nuns would respond through a grille that separated them from the outsiders.[1] Their voices would be heard, but their facial expressions would remain unseen.

The abbess, who was then in her fifties, testified first, and raising her right hand, she swore to tell the truth by the sign of the cross and on the words of the apostles. Doña Ynés remembered very well writing to her faraway brother and, after glancing at the letters that Juan de Guzmán handed to her, agreed that these indeed were the same two missives she and Francisca had penned. The abbess stiffly emphasized, "I have not been induced, nor suborned, nor terrorized into saying anything contrary to the truth" and added that she and her sister were very close and always had written to Francisco together. She also recalled that her brother "responded from the said Indies after having received the said letters."[2] Doña Ynés's taciturnity throughout the short interview was disappointing, though not unforeseen. Her acknowledgment of the authorship of the notes would have to suffice. The veracity of the content was not questioned and therefore not alluded to.

The abbess withdrew to call in her younger sister, doña Francisca, who confirmed everything doña Ynés had already stated. She recalled a letter from Francisco, informing them "now that doña Beatriz de Villasur his wife had died, he had married in the said Indies with doña Catalina de Vergara."[3] What the two women thought about this unplanned twist, doña Francisca did not reveal. Did they ever write their brother telling him that their letters were wrong, that doña Beatriz did not die? No one asked. How did they know that doña Beatriz was dead? No one asked. No one wanted to ask. It was all too clear that doña Ynés and doña Francisca lied to induce their stubborn brother to come home. It was a plot born out of a convenient and almost fatal illness, an idea that probably surged in their minds as they listened to a friend lament the hopelessness of their sister-in-law's condition. The anticipated death did not occur, but the distorted tidings were sailing toward their destination, never followed by a message relating doña Beatriz's miraculous recovery.

Other nuns in the convent came to testify, each one vowing that her association with doña Ynés and doña Francisca would not influence the truthfulness of the deposition. Catalina Ortega, a confidante of the two sisters and Noguerol's childhood friend, remembered hearing that doña Beatriz had died and "that they wrote it to their brother because he was married to her." Catalina Ortega was present when Noguerol visited his sisters shortly after he had returned from Peru. She did not describe the tone of the reunion; she only mentioned that Francisco was "speaking with the aforesaid that he had received their letters . . . about the death of doña Beatriz de Villasur his wife, and that he brought them with him."[4] As to the comportment of the duped *encomendero* as he had confronted his sisters with their fabrication, sor Catalina was mute.

Sister Francisca de la Peña, a young woman of thirty-two, had known doña Ynés and doña Francisca since she had entered the nunnery twenty-two years before. She scrutinized the letters before her and identified the virtually undecipherable script as the handwriting and signatures of the sisters. "At the time that the aforesaid wrote the two letters to the said Francisco Noguerol, it was public knowledge among all the nuns that the said two letters were sent . . . to the Indies advising him of the death of his wife." Word of Noguerol's second nuptials had reached the convent relatively soon after the celebration. "It seemed to her that when de la Gasca came he brought the news." Sor Francisca, like the other witnesses, did not offer more information than she was asked. Yet the report of Noguerol's marriage must have reverberated through the convent, because the nuns had known for some time that doña Beatriz had recovered from her illness.[5]

The inquest at San Pedro de las Dueñas did not unearth fresh evidence, but the defense accomplished its aim. The crucial letters were authenticated by their authors, as well as by other worthy religious women. In order to underscore the credibility and esteem of doña Ynés and doña Francisca, the group of men took the short country road to Grajal de Campos to collect more laudatory statements on the purity of the sisters' characters.

Seventy-year-old Francisco de Basurto praised the women as very honest, and he certainly would trust anything they said. The merchant Juan Fernández, whose daughter dwelled in the convent at San Pedro de las Dueñas, echoed the commendation, as did several clerics who had spoken with the nuns on numerous occasions. One of them, Francisco de la Mota, knew doña Ynés and doña Francisca especially well. For the past forty years he had administered Church sacraments in Grajal and frequently officiated Mass in the nearby convent. For some twenty years he had lived in the house of doña Costanza de Espinosa and was therefore privy to many joys as well as cares that affected the family. He could only eulogize the authors of the snare that caught their unsuspecting brother.[6]

The defense team hurried back toward Valladolid, carrying their latest bundle of vindicating declarations. They must have been content. Although neither Noguerol's sisters, nor anyone else, even insinuated any aberration in the correspondence, the unanimous profession of the nuns' trustworthiness was the trophy the lawyers strove for. With respect to the brazen duplicity, it could be argued, the two women acted out of love. True, they lied, but it was all for a good cause: to reunite their ailing mother with a son she had not seen for many years. In spite of the apparent contradiction, doña Ynés and doña Francisca were reputable women whose communication should have been accepted without a doubt, and Noguerol had been clearly justified in regarding their letters as satisfactory proof of his wife's death.

XXXVII

Shall Not Meet

They shall not meet nor communicate in
any public or suspicious place.
—Diocesan Court of León

The records are silent about the outcome of Noguerol's appeal. But the original verdict of 9 August 1557 clearly stated that his punishment consisted only of a fine and exile from Valladolid, Grajal, and Saldaña, not imprisonment. Francisco Noguerol de Ulloa was freed. It is evident, however, that the Council of the Indies did not pronounce a final ruling in the marriage question. Notwithstanding the favorable depositions substantiating Noguerol's assertion that he had remarried believing his first wife was dead, the secular court was not competent to render a judgment regarding the legitimacy of Noguerol's union with doña Catalina. Only the Church had jurisdiction over such matters.

Shortly after he had returned to Spain and before his arrest, Francisco had petitioned the diocesan court in León for annulment of his first marriage. The ecclesiastical judges of León, however, had ruled against Noguerol and had ordered him to return to doña Beatriz de Villasur. As the litigation before the Council of the Indies came to an end, Francisco, regardless of León's position, attempted to plead his case in the Church courts again.[1]

Doña Catalina de Vergara was from Villaflores, a village about thirty kilometers to the northeast of Salamanca. During the forced separation from her husband, doña Catalina had found needed refuge with her family, though she had often traveled to Valladolid where Noguerol was imprisoned. Although the Church in León had ordered "they shall not meet nor communicate in any public or suspicious place," the couple had remained in contact at least through shared attorneys. Following his release Francisco did not return to León, where the Santanders wielded some influence; instead, he turned toward Salamanca, hoping to find a more favorable attitude among the Church authorities there. The prestige that Francisco and Catalina lacked in León they possessed in Salamanca. They realized, however, that contested decisions in diocesan courts would lead only to delays rather than a final settlement. Only a bold stroke, an appeal to the highest authority in Christendom, could reunite them.[2]

A direct approach of the papacy was unusual, and few would dare to attempt it. The Spanish monarchy zealously exercised the extensive powers for supervision of the Church won by the Catholic monarchs and their grandson, Charles V. The Crown controlled the publication of papal bulls, the appointment to vacant benefices, and had little desire to allow papal intervention in decisions of Spanish diocesan courts. Furthermore, the late 1550s were marked by an inauspicious conflict between Pope Paul IV and King Philip II of Spain. The seventy-nine-year-old pontiff intensely disliked the Hapsburgs and Spain, and his challenge of Spanish power in Naples spurred a military confrontation in the fall of 1556. The Spanish forces, led by the Duke of Alba, the same man who later gained notoriety in the Low Countries, marched northward from Spanish-controlled south Italy and met only with minor resistance on the way. The Duke of Alba threatened to sack Rome, and the militarily weaker pope was forced to sign a peace treaty in September of 1557, though his hate of the foreigners had only deepened.[3]

It was during such strained relations between the Vatican and Spain that Francisco Noguerol and doña Catalina de Vergara directed a petition to the pope. It was a risky maneuver, dictated by desperation, that could incur the wrath of the monarchy as well as the Spanish Church. Even the Inquisition could be brought to bear against them, as bigamists. Yet this tactic seemed the only definitive solution. Doña Beatriz had nothing to lose in prolonging a conclusion to the issue; she had led a life of self-denial and abstinence for years and would never marry anyone else. But Francisco and Catalina, if they wanted to live together as husband and wife, had to act with alacrity.

XXXVIII

Carnal Intercourse

He can present to her the conjugal duty and coming together,
and carnal intercourse as is mandated.
—Apostolic Judge Pedro de Yllanes

A year had passed since Noguerol's release from prison, a year laden with efforts to reunite the unfortunate couple. Finally, the long-awaited courier from Rome arrived, and doña Catalina de Vergara, hopeful after months of patient waiting, went to Salamanca. On 5 November 1558 she handed don Pedro de Yllanes, the local Church *provisor*, an apostolic brief. Don Pedro took the roll in his hands and, in the traditional form, kissed it, placed it over his head, and swore that he would obey and execute its contents. The ceremony was short, though the preliminaries had been worked out several months in advance.[1]

The extensive, two-page document in Latin that had been signed in the pope's presence, and by his order, by Cardinal Gaddi on 27 July 1558 was directed to the ecclesiastical authorities at Salamanca. The brief contained a synopsis of the marital history of doña Catalina de Vergara and Francisco Noguerol de Ulloa, including the separation brought about because a certain Beatriz de Villasur had pretended to have contracted a prior marriage with Francisco. Doña Catalina had petitioned the pope to sanction her union and restore her husband to her. The plea was heard: Pope Paul IV decreed that the couple be rejoined.

Before the ruling could take effect, all parties involved in the case had to be notified of the papal decision. The Church *provisor* at León, Vázquez García de la Bandera, was officially informed and was given a copy of the brief. Doña Beatriz de Villasur's brother brought another copy to his sister, who received it in the presence of scribe Joan de Hinojedo. Francisco Noguerol de Ulloa accepted the brief while Sancho Martín, parish priest of Villaflores, looked on.[2]

Francisco Noguerol had also taken legal steps designed to unite him with his second wife. Simultaneously with doña Catalina de Vergara, he had petitioned the pope to restore him to doña Catalina, stating that they had been publicly married by word, had consummated the marriage, and had cohabited as man and wife for eight years. Francisco had been forced to separate from his wife because a Beatriz de Villasur had pretended to have been connected with him by marriage. Noguerol had invoked statutes governing the rules of the sacrament of marriage developed by Pope Boniface VIII, the precepts dictated by Church councils, as well as general legal practice in Spain in similar disputes.[3] Pope Paul IV had endorsed Noguerol's appeal as well, and Cardinal Gaddi issued a brief on 28 July 1558, ratifying the marriage with doña Catalina de Vergara. The judge in Salamanca again ordered that the letters of enforcement be sent to doña Beatriz de Villasur, as well as to the "very magnificent and reverend *señores provisores*" of the city of León" and to all other figures involved in the extensive case. The messenger of the diocesan court of Salamanca entrusted with delivering the documents to doña Beatriz de Villasur found a tightly closed door.

Doña Beatriz refused to accept the notification that her marriage was rendered invalid. Nevertheless, the public notary, Francisco Gómez, purportedly informed her in private.[4]

A public hearing of doña Catalina's case was scheduled and announced for 16 December 1558. On that day her attorney, Diego Pérez, pleaded before the apostolic judge in Salamanca for "fulfillment of justice." The solicitor charged that the earlier order separating doña Catalina from Francisco Noguerol, preventing "carnal access," was improper, and his client had taken the requisite steps to correct such injustice. A few days later Bartolomé Mateo de Benavides, Noguerol's *procurador*, reinforced doña Catalina's position and called for a fair verdict. The other protagonists did not act. Finally, the word came that Pedro de Yllanes would issue a decision on 24 December 1558.[5]

The apostolic judge appeared on the appointed day in the public hearing place of the diocesan court in Salamanca and announced to those present the restoration of Francisco Noguerol to doña Catalina de Vergara as "directed to us by His Holiness." Don Pedro, however, added a clause that provoked a loud protest from doña Catalina. The cause of her indignation was the judge's edict on sexual intercourse, an ambiguous proposition that would be difficult to monitor. The judge, forced to obey the pope's order, must have had doubts about the propriety of a union tainted by the existence of another woman claiming to be Noguerol's wife.

Doña Catalina's attorney swiftly attacked the unrealistic stipulation. "With regard to the said restitution ordering it to be done with the limitation that there be no copulation, . . . it is unjust, and very grievous in all that is by right. My party is married in fact, in the eyes of the Church, it is a bona fide marriage . . . and thus it should be ordered that the said restitution be and must be entire, and integral, in intercourse as in all the rest."[6]

The tempest caused by his verdict, as well as the seeming indifference of doña Beatriz de Villasur, led the judge to reconsider. On 21 January, Pedro de Yllanes publicly recognized that "regarding the joining together and obligation of carnal intercourse the sentence is incorrect, and is not as it should have been." The repentant judge agreed that "doña Catalina de Vergara appealed correctly, and thus in the rectification of the said grievance we revoke the part of the first decision. . . . To her the said Francisco Noguerol de Ulloa is restituted entirely . . . and that beyond the other marital benefits [*obsequios maritales*] he can present to her the conjugal duty and coming together, and carnal intercourse as it is mandated." And to assure doña Catalina's continual fulfillment, don Pedro ordered "in virtue of Holy obedience, fifty ducats for Holy works, each time he [Noguerol] acts in the contrary."[7]

XXXIX

To Sin Mortally

You have given occasion and cause for the aforesaid Noguerol and doña Catalina de Vergara to sin mortally and offend both God and man.—Miguel Ruiz

Many years later, in 1581, doña Catalina de Vergara wrote a letter to her banker, Simón Ruiz, one of the most important financiers in late-sixteenth-century Spain. "Illustrious Señor . . . I have need of a credit for Rome, of up to thirty escudos, that I have to give there, of those that remain in your power of the money that has been collected in Seville. Make the necessary transaction and take the commission. Please order that whoever takes the credit that the said thirty escudos should be given to Alonso de Ponte, who is *curial* [a member of the Curia] in Rome. And by this letter I ask you to send it with all brevity, for it would be a very distinguished service to me."[1]

What was the reason for transferring this sum to an official of the Roman Curia? Was the payment part of a long-standing debt to Rome, a debt dating to 1558? It is possible that some money had passed between the supplicants and the appropriate officials in Rome who might have been instrumental in swaying the pope to recognize their marriage. The papal brief, at whatever cost it had been obtained, had ended the couple's legal separation, though not without a last attempt by doña Beatriz to frustrate the intolerable and humiliating union. On 15 February 1559 a Miguel Ruiz, empowered to represent doña Beatriz, arrived in the diocesan court in Salamanca and asked for copies of all the previous proceedings. It was not until several months later, on 5 September 1559, that the *procurador* presented the case of his client before the Apostolic Judge Pedro de Yllanes.

"I Miguel Ruiz, in the name of doña Beatriz de Villasur, *vecina* of the *Villa* of Saldaña, *legitimate* wife of Francisco Noguerol *vecino* of the *Villa* of Grajal de Campos, in the suit and matrimonial case that the said my party has treated and treats with the said Francisco de Noguerol and with doña Catalina de Vergara, his *asserted* wife."[2]

The lawyer argued against the questionable legal proceedings of the

Church in Salamanca and called upon the court to heed the sentence pronounced by the Cathedral Church of León, "in favor of doña Beatriz, and against the wishes of her adversaries." Not only did the judges recognize the union between Francisco Noguerol and doña Beatriz de Villasur as a "true matrimony" but they also had ordered Francisco to return to his legitimate wife. Miguel Ruiz insisted that Noguerol had "married the said doña Beatriz de Villasur my party by words, they had made a true marriage, and had dealt with each other as husband and wife . . . by works and words, and in the absence, by letters."[3]

Ruiz was the first person during the protracted proceedings to state that his client had marital relations with Francisco, something that had been always denied by Noguerol and never previously mentioned by doña Beatriz. It seems more a tactical statement of a clever lawyer than a fact. Had it been true, doña Beatriz's case would have benefited from the start by being able to rival doña Catalina's chief weapon: consummation of the marriage.

Miguel Ruiz demanded that the apostolic judge of Salamanca approve and ratify the verdict rendered in León, and he admonished, "You should order that there be grave punishment and censure for both Francisco Noguerol and doña Catalina de Vergara, and that from this time forth they do not treat each other nor converse as husband and wife, nor be in places nor parts suspect."[4]

Miguel Ruiz attacked the "so-called sentence in favor of the said doña Catalina de Vergara," who had no right approaching the courts in this question because a sentence had already been issued upholding the cause of Beatriz de Villasur. "Doña Catalina de Vergara should not be restituted. The said suit should not be proven by her pretense of conjugal possession." Repeatedly, the lawyer of doña Beatriz reprimanded the court for allowing doña Catalina and Francisco to live together, knowing that an earlier interdict existed. The couple's full union was impeded by "divine law." Furthermore, Noguerol "had no authority to act himself to reunite with doña Catalina, for he could act only with the approval of the court of the diocese of León."[5]

The attorney reproached don Pedro de Yllanes: "You should know as a judge in this case, as it is fully and well enough proven on behalf of the said doña Beatriz, one cannot in any fashion in this world, order the restitution regarding carnal copulation." Doña Beatriz's advocate closed his long denunciation with a final rebuke: "You have given occasion and cause for the aforesaid Noguerol and doña Catalina de Vergara to sin mortally and offend both God and man."[6]

FATEFUL DECISIONS

XL
The Principal Houses

*The said Juan del Campo and Juan de Rubayo are encharged
with preparation and paving of the patio of the
principal houses that the said señor Noguerol de Ulloa has
on the plazuela of San Andrés.*—*Agustín de Tapia*

Villaflores, doña Catalina's native village, proved a safe haven during
the endless months of waiting for a decision by the ecclesiastical court
in Salamanca. Yet Villaflores did not suit the recently reunited couple as
a permanent residence. It was a small, unprepossessing agricultural
settlement that could not gratify such urban creatures as Francisco
Noguerol and his wife, who preferred a more stimulating community.
They might have considered other cities but in the end chose to settle in
Medina del Campo, the bustling cosmopolitan market town south of
Valladolid. The choice looked propitious at the time, and they could
not have foreseen the fate of Medina in later centuries, though the first
symptoms of decline appeared during their lifetime.[1]

Since the Reconquista of the Iberian Peninsula from the Moors,
Medina del Campo served as focus for merchants who traveled to the
fairs from all parts of Europe, to trade in wool, livestock, wines, and
the products of Islamic southern Spain. In 1421 the city gained a special
status, as an attempt was made to channel the sales of the Mesta, the
sheep ranchers' guild, through the Medina market in order to control
taxation. The merchants widely used letters of exchange in their transactions, and Medina's bankers established the rates of exchange of the
numerous currencies circulating in the city during the fairs. The city
boasted hundreds of *mesónes*, or inns, to accommodate the visitors;
dozens of notaries and bankers facilitated the commercial transactions;
beautiful churches, wealthy convents, affluent *cofradías*, and even a
public brothel, all formed part of the prosperous community. A great
fire had ravaged Medina in 1521 during the Comunero Revolt, but by
the late 1550s much of the urban center had been rebuilt.[2]

In the last part of the sixteenth century the city suffered several
setbacks. Philip II's decision in 1561 to establish a permanent capital in
Madrid weakened various cities in Castile, and the royal bankruptcy of
1575 seriously hurt Medina's bankers and investors. The growing trade
with the Indies, through Seville, gradually eclipsed the prominence of

Medina del Campo. Merchants and bankers gravitated to the south of Spain, as the profits from commerce with the colonies were increasing while the general economy of Castile was contracting.

Medina del Campo was plagued by recurring disease. The general lack of sanitation, a condition common to most settlements in Europe, was accentuated by overcrowding and inadequate clean water supply. The River Zapardiel, which cut through the city, mostly carried runoff water from the eastern plains, and there were not enough springs to keep the flow strong during the course of the year. Notwithstanding the usual meager trickle, the Zapardiel did occasionally flood, damaging nearby buildings. The riverbed served as a convenient place for dumping garbage, and often human refuse seeped in as well; yet people drank the contaminated water and washed in it. Medina's citizens voiced countless complaints in meetings of the town council about the filth and unhealthy conditions, but little was done to remedy the situation.[3]

The city, one of the largest in Castile, was densely populated. Furthermore, it regularly became overcrowded during the two annual fairs, when it swelled with merchants arriving from all corners of the peninsula, as well as from foreign lands. The inns were often packed beyond capacity, while the streets were piled with garbage. Crowding, transient population, filth, and polluted water served as an ideal breeding ground for most of the common, yet deadly, diseases of the sixteenth-century world.

Noguerol and his wife, however, found Medina del Campo a convenient niche. They would live close enough to Villaflores to oversee properties there, while the proximity to Valladolid and the Royal Chancellery was advantageous for Noguerol, whose legal proceedings and petitions to the Crown occupied much of his time. Medina's experienced bankers and skillful agents would assist with the collection of incomes in Spain, as well as the continued transactions in the Indies. The city's jealously guarded independence in both secular and ecclesiastical matters, and the distance from the diocese of León must have reassured the couple, whose marital situation remained insecure for as long as doña Beatriz grumbled.[4]

Had doña Catalina and her husband traveled from Villaflores taking the road to Cantalapiedra, then to Madrigal and northward to Medina del Campo, they would have perceived the fortress of La Mota in the distance as they approached the city, having the illusion of heading directly into the castle's keep. It was there that King Ferdinand and Queen Isabella paused on more than one occasion during their peripatetic reign. And it was La Mota that witnessed their daughter Juana's first signs of mental instability. Since 1539 the strong castle served as prison for Hernando Pizarro, who spent over twenty years in the fortress, as punishment, in part, for the execution of Diego de Almagro in 1538.[5]

By many accounts, Pizarro's life in La Mota was comfortable enough; he was allowed visitors and he did not even lack female companionship. Hernando's first few years in La Mota were enlivened by doña Isabel de Mercado, who bore him a daughter. When, however, Hernando's pretty young niece, Francisca, daughter and heiress of the conquistador of Peru and an Inca princess, arrived in Medina del Campo in 1552, the calculating uncle promptly married her. The jilted doña Isabel withdrew to a nearby convent, while the attractive bride was installed in La Mota. The unlikely pair had several children and dwelled in the prison together until Hernando was released by Philip II in 1561, about the time that Noguerol and doña Catalina were settling down in the vicinity.[6] It is easy to imagine the two couples meeting to reminisce about mutual friends and old times and battles. Notwithstanding Noguerol's early ties to Diego de Almagro, he did eventually join the Pizarro camp. The two warriors would have enjoyed their talk, and even their wives, in spite of the great difference in age, would have found topics of common interest. Although many men sailed to the Indies and came back to Medina del Campo, there were few women who knew Francisca's native land.

Had Francisco Noguerol and doña Catalina de Vergara arrived in Medina from Valladolid, the view before them would have been even more spectacular. After passing the small village of La Seca, they would have climbed a plateau; then, as they reached the southern edge, they would have seen Medina spread out before them on the plain below, surrounded by wheat fields. The city was split by the westward-flowing Zapardiel River, more an arroyo than a stream in the dry summer months. La Mota loomed on a rock outcrop on the north side of the Zapardiel. During the sixteenth century the city hall, which included the house of the *corregidor* as well as the jail, also stood on the north side, near the church of San Miguel, rather than on the main square, where it was transferred much later. The bridge of the Cordones, next to the San Miguel church, spanned the two riverbanks.

On the south side of the Zapardiel, the *calle* de la Rúa led from the bridge to the principal square and the cathedral *colegiata* of San Antolín. The tower and the already crumbling walls of the royal palace where Isabella the Catholic died only half a century before, in 1504, occupied the southwest corner of the plaza. A main street jutted southward from the plaza in the direction of Salamanca; another road headed southeast toward Avila. Most houses that lined the streets and the main square formed arcades; the upper floors served as residences, while the ground floors were dedicated to commercial activities. The fairs, held twice each year, in May and October, were concentrated in the spacious square. A chapel was constructed into the side of San Antolín church with a balcony overlooking the plaza, where by tradition, open-air Masses were celebrated to consecrate the transactions.[7]

Francisco and doña Catalina chose to build their principal residence on the plaza of San Andrés, on the north side of the Zapardiel, away from the clamor of the fairs. It took several years before the house, a substantial stone structure, was completed. As late as 8 February 1575, two master stone-cutters, Juan del Campo and Juan de Rubayo, were "encharged with the preparation and paving of the patio," which was to be lined with stone columns. The men were ordered to purchase and transport white stone from the quarries of San Miguel del Arroyo in the jurisdiction of Cuéllar, quite a distance from Medina.[8] That stone was extensively used in the walls, castle, churches, and houses of the city of Cuéllar, giving it a permanent white quality. Francisco and Catalina might have been reminded of the *sillar*, a white porous volcanic stone, employed in the buildings of Arequipa.

The wealth from the Indies assured Francisco and doña Catalina a prosperous and respectable existence, though it is unlikely that they ever fully integrated into the top level of society. Two obstacles stood in the way. First, Medina's upper crust was composed almost exclusively of members of seven old families, known as the *siete linajes*, most of whom could trace their origins back to certain local heroes of the early years of the Reconquista from the Moors. The *linajes* were frequently mentioned even in the town council meetings, and only descendants of the seven men could be worthy of prominence, a condition that neither Francisco nor his wife met.[9] More significant perhaps, was the delicate marital situation of the couple, which might have prevented a complete acceptance among the elite. Nor would Francisco's exploits in the Indies guarantee a place at the top. Noguerol was not a famed leader in the conquest of Peru or Chile. He enjoyed a certain notoriety and prestige among his contemporaries, but his accomplishments were minor, and silver alone could not blind the scrupulous patricians to pardon the flaws. Doña Catalina de Vergara, however, fared better, for the Vergaras were not strangers in Medina del Campo. Her brother's inn had prospered in his lifetime, and doña Catalina's children were not hindered from marrying into the *siete linajes*.

XLI

I Am Despoiled

Your viceroy . . . removed from me the said Collaguas Indians,
and their tribute . . . against all right, without cause
or any reason, from which I am despoiled.
—*Francisco Noguerol de Ulloa*

Before Francisco left Peru, probably in 1556, he had obtained permission from the *oidores* of the Audiencia of Lima to be absent from Arequipa for four years to conduct his business in Spain and at the same time to collect tribute from the Indians of the *repartimiento* of Los Collaguas. The viceroy, don Andrés Hurtado de Mendoza, Marqués de Cañete, who took office in 1556, at first had confirmed Noguerol's leave of absence; then, in 1559, he abruptly divested Francisco of his Indians and incorporated them into the patrimony of the Crown. The Marqués de Cañete had arrived in Lima flaunting a large retinue and soon lavished *encomiendas* on his favorites, even relatives, contrary to royal legislation. Denunciations of the viceroy's brazen largesse had roused general indignation in Spain, and calls for review of the prodigal viceroy's conduct echoed in the Council of the Indies. There existed a court order to sequester half of Noguerol's goods, which the Council of the Indies had issued in 1557, and Cañete had seized the opportunity to alleviate the criticism and to appease the king, and had appropriated one of the richest *encomiendas* in the Indies for His Majesty. Noguerol, caught in a subtle maneuver for self-preservation by a corrupt royal official, did not capitulate. He launched several petitions for restitution of the grant, with interest, as well as for extention of his leave of absence, citing unfinished lawsuits, "and having had many illnesses both he and his wife" as "just impediments" to returning to Arequipa. In 1560 the king did order restitution of Los Collaguas and granted Noguerol an extension of his leave for two years. By 1562, however, the issue of Noguerol's delay had become critical, and eager servants of the Crown were vying for the prized *encomienda*. The official Spanish policy mandated physical presence of the *encomendero* within the nearest city to the Indian *repartimiento*, and Noguerol would either have to resume his responsibilities in Arequipa or negotiate another license to collect tribute in absentia for several more years.[1]

Noguerol was not at all inclined to return to Peru, and even the thought of another transatlantic voyage must have nauseated the chronically seasick man. Both he and his wife preferred the unruffled stability of Medina del Campo to the uncertainties and rancor that they had known in Arequipa. Doña Catalina would never reconcile to abandoning her family again; she cherished the company of her children who, during her decade-long absence in the New World, had reached adulthood. Yet Francisco would not relinquish the handsome income from the Collaguas without a struggle.

Noguerol decided to negotiate with the Crown. In 1562 he petitioned the king for a license to collect tribute in Spain, complaining to His Majesty of the losses he had suffered because the Marqués de Cañete had appropriated his *encomienda* for the Crown in 1559: "Your viceroy . . . removed from me the said Collaguas Indians, and their tribute . . . against all right, without cause or any reason, from which I am despoiled. . . . I have received and receive a very notorious grievance, because I did not come, nor am I in these said kingdoms of my own free will, but forced and oppressed . . . to respond to the said accusations and face the suits that your *fiscal* and doña Beatriz de Villasur have entered against me." Francisco reminded Philip II that the monarch had rewarded others who had returned to Spain from Peru, men "like Tapia, *vecino* of Arévalo, and Captain Segura, and others, giving them license to collect tributes of their *repartimientos* for eight years," and he added pointedly, "They were not as early in that land as I, nor were they to be found later in the rebellion of Francisco Hernández Girón."[2] Noguerol naturally described the plunder he had suffered for defending the Crown against the rebels and demanded 20,000 ducats as compensation.

In this petition, while lamenting the injustices he had suffered, Francisco, perhaps unwittingly, betrayed his own duplicity. "It was some six years ago, more or less, being in the said realms, in my house and with Indians that in your royal name I have been entrusted, that a royal provision arrived directed to your audiencia and justices . . . ordering the sequestration of my goods . . . saying that I was married according to the order of the Holy Mother Church . . . with doña Beatriz de Villasur, and that I had turned to marry a second time, she being alive . . . with the said doña Catalina de Vergara. . . . Thusly the said provision came to my notice, and being so advised of it and of the accusations . . . both by your *fiscal* as well as by the said doña Beatriz . . . I came to this realm to respond to the said accusations with license from the Marqués de Cañete."[3]

Francisco's repeated protestations during his trial of having known nothing of doña Beatriz's charges until he reached Panama was an evident perjury. Did Noguerol also lie when he insisted that he remarried in "truthful ignorance?" Letters refuting doña Beatriz's demise could have reached Arequipa before the wedding took place, yet no evidence or even hints of such possibility ever surfaced.

Having reviewed Noguerol's petition, Philip II granted him, on 21 March 1562, the "full return with the fruits and rents" of the *repartimiento*, but regarding an indemnity for losses the *encomendero* sustained during the rebellion of Francisco Hernández Girón in 1554, the answer was a curt *"no hay lugar"* (there is no place).[4] For the next eight years Noguerol continued to receive remuneration from the *encomienda*. Furthermore, the king later also awarded him annual rents in the amount of 300,000 maravedis from sales taxes (the *alcabala*) of the city of Medina del Campo, although it is unclear why he had been favored with such income.[5]

XLII
And Gave Freedom

They have given to him, and gave freedom
from the said subjection and servitude.
—*Francisco Noguerol de Ulloa and doña Catalina de Vergara*

Noguerol's link with the Indies was not abruptly broken but continued for some time, in spite of the distances and the difficulties in communications. As late as the first of December of 1575, almost twenty years after he left Peru, Francisco met with his notary, Agustín de Tapia, regarding a shipment of seven silver bars that Alonso Gómez, treasurer of the cathedral of Lima, had sent five years earlier through Panama. The original source of the bullion was income from the *repartimiento* of Los Collaguas. The ingots, numbered and imprinted with Noguerol's name, had been registered in the port of Nombre de Dios on 2 March 1570, then transported on the ship *Nuestra Señora de la Consolación* to Seville. The silver was sold in 1575 by officials of the Casa de Contratación for 820,555 maravedis, and the money was deposited in a safety box.[1]

But before Noguerol's agent could transfer to him the proceeds from the sale of the metal, the last benefit from the Peruvian *encomienda*,

Philip II requisitioned all available cash at the Casa de Contratación in Seville, including Francisco's money. The king was facing grave financial difficulties, and precisely in 1575 he was forced to declare bankruptcy. Noguerol's fervent protests that the silver was his, from his Collaguas Indians "by reason of the *concordia* that was made between His Majesty and me," were to no avail.[2]

Francisco could console himself with the knowledge that his economic situation was significantly healthier than the king's. His investments in Spain generated a good income, even if occasionally dilatory, providing him and doña Catalina with secure prosperity. The time had come to sell any remaining property in Peru, and it was with that intent that Francisco returned to Agustín de Tapia, who drafted a power of attorney on 18 December 1575 for Diego Hernández de la Cuba, an *encomendero* in Arequipa, and Gonzalo Gómez de Buitrón, *mestizo* son of conquistador Gómez de León, authorizing the bearers to represent Noguerol. He added several clauses with specific instructions for the agents. They were to sell his *casas principales* in Arequipa, property that bordered the *ranchería* of Indians and the *calles Reales*. They were entrusted with collection of several outstanding debts, including 1,500 pesos in gold that the viceroy, the Marqués de Cañete, had appropriated "for the works of the monastery of San Francisco of Arequipa." Noguerol claimed this was his money "because of the agreement that His Majesty made regarding the *repartimiento* of Collaguas Indians." Furthermore, Francisco directed his representatives to gather some 25,000 pesos in gold and silver, from one Galleguillos, a majordomo who in his absence had collected tribute from the Collaguas Indians and had administered Francisco's haciendas for a period of four years. Diego Hernández de la Cuba and Gonzalo Gómez de Buitrón could deal with both the Collaguas and Ubinas Indians regarding any lawsuits that might be pending in the courts.[3]

Most of Francisco's and doña Catalina's assets had been invested in Spain in *censos* and *juros*. These bonds had become a favorite form of investment in sixteenth-century Spain because they provided easy credit to borrowers and a relatively secure means of income to investors. They were also a constant source of litigation and proved to be, in the long run, detrimental to the Spanish economy as a whole. Many contemporaries, especially churchmen, deplored the widespread use of *censos* and *juros*.[4]

The *censo* that Lope de Mendieta had bought in the 1550s from the Duke of Medina Sidonia was bringing in an annual return of 1,000 ducats (375,000 maravedis). The collection of the money was not always easy, as the payments were often in arrears, obliging Noguerol to send his agents to Andalusia to expedite the transaction. The 125,000 maravedis annual return from a *juro* of the *Villa* of Carmona proved equally encumbered, causing Noguerol's agents in the south to resign in exasperation. In 1576 Francisco entrusted these vexing matters to his longtime associate and experienced majordomo, Benito de Fresneda.[5]

Regularly, three times a year, Francisco collected 100,000 maravedis of royal rents in Medina del Campo, as granted by Philip II, income that proceeded from the sales tax.[6]

In addition to the royal rents, the *censo* on the estate of the Duke of Medina Sidonia, and the *juro* of the *Villa* of Carmona, Noguerol held a *censo* "on the persons and estate of Señor Francisco de Dueñas," one of the most prominent citizens of Medina del Campo. The *censo*, of 1,000 ducats, was placed by doña Ana Quadrado, the mother of Francisco de Dueñas. Noguerol received two payments per year, each of 139,687 maravedis, payable on Christmas Eve and the day of San Juan (June 24). Another *censo*, of don Juan de Bracamonte, señor of the *Villa* of Peñaranda, and his wife, doña Ana de Avila, yielded 600 ducats annually.[7]

On 29 August 1575 Noguerol purchased a short-term *censo* issued by the village of Peñaranda de Bracamonte. Francisco supplied the town with 2,500 ducats, valued at 937,500 maravedis, while the Alcalde Mayor Gómez Arias; *alcaldes ordinarios* Matheo Carmona and Andrés de San Miguel; *regidores* Francisco Gómez, Cristóval de la Huerta, Miguel Barvero, and Francisco Gutiérrez, as well as several merchants, lawyers, and even a shoemaker and an apothecary, pledged to ultimately pay off the debt.

On 3 September 1576, approximately one year after the loan, the townsmen Cristóval Martín and Simón Seco brought "a great quantity and sum of reales that are in some sacks" to Medina del Campo; the 2,500 ducats were returned, plus an interest of 66,964 maravedis. Following a formal legal procedure, the *censo* was terminated.[8]

Francisco Noguerol was a busy man; his investments were numerous and required much supervision to ensure a regular flow of income. The building and improving of the house where the couple resided, as well as the acquisition of other real estate in and around Medina del Campo, also needed attention. And there were other issues that Francisco and doña Catalina turned to. In a relatively short span of time they freed two slaves, a rather rare act.

On May 1575 Francisco met his notary regarding Ana Rodríguez, a black woman who had grown up in the household. She had served the couple faithfully, and for that reason and "other just causes that moved him," Noguerol freed her. The document of manumission bestowed on Ana complete freedom, as if she had not been born a slave. However, there followed an interesting stipulation: "the said Ana Rodríguez from now on goes from this said *villa* and is not nor resides in it" for a distance of a circle with a fifteen-league radius of Medina, and as an afterthought, the notary added in small letters above the line, "nor of the place of Villaflores, jurisdiction of Salamanca." If Ana failed to comply, she would forfeit her freedom and again become Noguerol's slave. As she could not read, the requirement was fully explained to her, and the witnesses, Benito de Fresneda, Diego García, and Gregorio López, signed for her.[9]

Why insist that Ana Rodríguez leave Medina del Campo and even stay away from Villaflores? It was a curious banishment, and perhaps it stemmed from doña Catalina's resentment of her husband's past indiscretion. Doña Catalina was certainly instrumental in granting freedom to another loyal servant, Francisco Noguerol, *mozo*, a *moreno* or light-skinned black, born in their house about twenty-two years before. The couple jointly commissioned Agustín de Tapia to draw up the papers on 14 February 1576, whereby "they have given to him, and gave freedom from the said subjection and servitude." They renounced all future claims and left out stipulations that might reverse the manumission.[10]

The recently freed Francisco Noguerol would have been born in Peru in 1554, not long before Francisco and doña Catalina had embarked on the voyage to Spain. The mother, one of their household slaves, had traveled with the infant and must have served doña Catalina during the early years of separation from her husband. The name of the slave, including the addition of the word *mozo* (the younger, but it can also just mean young man), implies possible paternity by the *encomendero*, although Noguerol never acknowledged the young Francisco as his son.

Why would doña Catalina have tolerated the presence of a bastard child, conceived after the couple had been married for several years? Perhaps, knowing that she would not have any more children herself and regretting the lost opportunity of raising to adulthood her son and daughter by Doctor Tejada, she had felt no animosity toward the little boy. In time, she might have grown fond of him, and that coupled with her Christian beliefs, had prompted her to beg her husband to free young Francisco. Freeing slaves, a valuable status symbol, was not a common occurrence. If their master relinquished them, they probably were old, infirm, and unable to work. But Ana Rodríguez and Francisco Noguerol *mozo* were both young and healthy, and they represented an estimable property that Noguerol and doña Catalina would not have surrendered without strong reason.

XLIII

Perpetual Memory

That there be a perpetual memory of our names.
—*Francisco Noguerol de Ulloa*

The fear of being forgotten pervaded the Spanish character of the sixteenth century. Death itself or the act of dying did not frighten the Spaniard nearly as much as oblivion, and some of the extraordinary exploits of the Age of Discovery were in part motivated by the often repeated triad: gold, God, and glory. The celebrated actors of reconnaissance and conquest have thrilled the popular mind: they and their endeavors have endured. The secondary figures, however, have been sentenced to obscurity.[1]

Noguerol hardly perceived himself as an insignificant soldier, although he must have recognized that his accomplishments in the Indies were less conspicuous than the deeds of some of his famous companions. But Francisco suffered from one weakness that many men feared: he had no legitimate children to carry the family name and history into the next generation, and the attempt to overcome this troublesome defect occupied his last years.

There were two ways in which Noguerol could solve the dilemma: he could set up an entailed estate, the *mayorazgo*, and he could endow the Church. Earlier, the entail had been largely a monopoly of the aristocracy, but in 1505 the Cortes of Toro had extended the privilege to the middle classes. By the mid-sixteenth century numerous families, becoming wealthy in the Indies, in government service, or in commerce, were founding *mayorazgos*. On the one hand, by concentrating wealth in a single heir, the system impoverished the younger children, yet it also promoted social mobility, as the more successful recipients climbed upward in society.[2]

Francisco Noguerol did establish a *mayorazgo* in 1576, and at the same time both he and doña Catalina erected a chapel where they desired to be entombed together. The chapel was intended as a burial site for future holders of the *mayorazgo* as well. For although Noguerol lacked legitimate offspring, he did not lack an heir.

Francisco's and Catalina's residence shared a small square with the Dominican monastery of San Andrés el Real, founded in 1406 by King Juan I of Castile. In the 1570s about twenty monks dwelled in San Andrés, as well as numerous other men: novices, servants, and lay brothers. The church had collapsed a few years earlier and had to be rebuilt. In March of 1576 the provincial of the Dominican order in Castile, authorized, from Valladolid, the brothers of San Andrés to search for endowments of chapels and chaplaincies, in order to help fund the reconstruction of the ruined temple. To Francisco and his wife, the neighboring priory offered immortality in the guise of a splendid chapel, and the couple swiftly proceeded to realize their dream.[3]

On 14 June 1576 Francisco Noguerol, "one of the conquerors of the realms and provinces of Peru," met with the prior, Friar Juan Sánchez, and other monks in the chapter hall of San Andrés. Francisco addressed the assembled brothers, declaring that he and his legitimate wife "in consideration of the fact that death is certain for all creatures," and desirous to serve God and of "someone to pray . . . for our souls and our successors, that there be a perpetual memory of our names, not for the honor of this world, but for the glory and honor of God our Lord . . . and for other reasons that animate us,"[4] wished to contribute to the building and the work of the church and monastery. Noguerol then presented the requisite license from Pedro Fernández, the provincial of the Dominican order.

Francisco met with the prior and the other monks several times in the following days to negotiate the minute details of the endowment. Finally, on 19 June 1576, the contract was ready. Francisco Noguerol de Ulloa affixed his distinctive signature to the agreement, and the prior, along with the friars present, signed on behalf of the monastery.

The monks guaranteed to Francisco and doña Catalina, and their heirs forevermore, the old sacristy and the so-called Ornazina chapel. The friars pledged a daily Mass of the Holy Spirit for the couple as well as for the conversion of the Indians of Peru. The Mass would take place at a specified time: in the six months from October through March it was to be heard at 11 o'clock, and from April through September at 10 o'clock. While work and embellishments of the chapel were in progress, the Mass was to be said before the altar of Our Lady. Noguerol and his wife also provided for four major chanted Masses with full sermons each year: on the eve of the Day of the Conception of Our

Lady, the Day of the Feast of Saint John the Evangelist, Resurrection Sunday, and on the second day of Pascua of the Holy Spirit.

The couple, jealous of their privileges, explicitly stated that no other chapel in the church should ever be in a more conspicuous place than their own. The monastery allowed the Noguerols to remove the heralds and arms that adorned the site and to replace them with their own. Did Francisco and doña Catalina ever wonder if some day in the future their perpetual resting place would be despoiled and would pass to a higher bidder? The principal donation to San Andrés was 500 ducats (187,500 maravedis), 300 to be paid immediately, the remainder after the construction of the chapel. In addition, 15,000 maravedis per year were to subsidize daily Masses until the donors' deaths. Another 1,500 maravedis would be dispensed yearly from the estate for the cloth and the cleaning of the chapel following the interment. The monastery would collect an annual rent of 100,000 maravedis, or one-third of the 300,000 maravedis *juro* that Noguerol received from the sales tax revenues of Medina del Campo.

Francisco spelled out in great detail how this income was to be disbursed. Half the money, some 50,000 maravedis, were set aside for the four annual chanted Masses; 3,000 maravedis were earmarked for the prior, for his supervision and administration of the endowment. The rest would defray the costs of daily Masses and prayers, and of the making of two huge standing wax candles designed to burn all day on Holy Thursday.

The convent and the prior were responsible for hiring a sacristan, an outsider, who would care for the silver, gold, jewels, ornaments, and cloths of the sepulcher of the chapel. The sacristan, in addition to the customary recompense, would each year be furnished with a hooded garment of Toledo cloth. The prior and the patron of the monastery pledged to audit the sacristan's activities. Francisco, concerned that the couple's eternal resting place might become a passageway between the outside and main part of the church, directed that a grille with a gate be installed.

Don Francisco and doña Catalina were anxious about two eventualities: the loss of the royal rent, and future failure of the Dominicans to uphold the contract. To protect the agreement in the first instance, they bound the prior to meet with the patron of the chapel and the town's *corregidor* if a monarch changed the payments. In such case, the endowment could be removed and reinvested at a similar rate to maintain the annual income. Should the Dominicans neglect their obligations or attempt to modify the provisions, then all "from that time forth will pass to the church of the place of Villaflores." Under the supervision of the bishop of Salamanca the endowment would be transferred, and the Dominicans would have to cede the original 500 ducats to the church of Villaflores, where a new chapel would be set up.[5]

Francisco strove to fend off oblivion and to glorify his success in the Indies by erecting an imposing memorial to himself and doña Catalina, and indeed he was, at least partially, successful. In the late eighteenth century the cleric-historian of Medina del Campo, Julián Ayllón, admired the handiwork: "He left a remarkable monument of his piety in a beautiful chapel that he founded in the church of San Andrés, of Dominican Fathers of this *Villa*, very well endowed, with decorous frescos on the walls and vaults, that represent the creation of man, and various apostles and saints."[6]

XLIV

Carry the Name

My wish is that the said don Diego Noguerol
that was previously called Tejada, and all the other people
that succeed in this vínculo, mayorazgo *and* patronazgo,
carry the name . . . Noguerol de Ulloa, with my arms.
—Francisco Noguerol de Ulloa

Age and illness were undermining the vigor of the old conquistador. Francisco was in his seventies, and his signature, once strong and energetic, seemed fragile and shaky. In the late summer of 1580 he met with the notary, Yñigo de Argandoña, in order to revise his will. In addition to Noguerol and the notary, four trustworthy men—two merchants, an innkeeper, and a barber—were present to witness the preparation, as well as the signing, closing, and sealing of the testament.

The total value of the assets in Francisco's estate reached 90,000 ducats. Noguerol had invested most of the property in *censos* and *juros*, although he also owned real estate: the mill of Pico in Guarena, a "quantity of land and some principal houses and two garden plots in Villaflores,"[1] and the land and houses on the plaza of San Andrés in Medina del Campo. Furthermore, Francisco had amassed silver, jewelry, and substantial furnishings. His debts, on the other hand, were

meager: 1,000 ducats each for dowries for doña María Osorio Noguerol and doña Blanca Noguerol Sandoval, his nieces, and a more substantial sum to doña Elena de Tejada, doña Catalina's daughter.

Noguerol's feebleness did not affect his wits as he dictated subtle
instructions to Yñigo de Argandoña. Uppermost on his mind were the
financial viability of the entailed estate and the future possessors of his
legacy. Francisco was childless; however, he explicitly and deliberately
disinherited his own relatives. The old man turned to his wife's family
and chose doña Catalina's grandson, Diego, as his principal heir. Don
Diego de Tejada was the youngest son of don Antonio de Tejada and
doña Juana de Salazar. His parents had both died, and his grandmother
and her husband cared for the child. Don Diego would not inherit the
estate, however, until the death of doña Catalina de Vergara.

Noguerol meticulously outlined the succession in the eventuality of
don Diego's death. If he left legitimate children, the *mayorazgo* would
pass to his eldest son, then along the traditional line of males, then
females, oldest to youngest. Should Diego die without issue, the estate
would shift to his sister, doña Catalina de Vergara, named after her
grandmother, and her descendants. If doña Catalina (the younger)
passed away without heirs, her aunt, doña Elena de Tejada and her
offspring would inherit the *mayorazgo*. If doña Elena remained childless, the estate would return to the other brothers of Diego and Catalina, first Juan de Tejada, and last Antonio de Tejada. Apparently,
neither Francisco nor doña Catalina fancied these two grandsons, for
in spite of the general preference throughout the will for male heirs,
Francisco skipped the two brothers of don Diego and named their sister
and aunt first before turning back to them. If all the above died without
progeny, then the *mayorazgo* fell to the next nearest relative of doña
Catalina de Vergara, Noguerol's wife, again males taking precedence
over females.

And "in case God Our Lord gives no relatives to doña Catalina de
Vergara . . . then the estate . . . goes to the Cofradía de la Santa
Caridad . . . to have and enjoy and use forevermore . . . to distribute the
income each year to the poor and in doing good works for my soul and
doña Catalina de Vergara's."[2] Noguerol, unflinching, ignored his own
relations, other than dowries for two nieces. His bitterness toward his
family was not assuaged with the passage of time, nor did the proximity
of death kindle forgiveness. Any relative of doña Catalina or charity
would be preferable to his own kin.

Francisco disinherited the Noguerols, but he was heedful that his
name not expire with his body: "My wish is that the said don Diego

Noguerol that was previously called Tejada, and all the other people that succeed in this *vínculo, mayorazgo* and *patronazgo,* carry the name . . . Noguerol de Ulloa, with my arms."[3] Should the heirs violate the stipulation, they would lose the estate, and the rents would henceforth be applied to the support of the poor in the Smallpox Hospital of Medina del Campo. None of the entailed estate was ever to be encumbered by the successors of Francisco Noguerol.

Francisco, once a victim of royal bankruptcy, attempted to safeguard the *juro* of Medina del Campo, the foundation stone of the endowment of both the chapel and the *mayorazgo,* from expropriation. He authorized the patron of his chapel and the prior of San Andrés, in case a future monarch tampered with the *juro,* to remove the deposit from the strongbox of the monastery and reinvest the original endowment in a more secure fashion.[4]

XLV
Interred in My Chapel

Whenever my God is served to carry me from
this present life, my body should be interred in my chapel.
—Francisco Noguerol de Ulloa

Francisco Noguerol de Ulloa lived for another year, but as the autumn air of 1581 swept the plains of Castile, the colorful protagonist of many and diverse battles lay dying, secure in his faith and content with the provisions safeguarding his legacy.

Following Francisco's death, doña Catalina de Vergara, dressed in mourning, met on the first day of October 1581 in a solemn public ceremony with the notary Yñigo de Argandoña; the *corregidor* of Medina del Campo, Doctor Gante del Campo; and the men who had witnessed Francisco Noguerol's testament. The notary produced the sealed document, opened it, and presented it for examination. The witnesses carefully checked the signature and swore that it was authentic.

Doña Catalina had little time to grieve following her husband's death as she faithfully executed his instructions. "Whenever my God is served to carry me from this present life, my body should be interred in my chapel . . . according to the wishes and command of my wife doña

Catalina de Vergara."[1] Francisco's widow did see to it that his remains were borne by the *señores beneficiados* of the Cabildo Mayor of Medina del Campo the short distance from his house to the monastery of San Andrés el Real, while escorted by a procession of several religious brotherhoods of Medina del Campo: the Santa Vera Cruz, the Caridad, the Angustias, the Ánimas de Purgatorio, and the Santíssimo Sacramento. Doña Catalina duly rewarded the bearers of her husband's body as well as each of the attendant brotherhoods. She also arranged for 1,000 Masses in various churches of the city and selected and clothed twelve paupers in fulfillment of Francisco's orders.

The reading and publishing of Noguerol's will required doña Catalina's presence, although there were few surprises for the widow. Francisco designated doña Catalina de Vergara the sole heir and executor of the testament, with full power to administer the estate that would eventually pass to her grandson don Diego. Noguerol took great care to spell out exactly how the property was amassed, stating explicitly that doña Catalina had carried into the marriage 20,000 ducats of her own, while his assets were worth 24,000 ducats. The remainder, that would add up to the current figure, constituted joint earnings. Was Noguerol preoccupied about a contesting of the will?

The old conqueror, clearly manifesting his affection for don Diego, his ultimate heir, bequeathed to the boy his swords, his coat of mail, his weapons, harnesses, straps, and other gear, as well as his horses—all the paraphernalia of his past glory.

Francisco remembered various servants with monetary gifts and freed two women slaves, though one would not gain her liberty until doña Catalina's death. Noguerol's longtime associate and majordomo, Benito de Fresneda, the man who had helped defend Noguerol against doña Beatriz and the Fiscal Agreda some thirty years earlier, and who had served as his agent in Seville overseeing the irksome Andalusian investments, received fifty ducats.[2]

In his will Noguerol contrived to resolve the question of the long-standing debts owed him in Arequipa, capital that he had been trying to retrieve since at least the mid-1570s, without success. He reconciled himself to the loss of this revenue, but not without a posthumous revenge. In an ingenious clause of his testament, Noguerol, under the guise of altruism, arranged for future discord and litigation. He empowered the *corregidor* of Arequipa and the guardian of the monastery of San Francisco in that city to join together and to assume collection of the "gold, silver, jewels, and precious stones" that were owed by Alonso de Galleguillos, Noguerol's majordomo, and others. Noguerol instructed the men to divide the booty into three equal parts: one portion was to be accorded to the Collaguas Indians he had held as *encomendero* "and their heirs." A similar share was destined for the Ubinas Indians, that he also at one time possessed. The last third was to be dispensed and used as the *corregidor* of Arequipa and the Franciscan guardian saw fit.[3]

Noguerol's clever stratagem pitted *encomenderos* against government officials, the Church against the Crown, as they battled each other into the next century. The old man must have chuckled, knowing well the repercussions of a provision fraught with obstacles and undermined by inherent rivalry. And his widow also must have appreciated the irony in such an arrangement, as she listened to her husband's words being recited by the notary.

The funeral procession was Noguerol's last journey. His will ensured that all present at the ceremony would remember that day, as well as his past exploits. Noguerol, who was born near the beginning of Spain's golden age of exploration and discovery, had ended his long career at the apex of the empire, when Philip II annexed Portugal. In his youth Francisco had shared a strong desire for independence with hundreds and thousands of other young men of his generation who had rushed overseas, full of expectations and illusions. Many of those who had valiently set forth died of sickness or starvation, or were shipwrecked on the journey; some had perished at the hands of native Americans defending their lands against the bearded invaders; others had lost their lives in fratricidal strife, which had pitted Spaniards against each other. Yet in spite of such obstacles, many had reached their destination and settled in towns they had built, married, and had children. Francisco's experiences were not unique. With the exception of his accidental bigamy, almost all the other events of his life were common for that time and place, certainly for other *encomenderos*. Even his return to Spain was not unusual. Many *indianos* came back to their home towns and their families, bringing with them lesser or greater wealth, impressing those who had never ventured beyond the Iberian shores. The true legacy that Francisco Noguerol de Ulloa left to posterity lies in the scattered and often fragmentary documents, which together give life to a distant age.

XLVI
From the Estate

Would never return to ask for anything else
from the estate.—Doña María Osorio Noguerol

>●<

In the first weeks following Noguerol's death, doña Catalina de Vergara attended to various matters, the normal religious observances that were expected, as well as the business and legal demands associated with the death of a spouse. And, as the sole proprietor, she supervised a complex set of economic activities. Yet she must have welcomed this bustle, a distraction from the sense of loss that enveloped her. Her marriage to Francisco of more than thirty years knew both felicity and adversity and had survived a potentially lethal contest that in the end solidified a relationship already strong. The couple had shared much on both sides of the Atlantic; they had fought together to preserve their marriage; and finally their years in Medina del Campo transpired in relative calm. Doña Catalina, though neither prostrate with grief nor alone, must have missed Francisco's company.

Shortly after the funeral, doña Catalina fulfilled Noguerol's obligation to settle dowries on his two nieces. She instructed Benito de Fresneda to deliver 1,000 ducats to María Osorio Noguerol, who was then married to García Rodríguez de Montalvo, a *regidor* of Medina del Campo. Doña María, who finally collected a dowry promised her in 1573, readily signed a receipt stating she would "never return to ask for anything else from the estate" and pledged that if she died without heirs, the 1,000 ducats would revert to the children of Elena de Tejada and Juan de Zuazo.[1]

Before the year was over, doña Catalina paid out another dowry, one that Francisco had promised his niece, doña Blanca Noguerol Sandoval, in Grajal de Campos in 1562. In the meantime, however, doña Blanca had passed away, and it was her husband who, in the name of the children, collected the 1,000 ducats.[2]

XLVII

He Had Consummated

He had consummated with me the marriage.
—*Doña Beatriz de Villasur*

Notice of Francisco Noguerol's death reached within a few weeks various corners of Spain and did not elude the ears of an interested party in a small commercial town to the north. Doña Beatriz de Villasur had been living quietly in Saldaña since the reunion of her husband and doña Catalina, collecting from Francisco 150 ducats annually, as mandated by the court. Doña Beatriz had never fully accepted the decision of the ecclesiastical judge in Salamanca, a decision she considered unjust and sinful, yet she could do little to interfere. She was a frail and ailing woman, but infinitely patient. Soon after Francisco died, doña Catalina terminated the support payment to doña Beatriz; after all, she had no obligations toward her rival. But she was wrong.

Doña Beatriz de Villasur grasped the chance she had been waiting for and went back to the courts shortly after Noguerol's death. She returned to Salamanca to appeal the ruling handed down by Pedro Yllanes in 1558 and succeeded in overturning that decision. She filed a petition in Medina del Campo on 16 February 1583 and, emboldened by Francisco's inability to counter her allegations, she announced "he [Noguerol] had consummated with me the marriage" and asserted that they had lived together as man and wife for two and a half to three years. He later went to the Indies and did not take his wife along. "There he earned as joint marital property [*bienes gananciales*] some 200,000 ducats in *juros* and rents, jewels, silver and gold." Doña Beatriz therefore demanded one-half of Noguerol's estate.[1]

Doña Catalina de Vergara, undaunted by the Church's reversal, rejected outright doña Beatriz's claims and resolved to end the issue once and for all. Doña Catalina hired an attorney, Luis de Salcedo, to defend her marriage and, most of all, the inheritance of her young grandson. Luis de Salcedo initiated the rebutter in his client's name on 11 March, stating that don Francisco was never married to doña Beatriz in the eyes of the Church, that he had never carried her to his house, and that they never began true married life. Without copulation, the marriage had never been validated and it was therefore impossible to speak of any combined possessions. "Thus, the said doña Beatriz de Villasur should never get half the joint property she asked for."[2]

The lawyer further argued: "If don Francisco Noguerol de Ulloa had received payment for dowry, it was very little, and he later spent it, and used it up, and thus you cannot say that with this dowry he had received and acquired the goods and estate, because it had been all previously virtually spent." Noguerol amassed his true estate after he had married doña Catalina, and there were no funds from Beatriz de Villasur left. Luis de Salcedo pointed out that "to the day he died," Noguerol paid an annual stipend to doña Beatriz, and she presently "has goods and an estate with which she can honestly live." In closing, the attorney asked the justice of the city of Medina del Campo for a term of three years in order to prepare, in the Indies, doña Catalina's defense.

Doña Beatriz de Villasur immediately appealed this extension at the Royal Audiencia and Chancellery in Valladolid. She was not a young woman anymore and could not afford the wait. The chancellery granted doña Beatriz's appeal, although only partially, reducing the period to two and a half years, a small concession in a race against time. Doña Catalina was also aware of the drawbacks if the dispute lingered on. She, too, was not young and feared the consequences of a prolonged battle. The estate was in jeopardy, and if the litigation continued into the next generation, Francisco's legacy could be fractioned and destroyed. The two women, pressured by age and willing to compromise, decided to negotiate.

Doña Beatriz hired and endowed with extensive powers to represent her Gregorio Díaz Bermúdez, a *vecino* of Saldaña, and Martín de Cárdenas, the prebend of the cathedral church of Salamanca. Both men journeyed back and forth between Saldaña and Medina del Campo in mid-1583 in order to mediate a final accord in a controversial and protracted contest. The principal obstacle, Francisco Noguerol de Ulloa, was gone, and his wives seemed disposed to come to terms.

In November of 1583 the two agents parted from doña Catalina, entrusted with her binding offer to doña Beatriz. They set out immediately for Saldaña to present it to their party. The arbitrators were satisfied with the deal they struck but needed doña Beatriz's approval and acceptance to seal the agreement.

The preamble of the document stressed the importance of reaching an understanding in the costly conflict, especially given the quality of the parties involved. Doña Catalina de Vergara proposed that in return for a financial settlement, doña Beatriz de Villasur and her heirs drop forever all charges against her and her heirs. Elaborate safeguards were written into the contract to prevent either party from reinitiating the dispute in the future, and the agents Díaz Bermúdez and Cárdenas were charged with ending the ongoing lawsuits.

The recompense doña Catalina promised her adversary in exchange for peace, though only a fraction of doña Beatriz's original demand, nevertheless far exceeded the amount Cristóval de Santander had paid to outfit his derelict son-in-law for overseas adventures. Doña Catalina de Vergara would altogether give doña Beatriz de Villasur 3,700 ducats, valued at 1,387,500 maravedis. The intermediaries carried with them to Saldaña 2,000 ducats in cash. The remaining 1,700 ducats were to be remitted on the day of Santiago in July 1584. Doña Catalina insisted that the agents contact doña Beatriz within fifteen days from the date of the document and then report to her how the offer was received. Should doña Beatriz refuse the proposition, then the 2,000 ducats were to be returned in full to doña Catalina, who warned the men that she was not disposed to increase the total sum. As a guarantee of full compliance with the terms of the bargain, doña Catalina requested a *carta executoria* from the king to enforce forever the propitious agreement.[3]

Gregorio Díaz Bermúdez and Martín Cárdenas sped from Medina del Campo to Saldaña to convey doña Catalina's offer to their client. Doña Beatriz de Villasur was not well and, perhaps knowing that her death was near, ratified the settlement without delay. On 22 November 1583 she swore in the presence of several witnesses her acceptance of the agreement, neglecting, however, to affix her name, claiming "I cannot sign because of the infirmity of my hands."[4] Whether the refusal was prompted by genuine disability or deliberate last defiance, it did not upset doña Catalina de Vergara, who contentedly signed the papers several days later. The nightmare of the past thirty years was finally coming to a close.

In less than a year doña Beatriz de Villasur was dead. She never collected the full amount due to her, but her nephew and only heir, Cristóval Adarzo de Villasur, did. On 22 September of 1584 doña Catalina de Vergara paid him 1,400 ducats; and a few months later she transferred the last 300 ducats to the man who addressed her as the "widow of the illustrious señor Francisco Noguerol de Ulloa," a designation that doña Beatriz would have never conceded. The dispute was indeed over.[5]

XLVIII

Has Not Fulfilled

*It appears to me that Francisco Morvelle has not
fulfilled his obligations carefully, although I have
well learned that he has not been so careless
that he forgot to collect.* —Doña Catalina de Vergara

❧●❧

Noguerol's widow inherited not only a substantial estate but also numerous annoyances. The rents from Andalusia, the *juro* of the *Villa* of Carmona, and the *censo* from the Duke of Medina Sidonia were regularly in arrears, but doña Catalina soon discovered one of the causes and did not hesitate to consult Simón Ruiz. She suspected that her agent had been less than honest. "It seems to me that Francisco Morvelle has not fulfilled his obligations carefully, although I have well learned that he has not been so careless that he forgot to collect." Simón Ruiz, who also relied on Morvelle as agent, offered to investigate the situation. Doña Catalina gratefully accepted, knowing that he would undertake the work for the sake of getting it done, not for the reward; after all, she told him, "in a house that prospers as much as yours, it is like a drop of water in the sea." Doña Catalina confided to the banker, "I have much need of the monies for the many things that have been offered to me, and continue to be offered."[1]

Francisco Noguerol had at one point acquired a *censo* from Francisco de Dueñas, a *regidor* of Medina del Campo, and his wife, doña Mariana Beltrán de Mella, a far less troublesome investment for doña Catalina to oversee. The elder Dueñas died, leaving the heirs the obligation to make payments. His son, don Rodrigo de Dueñas Beltrán, also a city *regidor*, promptly discharged the interest due to doña Catalina; however, by the following year, 1586, he too was dead. His mother, doña Mariana, who became tutor and guardian for her own minor children as well as her grandchildren, took charge of the estate. Doña Catalina and doña Mariana were well acquainted, and the smooth business transactions reflected their friendship.[2]

The royal rents of Medina del Campo, based on the income from the Rúa and Cuatro Calles, also proved a reliable source of income, and the collection was easy. On 23 June 1587, for example, doña Catalina received 100,000 maravedis from Juan de Salazar, the city's treasurer, as the first of the two annual payments. At the same time she asked the treasurer to take 19,733 and a half maravedis from the total owed her and pay it directly to the monastery of San Andrés.[3]

One of doña Catalina's last acts was a large payment to her son-in-law, Juan de Zuazo: the majority of the 16,000 ducats in dowry she and Francisco had promised in 1567 to her daughter Elena de Tejada. The total sum of this generous gift, in sharp contrast to the dowries Noguerol had presented his two nieces, was not due until the death of doña Catalina.[4]

Throughout her widowhood doña Catalina de Vergara skillfully administered the estate left in her care, preserving it for Francisco's chosen heir, her grandson don Diego. She diligently fulfilled the obligations set up by Noguerol and, at the same time, insisted that income due to her be paid promptly. Doña Catalina confronted difficulties with courage and firmness, undaunted by rebels, courts, or debtors. The adroitness she displayed during the delicate negotiations with doña Beatriz de Villasur bear witness to doña Catalina's capabilities and intelligence. She compromised without damaging Noguerol's legacy, while safeguarding it from future claims by discontented heirs of Francisco's first wife.

XLIX
As Good Brothers

*If there is any doubt that they might have,
let it be settled amiably and as good brothers.*
—*Doña Catalina de Vergara*

The muted bells of the Dominican monastery of San Andrés el Real tolled, echoed by those of San Miguel, and soon the bells of many other churches in Medina del Campo joined suit on a cold February day in 1592. The ringing began on the north side of the Zapardiel, then shifted to the south, announcing the death of the widow of don Francisco Noguerol de Ulloa. The body of doña Catalina de Vergara was slowly carried in a long funeral procession toward the monastery of San Andrés. The cortege was headed by the clerics of the *cabildo mayor* of Medina del Campo, bearing the crosses of the parish. They were followed by members of numerous *cofradías* of the city. Boys from the local Jesuit school sustained their banner as they escorted the bier.

The servants of the household had been given mourning dress, and they too joined in the procession. And the family was there, doña Elena de Tejada with her husband Juan de Zuazo, don Diego Noguerol de Ulloa and the other grandchildren, the nephews and nieces, and the cousins. The somber mourners, their footsteps muffled, moved steadily toward the principal doorway of the church. The prior of San Andrés stood at the entrance, waiting to receive the remains of doña Catalina de Vergara and to lead the cortege toward the family chapel. There, doña Catalina was laid next to Francisco Noguerol, at his right side, as she had wished.

Doña Catalina, perhaps apprehensive toward the end of her life about her marriage and worried about her salvation, invoked the intercession on her behalf by Saint Mary "the true advocate of sinners," and numerous other saints, "so that all will be my advocates before His Divine Majesty and all the Celestial Court will be in my aid before my God and Redeemer." She had asked for five hundred Masses in San Andrés "as quickly as possible after I die" and did not forget to order Masses for the conversion of Indians and for the souls of Noguerol's as well as her own parents. As was customary, doña Catalina provided that after her death twelve paupers be clothed and fed. Furthermore, mourners were treated to a banquet in remembrance of the couple. Doña Catalina had left instructions that six *cargas* of wheat for bread, twelve sheep to roast, and twelve skins of wine to accompany the meal be furnished.

Doña Catalina left monetary gifts for various relatives and servants, though her personal objects—her embroidered skirts and blouses, her lace, and her gold jewelry—were destined for her granddaughter and namesake, who also received 2,000 ducats.

Don Diego, the heir of the *mayorazgo*, was still a minor when doña Catalina died. In her will she changed Francisco's provision that had made Diego patron of the Noguerol chapel and transferred the office to her eldest grandson, Antonio Lisón de Tejada. She was concerned that this shift might lead to future animosity: "I order and encharge the said don Antonio Lisón de Tejada and don Diego Noguerol de Ulloa to take it thusly well, and that above all they are not displeased, that if there is any doubt that they might have, let it be settled amiably and as good brothers . . . let it be agreed to without lawsuits, and in this fashion they will have my blessing."[1]

EPILOGUE

Epilogue
Treasures Upon Earth

Lay not up for yourselves treasures upon earth,
where moth and rust doth corrupt, and where thieves break through
and steal.—Matthew 6:19

Even the most carefully laid plans can go awry, especially if long periods of time are involved. Noguerol's scheme began to unravel even before doña Catalina died. The substitution of don Antonio for don Diego as the patron of the chapel was not improper, since Diego was still a minor and an adult would be better suited to assume the duties of patron following doña Catalina's demise. It was, nonetheless, symptomatic of a problem: there were few direct descendants; Francisco had none, and don Diego was still too young to be relied on to have a full commitment to the Noguerol de Ulloa line that he was to head.

Don Diego did possess the *mayorazgo* when he reached adulthood, though only briefly, and he proudly used the high-sounding name don Diego Noguerol de Ulloa Lissón de Tejada. Shortly after the turn of the century, in violation of the line of succession designated by Francisco, the estate passed to don Antonio Noguerol de Ulloa, don Diego's older brother.[1]

Don Antonio was a town *regidor* of Medina del Campo and participated in local politics in the 1620s and early 1630s. In 1630 a census of the city was taken, and he was charged with the preparation of the returns for "the river bank and the plazuela de San Miguel, and the section of the Callejón, with the district of San Andrés and the Hospital of the Bishop." But don Antonio was inconsistent in his attendance at the meetings of the Ayuntamiento. In 1639 he was absent from Medina del Campo at a critical juncture in the city's history, and indeed, in the history of Castile.[2]

The late 1630s saw the revolt and independence of the Low Countries, of Portugal, even a threat of the disintegration of the Spanish portion of the peninsula, with a movement for the independence of Catalonia and Navarre. The Spanish king had armies in the field throughout Europe to stem the imminent collapse of the empire, but these armies were costly. Philip IV and his energetic first minister, the Count-Duke of Olivares, tried to block the centrifugal forces. Many

times the expenses for maintaining the empire far outstepped the revenues, and the government once again went bankrupt.

The Crown often resorted to forced loans to continue its policies,
and such was the case in 1637. The loans, assessed against the towns,
were given the onerous name of the *millónes*, after the sums that were
to be generated, but in a severely depreciated currency. The king ordered that Medina del Campo's heavy assessment of more than 2
million maravedis was to be supplied from a special sales tax on certain
products. Local citizens bitterly complained that such a tax would
force people to trade elsewhere, to the devastation of Medina's commerce. As a result, the town officials collected but a fraction of the
necessary amount.[3]

The wealth of Francisco Noguerol de Ulloa had not been forgotten.
On 27 November 1639 the *regidores*, faced with threats from the
central government, went to San Andrés el Real and demanded from
the recently chosen prior of the monastery, Juan Rodríguez, a loan of
780,000 maravedis from the capital of Noguerol's endowment.

The treasure was kept in the family chapel secured in the strongbox
by three locks. The *corregidor*, Juan de Zamora Cabreros, had one key,
the prior another; the third key was in possession of the patron, don
Antonio Noguerol de Ulloa, who was absent. The men nevertheless
removed the box and without scruples broke the third lock. The silver
and gold stored near Francisco's sepulcher was calculated to be worth
2,164,402 maravedis.

Noguerol, long after his death, was again despoiled to support a
bankrupt government. A *censo* was created, giving don Antonio a
return of 39,000 maravedis of rent on the 780,000 maravedis to cover
what in reality amounted to theft. The government promised to pay the
annual income and someday, if demanded, the principal as well. Don
Antonio was not alone; other loans were forced, other properties used.
But whatever was left would be henceforth repaid in depreciated currency.[4]

In the latter part of the seventeenth century the Dominicans tried to
close out the Noguerol *censo*, to redeem the one taken by the government in 1639. It does not appear this effort was totally successful. The
holder of the *censo* in 1705 was doña Leonarda Mardeus de Rocabertti
Noguerol de Ulloa, who was said to reside in Madrid, but her exact
whereabouts were unknown. The monastery needed proceeds from the
endowment for repair and construction. The city still owed the
780,000 maravedis from the forced loan of the previous century, but
the friars could not collect the full amount because the city treasurer

was in jail for absconding with municipal funds. By the early eighteenth century the city payment that Francisco Noguerol had held by royal privilege was also in arrears. In January 1716 officials searched the town records for information on the original grant but could not find any.[5]

The final blow to Francisco Noguerol's legacy came in the early nineteenth century. Again, part of the problem stemmed from the bankruptcy of the Spanish monarchy. The weak and vacillating Charles IV, then his son Ferdinand VII, were no match for Napoleon Bonaparte. When French troops marched into Spain in 1808, they easily toppled the government, and Napoleon placed his brother Joseph on the Spanish throne. It was not the ousted monarchy, but the people of Spain, who ultimately rose up and drove the foreigners out.

Because of its strategic importance and the assumption by some of the French that it was a center for the production of brandy, Medina del Campo was occupied briefly by military troops. The French commandeered as their quarters two monasteries: the Franciscan on the south side of the Zapardiel, and the Dominican on the north. The invaders stayed only a few days, but as they withdrew, the soldiers mercilessly set fire to both monasteries, burning nearby houses in the process. Much of San Andrés el Real was destroyed.[6]

The monks who fled were housed for a time in the palace of the Condesa de Bornos. Any plans of returning and rebuilding the ruined priory were dashed in 1836, as a liberal Spanish government abolished and expropriated the properties of the monastic orders.[7]

Today, there is not a trace of a plaza San Andrés or a Dominican monastery of the same name in Medina del Campo. An old couple can be seen cultivating a few vegetables in a fenced field where San Andrés el Real once proudly stood. In the center of that enclosure a few tall trees rise near, perhaps above, the very spot where don Francisco Noguerol de Ulloa and doña Catalina de Vergara were once laid to rest.

Glossary

alcabala: sales tax
alcaide: warden, or governor of a fortress
alcalde: mayor
alguacil: sheriff
arcabucero: arquebusier
arras: groom's marriage gift
audiencia: court; could exercise executive duties
bienes: goods
bienes capitales: goods brought into a marriage
bienes gananciales: joint earnings
bienes multiplicados: joint assets
caballero: horseman or knight
cabildo: municipal council
cacique: Indian chief; headman
calle: street
capellanía: chaplaincy
carta executoria: court enforcement order
carta de pago: acknowledgment of payment
carta recetoria: a writ to take certified testimony
cédula: royal order or decree
censo: interest-paying bond
cofradía: confraternity
contador: accountant
converso: "new" Christian, Jewish ancestry
demanda: an order or legal claim
doctrinero: cleric in charge of an Indian parish
encomendero: holder of an Indian grant
encomienda: grant of tribute-paying Indians
factor: treasury official; agent
fiador: one who guarantees or posts bond
fianza: bond for security
fiscal: crown prosecutor
fueros: laws; privileges
hidalgo: lesser untitled nobility; gentry
interrogatorio: questionnaire
juramento: oath
juro: income-producing government bond
justicia mayor: chief justice
legajo: bundle of documents
letrado: lawyer
mayorazgo: entailed estate

mejoría: melioration
merced: grant
morisco: "new" Christian, Moorish ancestry
nuncio cierto: certified envoy
obras pías: pious works
oidor: justice of the audiencia; judge
patronato: patronage
probanza: a legal proof
procurador: solicitor; attorney
provisor: ecclesiastical judge
rebeldía: failure to appear in court when summoned
regidor: town councilor
relator: court reporter
renta: income
repartimiento: Indian grant equivalent to *encomienda*
residencia: legal review of an official's tenure
solicitador de causas: court solicitor
testigo: witness
vecino: city resident, with legal status
veedor: inspector
vida maridable: cohabitation; married life
villa: town or city
visita: inspection
yanakuna: Indian servant, outside tribute system

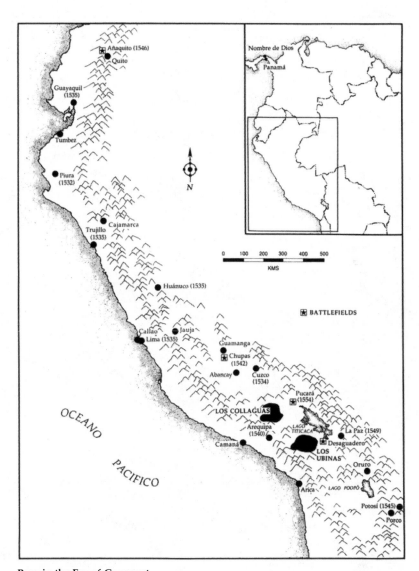

Peru in the Era of Conquest

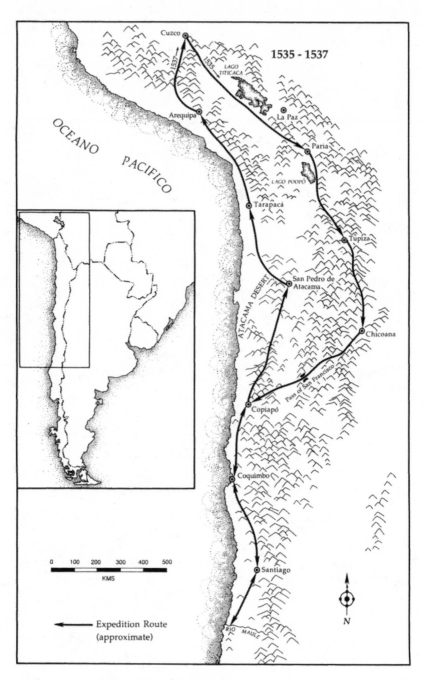

Diego de Almagro's Chilean Expedition

Spain in the Sixteenth Century

Currency and Measures

Currency

Spanish currency value and equivalencies changed several times during the sixteenth century. Inflation existed, especially following 1550, and buying power eroded continuously. The following equivalencies are approximate:

blanca (vellón, or copper-silver)	½ maravedi
maravedi	basic unit of currency
ducat (23¼K gold coin)	375 maravedis
escudo (22K gold coin)	350 maravedis (introduced 1537)
(escudo, also called corona)	400 maravedis (modified 1566)
castellano	490 maravedis
marco	50 castellanos
real	34 maravedis
peso (American gold coin)	450 maravedis

Measures

cántaro	measure of wine, about 32 pints
carga (varies)	measure of volume, 3 to 4 *fanegas*
fanega (varies)	about 1½ bushels, or 58 liters
league (distance)	about 3½ miles, or 5.57 kilometers

A Brief Chronological Table of Major Events

❧●❧

The Protagonists and the Indies

c. 1510	birth of Francisco Noguerol de Ulloa
1524–25	Pizarro's first expedition along Pacific coast
26 Feb. 1526	assassination of Mendo Noguerol
23 Mar. 1526	execution of Bishop Antonio de Acuña
1526–27	Pizarro's second expedition
7 May 1530	marriage contract with Beatriz de Villasur
27 Dec. 1530	Pizarro leaves Panama on third expedition
16 Nov. 1532	Spanish capture Inca Atahualpa at Cajamarca
12 Dec. 1534	Francisco writes Beatriz from Panama
3 July 1535	Diego de Almagro's Chilean campaign begins
18 Apr. 1537	Almagrists return and take Cuzco from Pizarrists
12 July 1537	battle of Abancay; Almagrist victory
6 Apr. 1538	battle of Las Salinas; victory of Hernando Pizarro
1540	city of Arequipa founded
26 July 1541	Francisco Pizarro assassinated in Lima
16 Sept. 1542	battle of Chupas; Almagro "the Younger" defeated
20 Nov. 1542	"New Laws" to protect Indians from the *encomenderos*
3 Nov. 1543	Viceroy Núñez Vela, Dr. Tejada, and wife leave Spain
25 Apr. 1545	Dr. Tejada dies at sea, returning to Spain
18 Jan. 1546	battle of Añaquito; Viceroy Núñez Vela defeated
7 June 1546	sisters report death of Beatriz de Villasur
21 Oct. 1547	battle of Huarina; royalists defeated
9 Apr. 1548	battle of Jaquijahuana; Gasca defeats Pizarro
10 Sept. 1548	Francisco receives Los Collaguas *encomienda*
5 Oct. 1549	dowry agreement, Catalina de Vergara and Francisco
May 1551	Francisco ships 65 bars of silver to Spain
13 Nov. 1553	Francisco Hernández Girón uprising in Cuzco
30 July 1554	case filed against Noguerol in Valladolid
8 Oct. 1554	battle of Pucará; *audiencia* defeats rebels
6 June 1555	court demands return to wife in Spain
22 Dec. 1556	Francisco appears before diocesan court in León
13 Feb. 1557	warrant issued for Francisco's arrest
30 Mar. 1557	Francisco jailed in Valladolid
9 Aug. 1557	first decision; appeal begins
5 Nov. 1558	presentation of apostolic brief in Salamanca
21 Jan. 1559	decision of diocesan authorities in Salamanca
14 June 1576	Francisco establishes *capellanía*, *mayorazgo*
Sept. 1581	death of Francisco Noguerol de Ulloa
1584	death of Beatriz de Villasur
Feb. 1592	death of Catalina de Vergara

Spain and Europe

26 Nov. 1504	death of Isabella the Catholic
1505	Cortes of Toro
3 June 1509	Henry VIII marries Catherine of Aragon
1515	birth of Saint Teresa of Avila
23 Jan. 1516	Ferdinand of Aragon dies
1516	Charles I becomes king of Spain
31 Oct. 1517	Luther's theses; Reformation begins
1519	Charles I elected Holy Roman Emperor Charles V
July 1520	uprising of the *comuneros* begins
23 Apr. 1521	defeat of *comuneros* at Villalar
1521	Diet of Worms; Luther and Charles V
1521–29	war between Spain and France
1525	Cathedral of Seville completed
24 Feb. 1525	battle of Pavia; Francis I captured
21 May 1527	future Philip II born in Valladolid
1528	publication of Castiglione's *Courtier*
1532	first printed edition of Machiavelli's *Prince*
1534	Ignatius de Loyola founds Society of Jesus
1545–63	Council of Trent
1547	death of Henry VIII; birth of Miguel de Cervantes
1550	Las Casas and Sepúlveda, Valladolid, debate just conquest
1553	Cieza de León publishes *Crónica del Perú*
25 July 1554	marriage of Mary Tudor and Spain's Prince Philip
1555–59	pontificate of Paul IV; first Index
13 Apr. 1555	death of Juana "La Loca," mother of Charles V
25 Oct. 1555	Charles V abdicates in favor of Philip II
17 Nov. 1558	Mary Tudor dies; Elizabeth I ascends English throne
21 May 1559	auto-da-fé in Plaza of Valladolid
1560	Domingo de Santo Tomás publishes Quechua dictionary
1562–65	French Florida fails; Spanish found St. Augustine
1566	Bartolomé de Las Casas dies
1567	Saint Teresa of Avila founds convent in Medina
10 Nov. 1567	Pedro de la Gasca dies
1567–73	Duke of Alba's "iron rule" in the Netherlands
7 Oct. 1571	battle of Lepanto
1575	Spanish government bankrupt
1577	El Greco established in Toledo; Juan de Juni dies
1577–80	Francis Drake's circumnavigation
25 Aug. 1580	Portugal invaded and conquered by Philip II
1582	death of Saint Teresa of Avila
29 Apr. 1587	Francis Drake's raid on Cádiz
21–29 July 1588	Spanish Armada attacks England
1591	deaths of Saint John of the Cross, humanist Luis de León
1598	death of Philip II of Spain

Notes

Abbreviations Used in Notes

AGI   Archivo General de Indias, Seville
AGS   Archivo General de Simancas
AHA   Archivo Histórico, Arequipa
AHNM   Archivo Histórico Nacional, Madrid
AHPV   Archivo Histórico Provincial, Valladolid
AMMC   Archivo Municipal, Medina del Campo
ANP   Archivo Nacional del Perú, Lima
ASFL   Archivo del Convento de San Francisco, Lima
BNL   Biblioteca Nacional, Lima
BPM   Biblioteca del Palacio, Madrid
RAH   Real Academia de la Historia, Madrid

Prologue: Justice Be Fulfilled

1. John Lynch, *Spain under the Habsburgs*, 2 vols. (London: Oxford University Press, 1965), 1:39–41; John H. Elliott, *Imperial Spain, 1469–1716* (New York: New American Library, 1966), p. 155. Very incomplete information on Mendo Noguerol's tenure at Simancas is to be found in the AGS: Cédulas de Cámara, 7 Apr. 1521; Cédulas, libro LIV, ff. 115, 156; libro LVI, f. 80; libro LXI, f. 182; Comunidades de Castilla, libro I, f. 508; and Estado, Castilla, leg. 8.

2. Hayward Keniston, *Francisco de los Cobos: Secretary of the Emperor Charles V* (Pittsburgh: University of Pittsburgh Press, 1959), pp. 92–93. Keniston offers a different version of the murder. He reports that the bishop entered the office of the jailer, threw embers from a brazier on top of the table, then crushed Mendo's skull with a brick hidden in the sleeve of his robe. This version seems unlikely on a number of counts. We have reported here only the bare outlines of the death of Mendo and the inquiry, trial, and execution of the bishop of Zamora. Roger Bigelow Merriman describes the assassination of the jailer and the events following in *The Rise of the Spanish Empire in the Old World and in the New*, 4 vols. (New York, 1918–34; rpt. 1962), 3:121. Most accounts refer to the important, although flawed, collection of documents on the *comunero* revolt in Manuel Dánvila y Collado's *Historia crítica y documentada de las Comunidades de Castilla*, 6 vols. (Madrid, 1897–99), 5:567, 570–74. Prudencio de Sandoval, *Historia del Emperador Carlos V*, 3 vols. (Madrid: Atlas, 1955–56), 1:449, also describes the events in Simancas. A full account is provided by Manuel Bachiller (1580), "Antigüedades y sucesos memorables sucedidos en esta muy noble y antigua villa de Simancas," published in the *Colección de documentos inéditos para la historia de España* (Madrid, 1842), 1:530–63. Bachiller wrote, "another son [of the *alcaide*] that was named Francisco Noguerol, went to the Indies and returned so rich, that in this time [1580] he is the richest and most powerful person in Medina del Campo,

where he has establihsed himself" (p. 562). The accounts of the assassination vary slightly in detail. The background of the *comunero* revolt is examined carefully by Henry Latimer Seaver, *The Great Revolt in Castile: A Study of the Comunero Movement of 1521–1522* (New York: Octagon Books, 1966).

3. Karl Adolf Constantin Höfler, *Don Antonio de Acuña genannt der Luther Spaniens* (Vienna, 1882), p. 85. We have never found Francisco Noguerol's exact date of birth, but we estimate, on the basis of his later statements, that he was born in 1510. We have no direct account of young Francisco's attitude at this date, but seven years later, in early 1533, he wrote his bride, consoling her on the loss of her sister and confessing his remorse at the earlier death of his own father (see chapter XIII); AGI, Justicia 1076.

4. Dánvila, *Comunidades de Castilla*, 5:573. We searched unsuccessfully for the will of Mendo Noguerol in the notarial records for Simancas in the AHPV. The extant burial registers for the church in Simancas, now housed in the diocesan archive in Valladolid, do not begin this early. The local clergyman in Simancas could provide little help beyond pointing to approximately where in the church Mendo was laid to rest in 1526.

5. This evidence is to be found in AGI, Justicia 1076.

I *She Who Died*

1. AGI, Justicia 1076.

2. The two letters from Noguerol's sisters are included in the court documents found in ibid. The handwriting of the originals is almost impossible to decipher, not a problem of paleography, but simply a matter of terrible penmanship. The scribes prepared certified copies of the two letters, but the originals were displayed to key witnesses to verify they had actually been written by the nuns.

3. *Dolor de costado*, an imprecise term used by physicians in early modern Spain that could refer to a variety of ailments afflicting the chest. It may have been tuberculosis, pneumonic plague, pneumonia, or any of a number of other infections.

4. Both letters are in AGI, Justicia 1076. Many of the papers of San Pedro de las Dueñas are now available to researchers. Several documents refer to Francisco Noguerol's sisters. See José María Fernández Catón, *Catálogo del archivo del monasterio de San Pedro de las Dueñas* (León: Centro de Estudios e Investigacion San Isidoro, 1977), pp. 7–14. The modern restoration of the convent is probably far removed from what it would have looked like in the middle of the sixteenth century, during the tenure of doña Francisca and doña Ynés.

5. AGI, Justicia 1076. The conventual life was all too common for Spanish young ladies of the sixteenth and seventeenth centuries. With the attraction of military service in Spain's far-flung empire, along with the allure of the Indies, there were simply too few eligible bachelors. Further, many parents could not afford a suitable dowry to secure a good marriage for their daughters. Life in the convent provided the alternative. Of Castile's population of some 6.5 million in 1591, the Church consumed about 1.1 percent of the total, with 20,369 nuns, a similar number of monks, and just over 33,000 secular clergymen, J. H. Elliot, *The Count-Duke of Olivares: The Statesman in an Age of Decline* (New Haven, Conn.: Yale University Press, 1986), p. 183.

6. AGI, Justicia 1076.

II Hardship and Risk

1. Much of the background information on Noguerol's career is gleaned from his own defense and *relación de méritos* in the AGI in Justicia 1076, Patronato 109, and Patronato 194. He refers more than once to his services with Alvaro de Luna, the Count of Benavente, and the Duke of Medina Sidonia. We note the extensive commercial activities of the Medina Sidonia family in Fernand Braudel, *The Mediterranean and the Mediterranean World in the Age of Philip II*, 2 vols. (New York: Harper Torchbooks, 1975), 1:257–58, 637–40. Income of the Duke of Medina Sidonia was about 50,000 ducats in 1525, 80,000 in 1558, and 150,000 in 1581 (2:714). See also Peter Pierson, *Commander of the Armada: The Seventh Duke of Medina Sidonia* (New Haven, Conn.: Yale University Press, 1989). It is unclear which duke Noguerol actually served, and Pierson's brief genealogical outline of the ancestors of the famous seventh duke does not shed much light on the subject: "Ferdinand of Aragon now took charge. There remained three brothers from the third Duke's second marriage [he died in 1507], on whom he settled the Medina Sidonia inheritance. Because the eldest was feebleminded, Ferdinand allowed him the title and set him aside; he arranged for the second, Don Juan Alonso de Guzmán to exercise all pertinent authority and rights. . . . From 1538 Don Juan Alonso shared the ducal title, and on his older brother's death in 1549, he became sole Duke, ranked sixth in the succession" (p. 10). It would seem that Noguerol served the fifth duke in name, but in reality his orders must have come from the future sixth duke. Don Juan Alonso de Guzmán, the sixth Duke of Medina Sidonia, died in 1558 and was succeeded by his grandson, don Alonso Pérez de Guzmán el Bueno, the future commander of the Invincible Armada.

2. This passage is based on various documents on behalf of Francisco Noguerol de Ulloa in AGI, Justicia 1076.

3. AGI, Patronato 194. The excitement of the young man in Panama is clear in his letter to his wife, AGI, Justicia 1076. See chapter XIII.

4. John Hemming, *The Conquest of the Incas* (London: Sphere Books, 1972), pp. 72–78. The details of the conquest and civil war period in Peru have been told many times. William H. Prescott's classic work, *History of the Conquest of Peru* (New York: Harper and Brothers, 1851), may still be read with enjoyment, although his description of the Inca empire is outmoded. The most readable modern account of the events, one that stresses the response of the native American, is Hemming, *Conquest of the Incas*. For biographical analysis of the Spaniards who participated in the ransom, see the study of James Lockhart, *Men of Cajamarca: A Social and Biographical Study of the First Conquerors of Peru* (Austin: University of Texas Press, 1972). A description of many of the gold and silver pieces that were assayed is found in Noble David Cook, "Los libros de cargo del tesorero Alonso Riquelme con el rescate de Atahualpa," *Humanidades* 2 (1968): 41–88.

5. There is no complete modern account of this ill-fated first expedition to Chile. One of the more useful earlier works is Tomás Thayer Ojeda, *Los conquistadores de Chile*, 3 vols. (Santiago, 1908–13). Thayer Ojeda reports (1:51) that Noguerol was born about 1511 and commanded the Chilean expedition's rearguard. He was the "son of the alcaide of Simancas, that the bishop of Zamora killed." Thayer Ojeda also provides a chronology of the first Chilean venture (2:13–21). See also H. R. S. Pocock, *The Conquest of Chile* (New York: Stein and Day, 1967), pp. 19–44;

Hemming, *Conquest of the Incas*, pp. 177–79; and Eugene E. Korth, *Spanish Policy in Colonial Chile: The Struggle for Social Justice, 1535–1700* (Stanford, Calif.: Stanford University Press, 1968). For this description we have used especially the chroniclers Pedro de Cieza de León, *Obras completas*, 2 vols. (Madrid: Instituto Gonzalo Fernández de Oviedo, 1984–85): 1:351–57, and Pedro Pizarro, *Relación del descubrimiento y conquista del Perú* (Lima: Universidad Católica, 1978), pp. 121–22, 156.

6. AGI, Justicia 436.
7. Cieza de León, *Obras completas*, 1:351–57; and Pizarro, *Relación del descubrimiento*, pp. 121–22, 156.
8. Pedro Pizarro, *Relación del descubrimiento*, pp. 182–83. Hemming, *Conquest of the Incas*, pp. 169–235, provides a detailed account of the Indian rebellion.
9. AGI, Justicia 436. Another copy of the *merced* can be found in Justicia 448. The grant is dated in Cuzco, 22 Jan. 1540.
10. AGI, Justicia 436.
11. Alonso Enríquez de Guzmán, *Vida y aventuras de un caballero noble desbaratado* (Lima: Cantuta, 1970), p. 116.
12. See Guillermo Lohmann Villena, "Las expresiones de última voluntad de Francisco Pizarro: Un incierto complejo documental," *Revista Histórica* 34 (1983–84): 17–40. Lohmann states, "It is shocking that a staunch Almagrist should appear at Pizarro's side at such an exceptional circumstance, normally enveloped by an air of familiarity" (p. 35). If indeed Noguerol was jubilant, his enthusiasm was tempered as another Spaniard, Lucas Martínez Vegaso, laid claim to part of the tributes of the natives (see chapter IV); AGI, Justicia 436.

III Neither Rectitude nor Tranquility

1. This chapter is based on a long letter (AGI, Patronato 194) constituting the equivalent of a service report of the young conquistador. It was published in its entirety by Raúl Porras Barrenechea, *Cartas del Perú (1524–1543)* (Lima, 1959), pp. 420–23.
2. AGI, Patronato 194. Spaniards often used slaves and their Indians to carry correspondence. During periods of civil warfare the use of such messengers probably increased.
3. Ibid.
4. Ibid.
5. Ibid.
6. Ibid.
7. Ibid.
8. Ibid.
9. Ibid.; an invaluable compilation of letters in English of other figures in the early colonial period, many of a personal nature, has been edited by James Lockhart and Enrique Otte: *Letters and People of the Spanish Indies: The Sixteenth Century* (Cambridge: Cambridge University Press, 1976).
10. Pedro Pizarro, *Relación del Descubrimiento*, pp. 215–18. AGI, Patronato 109; Noguerol did not himself state that he fought at Chupas, but several witnesses did testify to his presence there.

IV   The Healthiest in Peru

1. Cieza de León, *Obras completas*, 1:101. An urban history of Arequipa has yet to be written. Keith A. Davies provides an interesting discussion of the economic development of the region in the sixteenth and seventeenth centuries in *Landowners in Colonial Peru* (Austin: University of Texas Press, 1984).

2. AGI, Justicia 1076. Although we lack direct documentation regarding Noguerol's annulment proceedings in Lima, there are several references made by his attorneys in Spain, and more important, Francisco himself tells ecclesiastical authorities in León in 1556 that he was waiting for judgment on the dissolution of his bond to doña Beatriz de Villasur when he received letters informing him of her death (see chapter XIX). Various witnesses attest to the position of Francisco in Arequipa's society, as well as his marital status. For an overview of the role of the European elite, see James Lockhart, *Spanish Peru, 1532–1560: A Colonial Society* (Madison: University of Wisconsin Press, 1968); and for the evolution of the central coastal estates, consult Robert G. Keith, *Conquest and Agrarian Change: The Emergence of the Hacienda System on the Peruvian Coast* (Cambridge: Harvard University Press, 1976).

3. AGI, Justicia 436. Efraín Trelles Arestegui, *Lucas Martínez Vegazo: Funcionamiento de una encomienda peruana inicial* (Lima: Universidad Católica, 1983), examines the career of this controversial *encomendero*.

4. Víctor M. Barriga, ed., *Documentos para la historia de Arequipa*, 3 vols. (Arequipa, 1939–55), 2:105–106.

5. Magnus Mörner, *La corona española y los foraneos en los pueblos de indios de América* (Stockholm: Latinamerikanska-institutet i Stockholm, 1970) describes the structure of both small towns, and administrative centers, such as Arequipa. See also Constantino Bayle, *Los cabildos seculares en la América Española* (Madrid: Sapientia, 1952); John Preston Moore, *The Cabildo in Peru under the Hapsburgs* (Durham: Duke University Press, 1954); María Antonia Durán Montero, *Fundación de ciudades en el Perú durante el siglo XVI* (Seville: Escuela de Estudios Hispano-Americanos, 1978), pp. 112–14; and Ralph A. Gakenheimer, "Determinants of Physical Structure of the Peruvian Town of the Sixteenth Century" (Ph.D. diss., University of Pennsylvania, 1964).

6. AGI, Justicia 1076. The requirement to bear arms and to maintain men and equipment made the *encomendero*'s position similar, at least still in the 1540s in Peru, to the feudal *señores* of the reconquest towns in Spain, although unlike the *comendadores*, the *encomenderos* could not dispense justice. Crown officials, the *corregidor* and *justicia mayor*, rendered the initial judgments in legal matters. The general history of the *encomienda* in the New World has been examined by Silvio Zavala, *La encomienda indiana* (Madrid: Centro de Estudios Históricos, 1935); and Lesley B. Simpson, *The Encomienda in New Spain: The Beginnings of Spanish Mexico*, rev. ed. (Berkeley: University of California Press, 1966). For Peru see Trelles, *Lucas Martínez*; Manuel Burga, *De la encomienda a la hacienda capitalista: El valle del Jequetepeque de siglo XVI a XX* (Lima: Instituto de Estudios Peruanos, 1976); and Lockhart, *Spanish Peru*, pp. 11–33. For the Old World background of the institution of the *encomienda*, see Robert S. Chamberlain, "Castilian Backgrounds of the Repartimiento-Encomienda," in Carnegie Institution of Washington, *Contributions to American Anthropology and History* 5 (no.

25, 1939):19–66. Guillermo Lohmann Villena, *El corregidor de los indios en el Perú bajo los Austrias* (Madrid, 1957), continues to be useful. For a study of the Castilian official in the time of the Catholic monarchs, see Marvin Lunenfeld, *Keepers of the City: The Corregidores of Isabella I of Castile (1474–1504)* (New York: Cambridge University Press, 1987).

V This City Is Traitorous

1. C. H. Haring, *The Spanish Empire in America* (New York: Harcourt, Brace, & World, 1963), pp. 51–53, 82. For those wishing to follow the career of Bartolomé de las Casas, there is no better place to start than Lewis U. Hanke, *The Spanish Struggle for Justice in the Conquest of America* (Philadelphia: University of Pennsylvania Press, 1949).

2. Agustín de Zárate, *Historia del descubrimiento y conquista del Perú* (Lima: Miranda, 1944), p. 149; and Diego Fernández, *Historia del Perú*, in Juan Pérez de Tudela Bueso, ed., *Crónicas del Perú*, 5 vols. (Madrid: Atlas, 1963–65), 1:11–15.

3. Fernández, *Historia del Perú*, 1:15–16; Hemming, *Conquest of the Incas*, pp. 267–68; Prescott, *History*, 2:316; Francisco López de Gómara, *Hispania victrix: Historia general de las Indias*, 2 vols. (Madrid, 1946–47), chap. clxxi. The viceroy referred to Tejada as a dunce because he did not know Latin.

4. Fernández, *Historia del Perú*, 1:16–39; Prescott, *History*, 2:279–88; Cieza de León, *Obras completas*, 2:382–83.

5. AGI, Justicia 201B, Justicia 451, Justicia 1071, and Justicia 1147.

6. Juan Pérez de Tudela Bueso, ed., *Documentos relativos a don Pedro de la Gasca y a Gonzalo Pizarro*, 2 vols. (Madrid: Real Academia de la Historia, 1964), 2:92–95, 557–61. According to Zárate, *Descubrimiento y conquista*, p. 148, and Pedro Gutiérrez de Santa Clara, *Historia de las guerras civiles del Perú (1544–1548)*, in Pérez de Tudela, ed., *Crónicas*, 2:155, Tejada was from Logroño and was *alcalde de los hijosdalgo* of the Audiencia de Valladolid before leaving Spain. Much of the unusual background of the *oidor* can be traced in AGI, Justicia 451, Justicia 1069, and Justicia 1077.

7. AGI, Patronato 109.

8. The preceding section is based on Fernández, *Historia del Perú*, pp. 40–216; Gutiérrez de Santa Clara, *Las guerras civiles*, 3:409, 4:15; Zárate, *Descubrimiento y conquista*, pp. 295–99; and José Antonio del Busto Duthurburu, *La Pacificación del Perú* (Lima: Libreria Studium, 1984), pp. 65–83.

9. Pérez de Tudela, *Pedro de la Gasca*, 1:261–62; AGI, Patronato 109.

10. Pérez de Tudela, Pedro de la Gasca, 2:66–67.

11. Ibid., 1:260–61.

12. Ibid., 1:580–83.

VI This Is the Head

1. AGI, Patronato 109. The description of the events of this chapter is based largely on Zárate, *Descubrimiento y conquista*, pp. 307–12; Hemming, *Conquest of the Incas*, pp. 271–72; and the appropriate sections of Fernández, *Historia del Perú*, and Gutiérrez de Santa Clara, *Las guerras civiles*.

2. AGI, Justicia 201B. The rebel's head, along with that of his commander, the feared

and hated Carvajal, ended up in the Franciscan monastery in Lima. Just over six decades later, two men met in Cordova in Spain and chatted about the Peruvian rebellions and the fate of the leadership. One was the famous *mestizo* literary figure Garcilaso de la Vega, el Inca, and the other was a Franciscan missionary, Luis Gerónimo de Oré, who worked among the Collaguas Indians who had belonged to first Gonzalo Pizarro and then to Francisco Noguerol de Ulloa. They recalled that five skulls were housed in the Franciscan convent, one of Gonzalo Pizarro, another of Francisco de Carvajal, as well as that of a later rebel, Francisco Hernández Girón. For a description of the meeting see José Toribio Medina, *Biblioteca Hispano-chilena (1523–1817)*, 3 vols. (Santiago: José Toribio Medina, 1897–99), 1:115.

VII   Such Little Penitence

1. RAH, no. 9-4664, published by María Rostworowski de Diez Canseco, "La tasa ordenada por el Licenciado Pedro de la Gasca (1549)," *Revista Histórica* 34 (1985): 53–102. A more realistic view of the size of the grant when Noguerol assumed it can be found in Noble David Cook, *People of the Colca Valley: A Population Study* (Boulder, Colo.: Westview Press, 1982), pp. 11–17. For a general overview of how the *encomienda* system functioned in Peru in the early years, see Lockhart, *Spanish Peru*, pp. 11–33.
2. Pérez de Tudela, *Pedro de la Gasca*, 1:49.
3. Ibid., 1:13.
4. Ibid., 1:3 and 31.
5. AGI, Justicia 1076. Noguerol later insisted that he considered these letters a sufficient and certified evidence of his wife's death because they were written by exemplary and therefore highly credible religious women.

VIII   Kissed Her on the Cheek

1. AGI, Justicia 201B, Justicia 451, Justicia 1069, and Justicia 1070. Much of this information on the background of doña Catalina pertains to the inquiry into the role of Tejada during the Gonzalo Pizarro revolt. See Teodoro Hampe Martínez, "En torno al levantamiento pizarrista: la intervención del oidor Lisón de Tejada," *Revista de Indias* 44, no. 174 (1984): 389; Santiago Martínez, *Alcaldes de Arequipa desde 1539 a 1946* (Arequipa, 1946), pp. 72–73, mentions Francisca de Vergara of Villa Flor, Salamanca.
2. RAH, Colección Muñoz, A/110, 4845, h. 114–17.
3. Cristóbal de Burgos was a close friend and longtime supporter of Francisco Pizarro. He was engaged in the Peruvian venture almost from the beginning and was rewarded by Pizarro at Cajamarca. Cristóbal de Burgos, an enigmatic figure, had been a slave, perhaps a *morisco*, or a *converso*, who with his Peruvian wealth returned to Spain and purchased his freedom, then negotiated the grant of perpetual *regidor* of the city of Lima from Charles V. Gutiérrez de Santa Clara, *Las guerras civiles*, 2:371–73. He returned to take up his position as *regidor* but encountered opposition from other *regidores* who claimed there were already enough officials and furthermore argued that Burgos was illiterate. Nevertheless, he did persist and was successful, and he was later named *procurador*. He died about

1553. See the discussion of Burgos in Guillermo Lohmann Villena, *Los regidores perpetuos del Cabildo de Lima (1535–1821)*, 2 vols. (Seville: Diputación Provincial de Sevilla, 1983), 2:76–79; and Lockhart, *Men of Cajamarca*, pp. 35, 146.

4. Pérez de Tudela, *Pedro de la Gasca*, 2:93. It is difficult to ascertain the significance of this kiss, from the vantage point of the twentieth century. Townsend Miller, in his study of Queen Juana, suggests that in the sixteenth century such a kiss, especially by a nonrelative, was not to be taken lightly. "Whether Louis gave her the kiss on the cheek so shocking to Spanish sensibilities and etiquette is a matter of debate." From *The Castles and the Crown: Spain, 1451–1555* (New York: Capricorn, 1963), pp. 206–7. See also Bartolomé Bennassar, *The Spanish Character: Attitudes and Mentalities from the Sixteenth to the Nineteenth Century* (Berkeley: University of California Press, 1979), pp. 213–17.

5. AGI, Justicia 201B.

6. Ibid.

7. Pérez de Tudela, *Pedro de la Gasca*, 1:528.

8. Ibid., 1:274–75.

9. Martínez, *Alcaldes de Arequipa*, p. 73, names doña Francisca de Vergara as the wife of Gómez de León. He states that she was from "Villa Flor, Salamanca, the legitimate daughter of Juana Gómez and don Pedro Vergara." Doña Catalina was also from Villaflores, Salamanca, and her parents were Menezia de Vergara and Nicolás Gómez. Since both women came from the same village, and the names of their parents suggest perhaps a double marriage between the Gómez family and the Vergara's, we are assuming that doña Francisca and doña Catalina were first cousins. Hampe Martínez, "Levantamiento pizzarista," p. 398, suggests that Francisca was doña Catalina's niece, and it is likely that doña Catalina would have gone to live with a near relative following her husband's death.

10. AGI, Justicia 201B. On 20 May 1549 Pedro de Avendaño, the secretary of Pedro de la Gasca, in Lima, received part of the estate of Doctor Tejada from Cristóbal de Burgos, in whose power they were. These were some twenty-two legal books, primarily in Latin (BPM, Madrid, mss. 1960). Did Tejada know Latin better than Blasco Núñez Vela implied in his disparaging comments? Before settling in Arequipa, doña Catalina remained in Lima for a time in the house of Cristóbal de Burgos (see the letter from la Manta on 2 Jan. 1545, in RAH, 1830, h. 699, sent by Tejada to his spouse).

11. AGI, Justicia 1076. The ideal woman, from the standpoint of the male-dominated clergy, is well described by Luis de León, *La perfecta casada, 1589* (Madrid: Rialp, 1968). See Julia Fitzmaurice-Kelly, "Women in Sixteenth Century Spain," *Revue Hispanique* 70 (1927): 557–632; P. W. Bomli, *La Femme dans l'Espagne du siècle d'or* (The Hague: Martinus Nijhoff, 1950); Irene Silverblatt, *Moon, Sun, and Witches: Gender Ideologies and Class in Inca and Colonial Peru* (Princeton, N.J.: Princeton University Press, 1987); the same author's "Andean Women under Spanish Rule," in *Women and Colonization: Anthropological Perspectives*, ed. Mona Etienne and Elenor Leacock (New York: Praeger, 1980), pp. 149–85; Elinor Burkett, "Indian Women and White Society: The Case of Sixteenth Century Peru," in *Latin American Women: Historical Perspectives*, ed. Asunción Lavrin, (Westport, Conn.: Greenwood Press, 1978), pp. 101–28; Fernando Díaz Plaja, *La sociedad española* (Barcelona: Plaza & Janés, 1974); Marcelin Defourneaux, *Daily Life in Spain in the Golden Age* (London: Allen and Unwin, 1970), pp. 146–59;

Heath Dillard, *Daughters of the Reconquest* (New York: Cambridge University Press, 1985); Leon G. Campbell, "Women and the Great Rebellion in Peru, 1780–1783," *The Americas* 42 (1985): 163–96; and Luis Martín, *Daughters of the Conquistadores: Women of the Viceroyalty of Peru* (Alburquerque: University of New Mexico Press, 1983).

IX   The Crown Jewel

1. AGI, Justicia 1076. For details see chapter XXIX.
2. Ibid.
3. Lockhart, *Spanish Peru*, p. 156, indicates: "A dowry could also be a hedge against future indebtedness; sometimes husbands acknowledged receipt of a fictional dowry far in excess of the total worth of man and wife, so that if in the future the husband's property were seized for debts, or if claims heaped up after his death, the wife could always retain this large amount in the family as dowry goods." The rather sizable dowry described in the document does give rise to the suspicion that this particular receipt was designed to protect Noguerol's property, and it certainly was later used for this purpose (see chapter XXVI).
4. AGI, Justicia 1076. Unfortunately, we do not have the exact wedding date.
5. Ibid. Systematic study of those returning to Spain should yield interesting results. So far, we know few examples of the process. See Rafael Varón Gabai and Auke Pieter Jacobs, "Peruvian Wealth and Spanish Investments: The Pizarro Family during the Sixteenth Century," *Hispanic American Historical Review* 67 (1987): 657–95; and Ida Altman, *Emigrants and Society: Extremadura and Spanish America in the Sixteenth Century* (Berkeley: University of California Press, 1989), and the same author's "Spanish Hidalgos and America: The Ovandos of Cáceres," *The Americas* 43 (1987): 326–46.

X   They Would Kill Me

1. For a concise discussion of the perpetuity of the *encomienda*, see Hemming, *Conquest of the Incas*, pp. 385–400.
2. AGI, Justicia 1076.
3. Noguerol's activities may be traced in the *cabildo* sessions of the city of Arequipa, Archivo Municipal de Arequipa, Libros de Cabildo, Aug. 1551, Jan. 1552, and Apr., Oct., and Nov. 1553.
4. The following account of Noguerol's actions and tribulations in the rebellion of Francisco Hernández Girón is primarily extracted from his service report, prepared before the Audiencia of Lima before his departure for Spain; AGI, Patronato 109.
5. General descriptions of the Girón revolt can be found in the chroniclers. Noguerol's role and statement is found in AGI, Patronato 109.
6. AGI, Patronato 109.
7. Ibid. On doña Catalina's and doña Francisca's family ties, refer to n. 10 in chapter VIII.
8. AGI, Justicia 471.
9. Ibid.
10. AGI, Patronato 109.
11. Unfortunately, we were unable to find the exact date of departure from Peru or

arrival in Seville. The last notice of the couple in Lima is 18 Jan. 1555, and the first dated appearance of Noguerol in Spain is 22 Dec. 1556. Thus there are almost two years that are unaccounted for. According to a statement Francisco made in 1562, saying that "it was some six years ago, more or less" that he learned of doña Beatriz de Villasur's lawsuit against him while he was still in Peru and that he came to Spain with license from the Viceroy Marqués de Cañete (who took office in 1556), it would seem that the couple departed from Lima sometime in 1556 (see chapter XLI). Notice of their slave cargo transported back to Spain is found in the notarial records in Medina del Campo, where the couple later settled (see chapter XLII).

XI Silver Common As Copper

1. Mateo Alemán, *Guzmán de Alfarache*; we have used the 1623 James Mabbe translation, *The Rogue, or the Life of Guzmán de Alfarache*, 4 vols. (New York: Alfred A. Knopf, 1924), 4:264. First published in 1599, the tremendously popular novel reached its thirtieth edition within six years! The work of Mateo Alemán is described by José Fradejas Lebrero, *Novela corta del siglo XVI*, 2 vols. (Barcelona: Plaza & Janés, 1985), 1:266–79. Mateo's father was a physician for the jail, of Jewish origin; his mother was of Italian descent. Mateo was born in 1547 and would have been about nine when Noguerol and Catalina returned from the Indies. The first part of his novel *Guzmán de Alfarache* was published in 1599. See also Defourneaux, *Daily Life*, pp. 75–88.

2. The best description of Seville in the sixteenth century is found in Francisco Morales Padrón, *Historia de Sevilla: La ciudad del quinientos* (Seville: Universidad de Sevilla, 1983), pp. 21–23; see also Ruth Pike, *Aristocrats and Traders: Sevillian Society in the Sixteenth Century* (Ithaca, N.Y.: Cornell University Press, 1972), p. 21. Guzmán de Alfarache caught the excitement in his own return to Seville: "When we were come thither, out of the desire that we had to draw profit from those that returned from Peru, and to see our house become such another, as the Contractation house for the Indies; whither, and from whence, barres of gold and silver dayly come, and goe; and that it might bee all built of Plate, and pav'd with Gold" (4:261).

3. We shall see there are several conflicting statements as to the exact time that Noguerol discovered that his first wife was still alive.

XII On the First Ship

1. The verb *desposar* can mean both to betroth as well as to marry; the noun *desposorio* refers to betrothal. In the 1530s a marriage was legally valid when a couple freely consented to accept each other as man and wife in words of the present tense. It was to be done publicly and in the presence of a clergyman. For general work on marriage in early modern Europe, see John T. Noonan, Jr., *Power to Dissolve: Lawyers and Marriages in the Courts of the Roman Curia* (Cambridge, Mass.: Harvard University Press, 1972); Lawrence Stone, *The Family, Sex and Marriage in England 1500–1800*, abridged ed. (New York: Harper Torchbooks, 1979); Frances Gies and Joseph Gies, *Marriage and the Family in the Middle Ages* (New York: Harper & Row, 1987).

2. The *censo*, or bond, was initially brought to Spain in the late Middle Ages by Italian

merchants and by the sixteenth century was widely used. *Censos* were loans given to individuals or towns in return for annuities until the debt was repaid. The most common were the *censo al quitar*, a short-term loan in which the title to the property was transferred to the *censo* holder for a limited time, until the debt was canceled; the other, the *censo enfiteutico*, was a long-term loan, did not entail a transfer of title, and could be passed by inheritance. *Juros* were loans to the state. See Elliot, *Imperial Spain*, p. 186; Richard L. Kagan, *Lawsuits and Litigants in Castile, 1500–1700* (Chapel Hill: University of North Carolina Press, 1981), p. 132; and Henry Kamen, *Spain, 1469–1714: A Society in Conflict* (New York: Longman, 1983), p. 108.

3. AGI, Justicia 1076. It is here, in Valladolid in the summer of 1554, that the case of transatlantic bigamy actually gets under way. The best account of the way that the sixteenth-century Spanish legal system operated is to be found in Kagan, *Lawsuits and Litigants*.

XIII · I Promise You

1. For bigamy and the role of the Inquisition, see Henry Kamen, *Inquisition and Society in Spain in the Sixteenth and Seventeenth Centuries* (Bloomington: Indiana University Press, 1985). Generally, the Inquisition ruled in cases that also involved heresy. The secular courts usually claimed jurisdiction in the charge of bigamy. In the period Kamen studied, about 6 percent of all cases brought before the Inquisition dealt with bigamy (pp. 183–85). Kamen states: "From the mid-sixteenth century five years in the galleys became the standard punishment for men—a much lighter penalty than that meted out by secular courts. Women, no less than men, were frequent bigamists" (p. 206). For specific cases of attempts to end marriages, see Noonan, *Power to Dissolve*. For the importance of Medina del Campo, see Alberto Marcos Martín, *Auge y declive de un nucleo mercantil y financiero de Castilla la Vieja: Evolución demográfica de Medina del Campo durante los siglos xvi y xvii* (Valladolid: Universidad de Valladolid, 1978).

2. AGI, Justicia 1076.

3. Ibid. See Patricia Seed, *To Love, Honor, and Obey in Colonial Mexico: Conflicts over Marriage Choice, 1574–1821* (Stanford, Calif.: Stanford University Press, 1988).

4. In the 1530s the dowry was not inconsequential. By mid-century, with inflation, the buying power was rapidly diminishing. See Earl J. Hamilton, *American Treasure and the Price Revolution in Spain, 1501–1650* (Cambridge, Mass.: Harvard University Press, 1934).

5. AGI, Justicia 1076. There may be some confusion for a modern reader given that the documents presented by doña Beatriz often imply betrothal rather than marriage. A marriage consisted of several steps, the first being a formal contract between the parents of the couple regarding financial settlement; next a betrothal, where the bride and groom exchanged words of mutual acceptance; then it was required to publish banns in order to prevent a union where there were obvious impediments; next came a Church ceremony; and last, consummation. See Stone, *The Family, Sex and Marriage*, p. 30. The exchange of words of the present, however, was binding, and in the eyes of the Church it constituted a marriage. To help clarify, author Beatrice Gottlieb suggests we should think of marriage "as a process that takes place over time, consisting of several steps. This is the key to

understanding much of what is confusing about earlier European marriage practices. The most important element in the process is betrothal; the ways in which it can be important, however, are not immediately apparent to those of us who are unaccustomed to thinking of marriage as a process." Beatrice Gottlieb, "The Meaning of Clandestine Marriage," in *Family and Sexuality in French History*, ed. Robert Wheaton and Tamara K. Hareven (Philadelphia: University of Pennsylvania Press, 1980), p. 49. Francisco Noguerol himself stated in 1557: "I in reality married by words the said doña Beatriz de Villasur, in front of all the aforesaid and many learned people who were found present, and by the hand of the clergyman, although I was not consenting of my free will." AGI, Justicia 1076.

6. AGI, Justicia 1076.
7. Ibid.
8. Ibid. The origins of the fair in Villalón date to 1294, when Ferdinand III authorized weekly Saturday fairs. The broader importance of the city's fairs was recognized as Juan II in 1436 transferred the fair of Medina del Ríoseco to Villalón. At about the same time, jurisdiction of the city was turned over to don Rodrigo Alonso Pimentel, the Count of Benavente. Between 1491 and 1492 Ferdinand and Isabella attempted to shift commercial activities to Medina del Campo but failed because of pressures from the Count of Benavente. Jesús Urrea Fernández and José Carlos Brasas Ejido, *Antiguo partido judicial de Villalón* (Valladolid: Disputación Provincial de Valladolid, 1981), pp. 119–21. The town retains its distinctive commercial flavor. Of special architectural note is the 1523 rollo, one of the finest remaining in Spain.
9. AGI, Justicia 1076. This important, although short, correspondence allows insight into early sixteenth-century commercial relationships. For trade and commerce, especially as it relates to Medina del Campo, see Henri Lapeyre, *Une famille de marchands, les Ruiz: Contribution a l'étude du commerce entre la France et l'Espagne au temps de Philippe II* (Paris: A. Colin, 1955).
10. AGI, Justicia 1076. We were unable to determine the exact nature of the difficulties that Noguerol faced at this point.
11. Ibid.
12. Ibid.

XIV   Relieve My Conscience

1. The best study of the way the Spanish legal system functioned, at the level of the individual, is Kagan's *Lawsuits and Litigants*. Kagan stresses the increasing tendency during the period of Spaniards to use the courts to solve grievances. For the work of the Council of the Indies, see Haring, *The Spanish Empire*, pp. 94–109. "In its judicial capacity, the Council sat as a court of last resort in important civil suits appealed from the colonial *audiencias*, and in civil and criminal cases from the judicial chamber of the *Casa de Contratación*. Reserved to it in first instance were all other cases arising in Spain, and concerned with the Indies, as were all matters relating to *encomiendas* of Indians" (p. 98). See also the standard work on the council by Ernesto Schafer, *El Consejo Real y Supremo de las Indias*, 2 vols. (Seville: M. Carmona, 1935–47).
2. Kagan, *Lawsuits and Litigants*, p. 262, points out how little is known of the Castilian lawyer: " No general history of the legal profession exists, and biographical studies of practicing lawyers, as distinguished from judges and jurists, have yet to appear."

3. AGI, Justicia 436, and Justicia 1076.
4. AGI, Justicia 1076.
5. Ibid.
6. Ibid.
7. Ibid.
8. Ibid.

XV   Used Force

1. AGI, Justicia 1076. The distance from Grajal de Campos to Saldaña is not great, about thirty-five kilometers over gently rolling wheatlands. A reasonably good and direct road connected the two places. Furthermore, Sahagún is only five kilometers distant from Grajal. There was regular commercial contact between Sahagún and Saldaña, and rumors of famous sons in the Indies would have made the route quickly.
2. Ibid.
3. Ibid.; refer to Seed's *To Love, Honor, and Obey*. A free consent between marriage partners became, following Gratian's compilation of laws, the *Concordia discordantium Canonum* in 1142, one of the key elements to true marriage, and coercion of one partner was often used as a justification for annulment. See Noonan, *Power to Dissolve*, and Gottlieb, "Clandestine Marriage."
4. AGI, Justicia 1076.
5. The difficulty of communications between Spain and the Indies has been described by many, even contemporary observers, as we shall note. Unfortunately, the journey from the West Indies to Peru was as time-consuming and dangerous as the Atlantic crossing.
6. AGI, Justicia 1076.
7. Ibid.
8. Ibid.

XVI   Justice Will Not Be Lost

1. Kagan, *Lawsuits and Litigants*, p. 11.
2. Licentiate Martín Ruiz de Agreda was appointed *fiscal* on 13 June 1551 and served until 26 May 1558, when he was promoted to councilor. His defense of the king's interests led him to higher office as councilor for the Council of Castile on 25 Aug. 1560. See Schafer, *Consejo de las Indias*, 1:355 and 367.
3. AGI, Justicia 1076.
4. Ibid.
5. Ibid., or so we read in the letters of the nuns and the testimony of Noguerol's witnesses.
6. Ibid.
7. Ibid.
8. Ibid. We, too, checked the ship's register to see if the cargo was properly accounted for. See AGI, Contratación 2146. It is also interesting to note that Diego de Zárate was Lope de Mendieta's father-in-law.
9. AGI, Justicia 1076.
10. Ibid.

11. Ibid. Villaflores in the sixteenth century was a more prosperous place than it is today. There exists an early seventeenth-century contemporary description in Antonio Casaseca Casaseca and José Ramón Nieto González, eds., *Libro de los lugares y aldeas del obispado de Salamanca (manuscrito de 1604–1629)* (Salamanca: Universidad de Salamanca, 1982), pp. 195–96.

12. AGI, Justicia 1076.

XVII She Should Receive

1. AGI, Justicia 1076.
2. Ibid.
3. Dissolution of a consummated marriage was difficult. If uncompleted, the union could be broken to allow one to enter the Church, or for "grave cause." The pope alone had the authority to annul a marriage, by "un acto de la suprema potestad apostólica." If one spouse died, the other could remarry. If later it was discovered an error had been committed, the husband had to return to the first wife. See "Matrimonio" in the *Enciclopedia Universal Ilustrada Europeo-Americana*, 70 vols. (Madrid: Espasa, 1958), 33:1012–1147.
4. AGI, Justicia 1076. According to Noonan, *Power to Dissolve*, p. 22, it was not uncommon "for a wife to obtain from the court an order directing her husband to pay her living expenses during the suit (*alimenta*, the original alimony) and the expenses of litigation."
5. That he knew in Peru of action in Spain against him is clear from his prepared service report made before the Royal Audiencia in Lima, AGI, Patronato 109; see also chapter XLI.

XVIII No Case Is So Expensive

1. AGI, Justicia 1076.
2. Ibid. Guzmán de Alfarache had little good to say of lawyers. Typical of his complaints: "I told him; Sir, you are my friend; the Law is costly, and therefore let me advise you not to enter into it; you are fairly offered, and therefore (if you be wise) take your mandillion, lest you spend your cloake, to recover your coat; you will get nothing in the end by the bargaine; cloake, and coat, and whatsoever else you pretend, will goe all away in fees, so that the Lawyer at last will have all, and you your selfe nothing" (Alemán, *Guzmán de Alfarache*, 3:230).
3. AGI, Justicia 1076.
4. Ibid.
5. Ibid.; was this slip on the part of the council a simple error of the pen, or was it an intended act, in order to prolong the feuding? It seems highly unlikely that this could have been a mere oversight.
6. Ibid.
7. Ibid.

XIX In Truthful Ignorance

1. AGI, Justicia 1076.
2. Ibid.

3. The Santander family must have had important connections in León. Certainly, Noguerol did not find a sympathetic hearing in the diocesan court at León.
4. AGI, Justicia 1076.

XX He Should Be Jailed

1. AGI, Justicia 1076.
2. The Cortes that met at Toro in 1505 passed eighty-three laws, later ratified by King Ferdinand, which superseded previous regulations and became the prevailing legislation of the sixteenth century. The ordinance dealt primarily with issues of inheritance, succession to an entail (*mayorazgo*), relationship between married children and parents, marriage (prohibiting clandestine marriages under penalty of losing all property), adultery, dowry, and certain rights of women. For example, women could not conduct business without license of their husband, although a judge could compel a husband to give his wife license to act if there was a legitimate reason; or if a husband was absent for a long period of time, a judge could give the wife license to conduct business in his absence. A copy of the Laws of Toro (1505) can be found in *Los códigos españoles concordados y anotados*, 12 vols. (Madrid, 1872–84). We have used the facsimile edition of the *Compendio de los comentarios extendidos por el maestro Antonio Gómez, a las ochenta y tres leyes de Toro* (Madrid: Joseph Deblado, 1785), published in Valladolid in 1981. Yñigo López de Mondragón also represented Diego de Alvarado and his companions in a suit against Hernando Pizarro, receiving 20 ducats each year in fees. Schafer, *Consejo de Indias*, 1:59.
3. AGI, Justicia 1076.
4. Ibid.

XXI In Search of the Fugitive

1. AGI, Justicia 1076.
2. Ibid. What, indeed, was Gaspar doing at the convent? None of the witnesses offered an explanation.
3. Ibid.
4. Ibid.
5. Ibid.
6. Ibid.
7. Ibid.

XXII I Have Presented Myself

1. AGI, Justicia 1076.
2. Ibid. Licentiate Santander had a long career as court reporter (*relator*) of the Council of the Indies. He was appointed on 31 July 1545 and served until his death on 8 April 1569. He had much paperwork to handle as sole *relator*, until a second was added in 1566. The reporters often took their principal papers home with them after they finished a case. (Schafer, *Consejo de Indias*, 1:117, 366, and 374). Court *relatores* were trained lawyers who had an important position in the courts and were charged with summarizing the arguments presented by the litigants. Because

they were expected to live from fees paid by the litigants and in practice were paid only by the winning party, they were open to bribes, although, if such abuses were found, the *relatores* were punished. For more information, see Kagan, *Lawsuits and Litigants*, pp. 40–41.

XXIII Are You Married?

1. AGI, Justicia 1076.
2. Ibid.
3. Noonan in *Power to Dissolve*, pp. 1–79, offers another interesting case of bigamy in the chapter "The Steady Man." Charles of Lorraine married his cousin Nicole in 1621, and after a long separation from his wife, he married Béatrice of Cusance in 1637. Charles tried to have his first marriage annuled, on the basis of coercion but was unsuccessful. He lived with his second wife, regardless of the Church's displeasure, and finally both were excommunicated until they did separate. Eventually, in 1657 Nicole died. By that time Charles had cooled toward Béatrice and to her chagrin took no immediate action to "ratify his marriage" with her. In the end they did marry again, legally, in 1664, but two weeks later Béatrice died, and the grief-stricken Charles married within a year a thirteen-year-old girl. He was sixty-two.
4. Martin Ingram, "Spousals Litigation in the English Ecclesiastical Courts c. 1350– c. 1640," in *Marriage and Society: Studies in the Social History of Marriage*, ed. R. B. Outhwaite (London: Europa Publications, 1981), pp. 46–47, points out that it was customary for a couple "to exchange gifts or tokens symbolic of a binding union, including sometimes a ring by the man."
5. AGI, Justicia 1076. It seems that Agreda was prodding Santander in Noguerol's confession. For the *fiscal*, the most important issue, of course, was whether or not the king had been defrauded of the revenues on the treasure that Noguerol shipped back to Spain.

XXIV This Claim

1. AGI, Justicia 1076.
2. Ibid.
3. Ibid. There were numerous ways that sixteenth-century lawyers attempted to delay the working of the courts, as Kagan points out in *Lawsuits and Litigants*, pp. 43– 48, 83–84.

XXV Foul Odors and Vapors

1. AGI, Justicia 1076.
2. Ibid.
3. Ibid.
4. Ibid.

XXVI I Consent

1. AGI, Justicia 1076. See also chapter IX, n. 4, Lockhart's observation regarding receipts for "fictional dowries."

2. Ibid.
3. Ibid.

XXVII   No Hope of Survival

1. Again, Kagan's *Lawsuits and Litigants* provides the finest account in English of the Spanish legal process.
2. AGI, Justicia 1076.
3. Ibid.

XXVIII   Give Me the City

1. Luis Antonio Ribot García, et al., *Valladolid, corazón del mundo hispánico, siglo XVI* (Valladolid: Ateneo de Valladolid, 1981), pp. 38–40; see also J. J. Martín González, *Monumentos civiles de la ciudad de Valladolid* (Valladolid: Institución Cultural Simancas, 1983).
2. AGI, Justicia 1076.
3. Ibid.

XXIX   A Wise Man

1. AGI, Justicia 1076.
2. Ibid.
3. Ibid.
4. Ibid.
5. Ibid.
6. Ibid.
7. Ibid.
8. Ibid.
9. Ibid. Captain Gabriel de Rojas enjoyed a colorful career in the New World. He was born in Cuéllar, province of Segovia in Spain, came to the Indies around 1514, and distinguished himself in Nicaragua. He arrived in Peru, invited by his friend Francisco Pizarro in 1533, went to Jauja, and played a key role in the defense of Cuzco during the uprising of Manco Capac, commanding one of the three cavalry contingents that had attacked the native insurgents. In one of the many skirmishes with the Indians he was wounded by an arrow that penetrated his nose and palate. When Diego de Almagro returned from Chile, Gabriel de Rojas joined him in the conflict with the Pizarros, and Almagro named him his deputy in Cuzco. Following the Almagrist defeat at the battle of Salinas (1538), Captain Rojas was imprisoned by Gonzalo Pizarro but was soon freed and served the Pizarros again. During the uprising of Gonzalo Pizarro, however, he at first supported the Viceroy Blasco Núñez Vela, and Gonzalo imprisoned him but later released him, and the captain supported the rebels. When Pedro de la Gasca arrived, he joined him, as so many others had done. He died in Cuzco in 1548. Much of this sketch is based on Manuel de Mendiburu, *Diccionario histórico biográfico del Perú*, 11 vols. (Lima, 1931–36), 9:466–71; and Hemming, *Conquest of the Incas*, pp. 191–92, 204. Mendiburu praises the brave captain, but he reproaches him for "his flexibility to adjust to anything, and accept posts regardless of how contradictory they might have

been." Indeed, compared with Gabriel de Rojas, Francisco Noguerol was a steady man.

10. AGI, Justicia 1076.
11. Ibid.
12. Ibid.
13. Ibid.
14. Ibid.
15. See Domingo de Santo Tomás, *Gramática o arte de la lengua general de los indios de los reinos del Perú* (Lima: San Marcos, 1951), and the same author's *Lexicón, o vocabulario de la lengua general del Perú* (Lima: San Marcos, 1951). An assessment of the importance of this Dominican friar can be found in John Murra, *Formaciones económicas y políticas del mundo andino* (Lima: Instituto de Estudios Peruanos, 1975), pp. 306–11. The work of Domingo de Santo Tomás was first published in Valladolid in 1560.
16. AGI, Justicia 1076.
17. Ibid.
18. Ibid.
19. Ibid.
20. According to law, an *encomendero* who married a woman with an *encomienda* would have to relinquish one of the grants. Los Collaguas was obviously the more lucrative *repartimiento*, and that was the one the couple had retained.

XXX Shock and Great Sadness

1. AGI, Justicia 1076.
2. Ibid.
3. Ibid.
4. Epidemics of the period have received increasing scholarly attention. See especially Vicente Pérez Moreda, *Las crisis de mortalidad en la España interior (siglos XVI–XIX)* (Madrid: Siglo Veintiuno, 1980); and José Antonio Salas Ausens, *La población en Barbastro en los siglos XVI y XVII* (Zaragoza: Institución "Fernando el Católico," 1981).
5. AGI, Justicia 1076.
6. Ibid.
7. For more information on the role of Indian women in Peruvian colonial society, see Burkett, "Indian Women and White Society." She points out, "The second major change in the lives of village women was in the character of the labor demands, both legal and illegal, made by the *encomenderos*. . . . Thus Spanish demands for women for personal service were a new element in that society. A key question, of course, is the meaning of personal service. On a legalistic basis such service meant cooking, cleaning, sewing, and performing other household tasks. Yet it would appear, if from no other evidence than the number of children whom Indian women bore by their masters, that service included sexual duties as well" (p. 109).
8. AGI, Justicia 1076.
9. Ibid.
10. Ibid.
11. Ibid.

12. Ibid.
13. Ibid.

XXXI   Never Forgive the Nuns

1. AGI, Justicia 1076; for at least one of a long Noguerol line in Galicia, see Javier Ruiz Almansa, *La población de Galicia, 1500–1945* (Madrid: Consejo Superior de Investigaciones Científicas, 1948), pp. 52 and 116.
2. AGI, Justicia 1076.
3. Ibid.
4. Ibid.
5. Ibid.
6. Ibid.
7. Ibid.

XXXII   He and She Knowing

1. AGI, Justicia 1076.
2. Ibid.
3. Ibid.
4. Ibid.
5. Ibid.
6. Ibid.

XXXIII   Married Life Together

1. AGI, Justicia 1076. Although the Spanish term *posesión* literally translates as "possession," it really has a much broader meaning that is impossible to express with one word. In the present instance it implies having the company, intellectual as well as physical, of a spouse.
2. Ibid.

XXXIV   Compel and Force

1. AGI, Justicia 1076.
2. Ibid.
3. Ibid.
4. Ibid. Noguerol's innocence regarding the charges of illegal shipment of treasure back to Spain was not to be challenged again. Fiscal Agreda was probably correct in arguing that the fine stemming from Noguerol's marriage to two women could have been higher. But this case was unusual because of the seemingly trustworthy letters from nuns testifying to the death of the first wife.
5. Ibid.
6. Ibid.

XXXV   Leave the House

1. AGI, Justicia 1076.
2. Ibid.
3. Ibid.

XXXVI   Contrary to the Truth

1. Fernández Catón, *Monasterio de San Pedro de las Dueñas*, pp. 7–9; AGI, Justicia 1076.
2. AGI, Justicia 1076.
3. Ibid.
4. Ibid.
5. Ibid.
6. Ibid. The testimony of nuns was almost always given much credit, and that of the abbess even more. See Judith C. Brown, *Immodest Acts: The Life of a Lesbian Nun in Renaissance Italy* (New York: Oxford University Press, 1986), for an ecclesiastical investigation into the actions in a convent in Italy some six decades after this inquiry focusing on the letters written by doña Ynés and doña Francisca Noguerol.

XXXVII   Shall Not Meet

1. The relationship between Church and state in Spain regarding the marital relationship is outlined in Kagan, *Lawsuits and Litigants*, pp. 33–34; AGI, Justicia 1076, and Patronato 109.
2. Casaseca and Nieto, *Aldeas del obispado de Salamanca*, pp. 195–96. Noguerol would continue to need access to the court at Valladolid, to pursue other legal claims; AGI, Patronato 109.
3. Kamen, *Spain*, pp. 45–46, 177–78; see also Ludwig von Pastor, *The History of the Popes* (London: Routledge & Kegan Paul, 1924), 14:65–67, 138.

XXXVIII   Carnal Intercourse

1. AGI, Patronato 109.
2. Ibid.
3. Noonan, *Power to Dissolve*, pp. 24–25, provides a useful brief description of the evolution of canon law from the twelfth to the sixteenth century. One of the earliest compilations of canon law was collected by Gratian in 1142; in 1232 five books of case law, the *Decretals* of Gregory IX, were added; the fourth dealt with marriage. In 1300 Pope Boniface VIII completed the collection with book six. In 1317 the Constitutions of Clement V (the *Clementines*) and later in 1330 more additions by Pope John XXII were attached. "The canons emanating in broad statutory form from the Council of Trent between 1548–64 were the last word, building on earlier decisions and sometimes overriding them. Together, these several documents of the past five centuries answered to the description 'law.'" See also Peter Partner, *Renaissance Rome, 1500–1559* (Berkeley: University of California Press, 1976), esp. pp. 41–46.
4. AGI, Patronato 109.
5. Ibid.
6. Ibid.
7. Ibid.

XXXIX   To Sin Mortally

1. AHPV, Colección de cartas, Simón Ruiz, C 66–299. Medina del Campo, 12 Nov. 1581. The best study of banking in general in sixteenth-century Spain is Ramón

Carande, *Carlos V y sus banqueros*, 3 vols. (Madrid: Revista de Occidente, 1949–67); regarding the Ruiz family, see the important work of Lapeyre, *Une famille de marchands, les Ruiz*.

2. AGI, Patronato 109. Emphasis is ours.
3. Ibid.
4. Ibid.
5. Ibid.
6. Ibid.

XL   The Principal Houses

1. Casaseca and Nieto, *Aldeas del obispado de Salamanca*, provides a fine description of the region around Salamanca.

2. Ildefonso Rodríguez y Fernández, *Historia de la muy noble, muy leal y coronada villa de Medina del Campo* (Madrid: San Francisco de Sales, 1903–1904), continues to be a mine of information on the history of the city. See also Marcos Martín, *Auge y declive*; and for the architectural and artistic history of Medina, Estéban García Chico, *Catálogo monumental de la Provincia de Valladolid: Medina del Campo* (Valladolid: Diputación Provincial de Valladolid, 1961); and Falah Hassan Abed Al-Hussein, "Trade and Business Community in Old Castile: Medina del Campo, 1500–1575" (Ph.D. diss., University of East Anglia, 1982).

3. Much of this section is based on examination of the *cabildo* records of Medina for the period that Francisco and Catalina lived there. A good general history of Medina del Campo from the late fifteenth century could be written on the basis of these, and the notarial records now in the AHPV.

4. The one clue that led us to follow Noguerol's footsteps to Medina del Campo was a note collected in the BNL, B 1173, in 1974, while engaged in other research. B 1173 includes part of a 1601 copy of his will that refers to Arequipa (incorrectly dated 1701 in the card catalogue of the manuscript collection). The clause was part of Noguerol's original testament dated in Medina del Campo on 8 Aug. 1580. The use of notarial records is difficult. The problems of research have been succinctly evaluated by Lockhart in *Spanish Peru*, pp. 269–71. Most but not all of Medina del Campo's registers were transferred to Valladolid. The city was large, and there were numerous scribes. Several hundred bundles, with up to two thousand pages each, often not numbered or indexed, exist for the sixteenth century. Finding the correct notary, then document, is based partly on luck and partly on educated guesswork.

5. Cesare Borgia was briefly imprisoned in the castle of La Mota and was able to escape, though not without injuries. See Ivan Cloulas, *The Borgias* (New York: Franklin Watts, 1989), pp. 262–63; and Miller, *Castles and the Crown*, p. 267.

6. Hemming, *Conquest of the Incas*, pp. 285–87.

7. See Eufemio Lorenzo Sanz, ed., *Historia de Medina del Campo y su tierra*, 3 vols. (Valladolid: Andrés Martín, 1986).

8. AHPV, Protocolos, Agustín de Tapia 7013. Regarding his own research for the *Men of Cajamarca*, James Lockhart stressed the need for careful examination of records in the places the conquistadores settled when they returned to the homeland. "All the archival collections and subsections thought likely to contain concentrated relevant material were examined, with one large exception: the local archives of the many places to which the conquerors returned in Spain. These could doubtless tell

us much, yet to investigate them thoroughly would be the work of years. Perhaps the desired data can come out of research aimed primarily at Spanish regional history. Without any doubt more information will come to light. It is hoped, indeed, that this study will help scholars working on related materials to see the potential value of scraps they might have discarded" (p. xv). The reader may wish here to return to the statement in the prologue of Lazarillo de Tormes, on our dedicatory page: "nothing should be thrown away or given up completely."

9. The *siete linajes* are discussed by Gerardo Moraleja Pinilla, *Historia de Medina del Campo* (Medina del Campo: Mateo Alaguero, 1971); and Rodríguez y Fernández, *Historia de Medina del Campo*, pp. 63–80.

XLI   I Am Despoiled

1. AGI, Patronato 109; Lima 119. At various points throughout the long legal process Noguerol was called on to provide adequate bonds, which were to cover any losses to the Crown should the *encomendero* fail to resume residency in Peru and assume his responsibilities there. An outline of Viceroy Cañete's administration in Peru may be found in Rubén Vargas Ugarte, *Historia del Perú: Virreinato (1551–1600)* (Buenos Aires: A. Baiocco, 1949), pp. 65–118.
2. AGI, Patronato 109.
3. Ibid.
4. Ibid.
5. Ibid., Justicia 1076.

XLII   And Gave Freedom

1. AHPV, Protocolos, Agustín de Tapia 7013 and 7014. Elinor C. Burkett, in "The Notarial Archives: Facts Beyond the Fad," in John Jay TePaske, ed., *Research Guide to Andean History: Bolivia, Chile, Ecuador and Peru* (Durham, N.C.: Duke University Press, 1981), p. 295, warns the researcher not to become "lost in the detail. Despite their repetitive and formal nature, the documents are fascinating as a real sample of life on a day-to-day level. The minutiae they provide is intriguing, making it difficult not to drown in the information."
2. AHPV, Protocolos, Agustín de Tapia 7014.
3. Ibid. 7013 and 7014. Gómez de León was the first husband of doña Francisca de Vergara. He died at the battle of Huarina in 1547.
4. Kagan, *Lawsuits and Litigants*, p. 132; Kamen, *Spain*, p. 108. Hassan Abed Al-Hussein, "Trade and Business Community," pp. 131–38, discusses the *censos* and the *juros* in the context of Medina del Campo. For a definition of *censo*, see chapter XII, n. 2.
5. AHPV, Protocolos, Agustín de Tapia 7014 and 7019.
6. Ibid. 7013, 7014, and 7019.
7. Ibid.
8. Ibid. 7014.
9. Ibid. 7013.
10. Ibid. 7013 and 7014. Hassan Abed Al-Hussein, "Trade and Business Community," n. 33/34, reports that "manumission, it seems, always took place at the death of the merchant or his wife."

XLIII Perpetual Memory

1. The prototype of the conquistador has recently been studied by Francisco de Solano, "El conquistador hispano: Señas de identidad," in *Proceso histórico al conquistador*, ed. Francisco de Solano (Madrid: Alianza Editorial, 1988), pp. 15–36. Standard studies include F. A. Kirkpatrick, *The Spanish Conquistadores* (Cleveland: World Publishing, 1967); and Jean Descola, *The Conquistadors* (New York: Viking, 1957). Of value is Jacques Lafaye, *Les conquistadors* (Paris: Le Seuil, 1973). Charles Gibson, *Spain in America* (New York: Harper and Row, 1966), p. 36, brilliantly sums up the often conflicting characteristics of the Spanish conquerors: "In conquest Spaniards demonstrated an almost superhuman determination to overcome obstacles and a supreme indifference to difficulties. Spanish fatalism, the obsession with death, and the mockery of life recur under everchanging conditions. Material and spiritual goals mingle in fascinating patterns. Combinations of lust and sentimentality, of honorable and base conduct, of altruism and selfishness occur and reoccur. The Spaniard appears as a man of epic qualities who descends to the depths of inhumanity. Valiant, cruel, indefatigable, ferocious, courageous, and villainous—Spanish character alternates among extremes and displays that 'coexistence of contrary tendencies' for which it is so celebrated." Bennassar, *Spanish Character*, p. 248, helps illuminate contrary tendencies regarding a preoccupation with death and a disregard of danger: "Thus the contemplation of death encouraged the absence of respect for life by developing a sort of exemption from risk . . . this by no means excluded joy of life."

2. Elliot, *Imperial Spain*, pp. 109–111; Lynch, *Spain under the Habsburgs*, pp. 103–104; and Kamen, *Spain*, p. 104. Keniston, *Francisco de los Cobos*, pp. 241–47, describes the secretary's similar *mayorazgo*, while Hassan Abed Al-Hussein, "Trade and Business Community," pp. 199–200, does the same for the *mayorazgo* in Medina del Campo.

3. AHPV, Protocolos, Agustín de Tapia 7014 and 7020, and Yñigo de Argandoña 7069 and 7071.

4. AHPV, Protocolos, Agustín de Tapia 7014. Julius Rivera, *Latin America: A Sociocultural Interpretation* (New York: Meredith, 1971), p. 6, states the desire for remembrance well: "Latin Americans fear oblivion and defy death; they even welcome death but refuse to be forgotten."

5. AHPV, Protocolos, Agustín de Tapia 7014 and 7020. The personal religious implications of these moves on the part of the couple are best delineated by William A. Christian, *Local Religion in Sixteenth-Century Spain* (Princeton, N.J.: Princeton University Press, 1981). For France, Michel Vovelle with Gaby Vovelle have used in part testaments to study religion of the commoners in *Vision de la mort el de l'audelà en Provence du XVe au XXe siècle* (Paris: A. Colin, 1970). See also Bennassar, *Spanish Character*, pp. 237–48 on Spanish preoccupation with dying well.

6. Rodríguez y Fernández, *Historia de Medina del Campo*, pp. 874–75.

XLIV Carry the Name

1. AHPV, Protocolos, Yñigo de Argandoña 7068.
2. Ibid.
3. Ibid.
4. Ibid.

XLV Interred in My Chapel

1. Also based on Noguerol's will, AHPV, Protocolos, Yñigo de Argandoña 7068. It seems Francisco died at the end of September 1581, but we lack the exact date.
2. Ibid. From the thirteenth to the eighteenth centuries, pious clauses constituted substantial parts of most European wills, not just those of Spain. See Philippe Ariès, *Western Attitudes toward Death: From the Middle Ages to the Present* (Baltimore: Johns Hopkins University Press, 1974), pp. 63–64.
3. BNL, B 1173. For a general study of restitution made by conquistadores to native Americans in Peru, based on last wills, see Guillermo Lohmann Villena, "La restitución por conquistadores y encomenderos: Un aspecto de la incidencia Lascasiana en el Perú," *Anuario de Estudios Americanos* 23 (1966): 21–89.

XLVI From the Estate

1. AHPV, Protocolos, Agustín de Tapia 7019.
2. Ibid. 7019 and 7022.

XLVII He Had Consummated

1. AHPV, Protocolos, Agustín de Tapia 7021.
2. Ibid.
3. Ibid.
4. Ibid.
5. Ibid. 7022.

XLVIII Has Not Fulfilled

1. AHPV, Colección de Cartas, Simón Ruiz, C 91–267, 16 Sept. 1584.
2. AHPV, Protocolos, Agustín de Tapia 7021, and Yñigo de Argandoña 7072.
3. AHPV, Protocolos, Agustín de Tapia 7020, for earlier collection of the revenue; and Yñigo de Argandoña 7073.
4. AHPV, Protocolos, Yñigo de Argandoña 7075.

XLIX As Good Brothers

1. AHPV, Protocolos, Agustín de Tapia 7029. Doña Catalina de Vergara's signed will was opened on 4 Feb. 1592; she must have died shortly before then, but we are missing the exact date of her death. The testament is the foundation for this chapter. We assume that in the short term her wishes were carried out and the burial took place in the fashion outlined in the text.

Epilogue: Treasures Upon Earth

1. AMMC, legajo 368, caja 507. There is no indication why Antonio de Tejada inherited the *mayorazgo*, since there should have been several people with prior claim, according to Noguerol's will. We know that doña Elena de Tejada's children were alive and certainly should have received the *mayorazgo* before their cousin. Archivo Diocesano de Valladolid, Parroquia de Santiago, Medina del Campo,

Libro de Defunciones. Three Lisón de Tejadas died in the parish in a relatively short period of time: Juan in 1587, Antonio in 1589, and a second Juan in 1603.

2. AMMC, Libro de Acuerdos, 1630–34.

3. See Kamen, *Spain*, pp. 196–256; Lynch, *Spain under the Habsburgs*, 2:79–86; and AMMC, legajo 371, caja 511.

4. AMMC, legajo 371, caja 511. It is ironic that one of the compelling reasons prompting the central government to pressure the towns for new funds was the need to block the French siege of the fortress of Fuenterrabía from July to September 1638. Noguerol had served there as a young man just over a century before. See Elliott, *The Count-Duke of Olivares*, pp 537–41.

5. AMMC, legajo 369, caja 508; legajo 410, caja 571.

6. Rodríguez y Fernández, *Historia de Medina del Campo*, pp. 874–75.

7. Ibid., pp. 471, 479, 494. Moraleja Pinilla, *Historia*, pp. 445–52. The fire broke out on 20 Sept. 1810. It is not impossible that remnants of the Noguerol chapel in San Andrés el Real were carted away, to be sold in a faraway land, perhaps even in the New World.

Bibliography

Alemán, Mateo. *The Rogue, or the Life of Guzmán de Alfarache*. 4 vols. New York: Alfred A. Knopf, 1924.

Altman, Ida. *Emigrants and Society: Extremadura and Spanish America in the Sixteenth Century*. Berkeley: University of California Press, 1989.

Altman, Ida L. "Spanish Hidalgos and America: The Ovandos of Cáceres." *The Americas* 43 (1987): 326–46.

Anonymous. *Lazarillo de Tormes (1554)*. In *Two Spanish Picaresque Novels*, translated by Michael Alpert, pp. 21–79. Baltimore, Md.: Penguin Books, 1969.

Ariès, Philippe. *Western Attitudes toward Death: From the Middle Ages to the Present*. Baltimore: Johns Hopkins University Press, 1974.

Bachiller, Manuel (1580). "Antigüedades y sucesos memorables sucedidos en esta muy noble y antigua villa de Simancas." In *Colección de documentos inéditos para la historia de España*, 1:530–63. Madrid: Academia de la Historia, 1842.

Barriga, Víctor M., ed. *Documentos para la historia de Arequipa*. 3 vols. Arequipa, 1939–55.

Bayle, Constantino. *Los cabildos seculares en la América Española*. Madrid: Sapientia, 1952.

Bennassar, Bartolomé. *The Spanish Character: Attitudes and Mentalities from the Sixteenth to the Nineteenth Century*. Berkeley: University of California Press, 1979.

Bomli, P. W. *La Femme dans l'Espagne du siècle d'or*. The Hague: Martinus Nijhoff, 1950.

Braudel, Fernand. *The Mediterranean and the Mediterranean World in the Age of Philip II*. 2 vols. New York: Harper Torchbooks, 1975.

Brown, Judith C. *Immodest Acts: The Life of a Lesbian Nun in Renaissance Italy*. New York: Oxford University Press, 1986.

Burga, Manuel. *De la encomienda a la hacienda capitalista: El valle del Jequetepeque del siglo XVI a XX*. Lima: Instituto de Estudios Peruanos, 1976.

Burkett, Elinor C. "Indian Women and White Society: The Case of Sixteenth Century Peru." In *Latin American Women: Historical Perspectives*, ed. Asunción Lavrin, pp. 101–28. Westport, Conn.: Greenwood Press, 1978.

———. "The Notarial Archives: Facts Beyond the Fad." In *Research Guide to Andean History: Bolivia, Chile, Ecuador and Peru*, ed. John Jay TePaske, pp. 284–99. Durham, N.C.: Duke University Press, 1981.

Busto Duthurburu, José Antonio del. *Diego de Almagro*. Lima, 1964.

———. *Francisco Pizarro. El Marqués Gobernador*. Madrid: Rialp, 1966.

———. *La Pacificación del Perú*. Lima: Libreria Studium, 1984.

Campbell, Leon G. "Women and the Great Rebellion in Peru, 1780–1783." *The Americas* 42 (1985): 163–96.

Carande, Ramón. *Carlos V y sus banqueros*. 3 vols. Madrid: Revista de Occidente, 1949–67.

Casaseca Casaseca, Antonio, and José Ramón Nieto González, eds. *Libro de los lugares y aldeas del obispado de Salamanca (manuscrito de 1604–1629)*. Salamanca: Universidad de Salamanca, 1982.

Chamberlain, Robert S. "Castilian Backgrounds of the Repartimiento-Encomienda." In Carnegie Institution of Washington, *Contributions to American Anthropology and History* 5, no. 25 (1939): 19–66.

Christian, William A. *Local Religion in Sixteenth-Century Spain*. Princeton, N.J.: Princeton University Press, 1981.

Cieza de León, Pedro de. *Obras completas*. 2 vols. Madrid: Instituto Gonzalo Fernández de Oviedo, 1984–85.

Clavero, Bartolomé. *Mayorazgo. Propiedad feudal en Castilla, 1369–1836*. Madrid: Siglo Veintiuno, 1974.

Cloulas, Ivan. *The Borgias*. New York: Franklin Watts, 1989.

Los códigos españoles concordados y anotados. 12 vols. Madrid, 1872–84.

Cohen, Martin. *The Martyr: The Story of a Secret Jew and the Mexican Inquisition in the Sixteenth Century*. Philadelphia: Jewish Publication Society of America, 1973.

Colección de documentos inéditos para la historia de España. 113 vols. Madrid: Academia de la Historia, 1842–95.

Cook, Noble David. *Demographic Collapse: Indian Peru, 1520–1620*. New York: Cambridge University Press, 1981.

———. "Los libros de cargo del tesorero Alonso Riquelme con el rescate de Atahualpa." *Humanidades* 2 (1968): 41–88.

———. *People of the Colca Valley: A Population Study*. Boulder, Colo.: Westview Press, 1982.

Dánvila y Collado, Manuel. *Historia crítica y documentada de las Comunidades de Castilla*. 6 vols. Madrid, 1897–99.

Davies, Keith A. *Landowners in Colonial Peru*. Austin: University of Texas Press, 1984.

Davis, Natalie Zemon. *Fiction in the Archives: Pardon Tales and Their Tellers in Sixteenth-Century France*. Stanford, Calif.: Stanford University Press, 1987.

———. *The Return of Martin Guerre*. Cambridge, Mass.: Harvard University Press, 1983.

Defourneaux, Marcelin. *Daily Life in Spain in the Golden Age*. London: Allen and Unwin, 1970.

Descola, Jean. *The Conquistadors*. New York: Viking, 1957.

Díaz Plaja, Fernando. *La sociedad española*. Barcelona: Plaza & Janés, 1974.

Dillard, Heath. *Daughters of the Reconquest*. New York: Cambridge University Press, 1985.

Domínguez Ortiz, Antonio. *La sociedad española en el siglo xvii*. Madrid: Consejo Superior de Investigaciones Científicas, 1963.

Durán Montero, María Antonia. *Fundación de ciudades en el Perú durante el siglo XVI*. Seville: Escuela de Estudios Hispano-Americanos, 1978.

Elliot, John H. *The Count-Duke of Olivares: The Statesman in an Age of Decline*. New Haven, Conn.: Yale University Press, 1986.

———. *Imperial Spain, 1469–1716*. New York: New American Library, 1966.

Enciclopedia Universal Ilustrada Europeo-Americana. 70 vols. Madrid: Espasa, 1958. 33:1012–47. "Matrimonio."

Enríquez de Guzmán, Alonso. *Vida y aventuras de un caballero noble desbaratado*. Lima: Cantuta, 1970.

Fernández, Diego. *Historia del Perú.* In *Crónicas del Perú,* ed. Juan Pérez de Tudela Bueso, 1:1–2:131. 5 vols. Madrid: Atlas, 1963–65.

Fernández Catón, José María. *Catálogo del archivo del monasterio de San Pedro de las Dueñas.* León: Centro de Estudios e Investigación San Isidoro, 1977.

Fitzmaurice-Kelly, Julia. "Women in Sixteenth Century Spain." *Revue Hispanique* 70 (1927): 557–632.

Flusche, Della M., and Eugene H. Korth. *Forgotten Females: Women of African and Indian Descent in Colonial Chile, 1535–1800.* Detroit: Blaine Ethridge, 1983.

Fradejas Lebrero, José. *Novela corta del siglo XVI.* 2 vols. Barcelona: Plaza & Janés, 1985.

Gakenheimer, Ralph A. "Determinants of Physical Structure of the Peruvian Town of the Sixteenth Century." Ph.D. diss., University of Pennsylvania, 1964.

García Chico, Estéban. *Catálogo monumental de la Provincia de Valladolid: Medina del Campo.* Valladolid: Diputación Provincial de Valladolid, 1961.

Gibson, Charles. *Spain in America.* New York: Harper & Row, 1966.

Gies, Frances and Joseph Gies. *Marriage and the Family in the Middle Ages.* New York: Harper & Row, 1987.

Ginzburg, Carlo. *The Cheese and the Worms: The Cosmos of a Sixteenth-Century Miller.* New York: Penguin, 1982.

Gómez, Antonio. *Compendio de los comentarios extendidos por el maestro Antonio Gómez, a las ochenta y tres leyes de Toro.* Madrid: Joseph Deblado, 1785. Valladolid: Lex Nova, 1981.

Gottlieb, Beatrice. "The Meaning of Clandestine Marriage." In *Family and Sexuality in French History,* ed. Robert Wheaton and Tamara K. Hareven, pp. 49–83. Philadelphia: University of Pennsylvania Press, 1980.

Gutiérrez de Santa Clara, Pedro. *Historia de las guerras civiles del Perú (1544–1548).* In *Crónicas del Perú,* ed. Juan Pérez de Tudela Bueso, pp. 2:132–4:225. 5 vols. Madrid: Atlas, 1963–65.

Hamilton, Earl J. *American Treasure and the Price Revolution in Spain, 1501–1650.* Cambridge, Mass.: Harvard University Press, 1934.

Hampe Martínez, Teodoro. *Don Pedro de la Gasca: Su obra política en España y América.* Lima: Pontifícia Universidad Católica del Perú, 1989.

———. "En torno al levantamiento pizarrista: La intervención del oidor Lisón de Tejada." *Revista de Indias* 44, no. 174 (1984): 385–414.

Hanke, Lewis U. *The Spanish Struggle for Justice in the Conquest of America.* Philadelphia: University of Pennsylvania Press, 1949.

Haring, C. H. *The Spanish Empire in America.* New York: Harcourt, Brace, & World, 1963.

Hassan Abed Al-Hussein, Falah. "Trade and Business Community in Old Castile: Medina del Campo, 1500–1575." Ph.D. diss., University of East Anglia, 1982.

Hemming, John. *The Conquest of the Incas.* London: Sphere Books, 1972.

Höfler, Karl Adolf Constantin. *Don Antonio de Acuña genannt der Luther Spaniens.* Vienna, 1882.

Ingram, Martin. "Spousals Litigation in the English Ecclesiastical Courts c.1350–c.1640." In *Marriage and Society: Studies in the Social History of Marriage,* ed. R. B. Outhwaite, pp. 35–57. London: Europa Publications, 1981.

Kagan, Richard L. *Lawsuits and Litigants in Castile, 1500–1700.* Chapel Hill: University of North Carolina Press, 1981.

Kamen, Henry. *Inquisition and Society in Spain in the Sixteenth and Seventeenth Centuries.* Bloomington: Indiana University Press, 1985.

———. *Spain, 1469–1714: A Society in Conflict.* New York: Longman, 1983.

Keith, Robert G. *Conquest and Agrarian Change: The Emergence of the Hacienda System on the Peruvian Coast.* Cambridge, Mass.: Harvard University Press, 1976.

Keniston, Hayward. *Francisco de los Cobos: Secretary of the Emperor Charles V.* Pittsburgh: University of Pittsburgh Press, 1959.

Kirkpatrick, F. A. *The Spanish Conquistadores.* Cleveland: World Publishing, 1967.

Korth, Eugene E. *Spanish Policy in Colonial Chile: The Struggle for Social Justice, 1535–1700.* Stanford, Calif.: Stanford University Press, 1968.

Lafaye, Jacques. *Les conquistadors.* Paris: Le Seuil, 1973.

Lanning, John Tate. *Pedro de la Torre, Doctor to Conquerors.* Baton Rouge: Louisiana State University Press, 1974.

Lapeyre, Henri. *Une famille de marchands, les Ruiz: Contribution a l'étude du commerce entre la France et l'Espagne au temps de Philippe II.* Paris: A. Colin, 1955.

Lavrin, Asunción, ed. *Latin American Women: Historical Perspectives.* Westport, Conn.: Greenwood Press, 1978.

———, ed. *Sexuality and Marriage in Colonial Latin America.* Lincoln: University of Nebraska Press, 1989.

León, Luis de. *La perfecta casada (1589).* Madrid: Rialp, 1968.

Leonard, Irving. *Books of the Brave.* Cambridge, Mass.: Harvard University Press, 1949.

Le Roy Ladurie, Emmanuel. *Montaillou: The Promised Land of Error.* New York: Vintage, 1979.

Lockhart, James. *Men of Cajamarca: A Social and Biographical Study of the First Conquerors of Peru.* Austin: University of Texas Press, 1972.

———. *Spanish Peru, 1532–1560: A Colonial Society.* Madison: University of Wisconsin Press, 1968.

Lockhart James, and Enrique Otte, eds. *Letters and People of the Spanish Indies: The Sixteenth Century.* Cambridge: Cambridge University Press, 1976.

Lohmann Villena, Guillermo. *El corregidor de los indios en el Perú bajo los Austrias.* Madrid, 1957.

———. "Las expresiones de última voluntad de Francisco Pizarro: Un incierto complejo documental." *Revista Histórica* 34 (1983–84): 17–40.

———. *Los regidores perpetuos del cabildo de Lima (1535–1821).* 2 vols. Seville: Diputación Provincial de Sevilla, 1983.

———. "La restitución por conquistadores y encomenderos: Un aspecto de la incidencia Lascasiana en el Perú." *Anuario de Estudios Americanos* 23 (1966): 21–89.

López de Gómara, Francisco. *Hispania victrix: Historia general de las Indias.* 2 vols. Madrid, 1946–47.

Lunenfeld, Marvin. *Keepers of the City: The Corregidores of Isabella I of Castile (1474–1504).* New York: Cambridge University Press, 1987.

Lynch, John. *Spain under the Habsburgs.* 2 vols. London: Oxford University Press, 1965.

Marcos Martín, Alberto. *Auge y declive de un núcleo mercantil y financiero de Castilla la Vieja: Evolución demográfica de Medina del Campo durante los siglos xvi y xvii.* Valladolid: Universidad de Valladolid, 1978.

Martín, Luis. *Daughters of the Conquistadores: Women of the Viceroyalty of Peru.* Albuquerque: University of New Mexico Press, 1983.

Martín González, J. J. *Monumentos civiles de la ciudad de Valladolid*. Valladolid: Institución Cultural Simancas, 1983.

Martínez, Santiago. *Alcaldes de Arequipa desde 1539 a 1946*. Arequipa, 1946.

———. *Fundadores de Arequipa*. Arequipa, 1936.

Medina, José Toribio. *Biblioteca Hispano-chilena (1523–1817)*. 3 vols. Santiago: José Toribio Medina, 1897–99.

Mendiburu, Manuel de. *Diccionario histórico biográfico del Perú*. 11 vols. Lima, 1931–36.

Merriman, Roger Bigelow. *The Rise of the Spanish Empire in the Old World and in the New*. 4 vols. New York: Macmillan, 1918–34; rpt.: Cooper Square, 1962.

Miller, Townsend. *The Castles and the Crown: Spain, 1451–1555*. New York: Capricorn, 1963.

Moore, John Preston. *The Cabildo in Peru under the Hapsburgs*. Durham, N.C.: Duke University Press, 1954.

Moraleja Pinilla, Gerardo. *Historia de Medina del Campo*. Medina del Campo: Mateo Alaguero, 1971.

Morales Padrón, Francisco. *Historia de Sevilla: La ciudad del quinientos*. Seville: Universidad de Sevilla, 1983.

Mörner, Magnus. *La corona española y los foráneos en los pueblos de indios de América*. Stockholm: Latinamerikanska-institutet i Stockholm, 1970.

Murra, John. *Formaciones económicas y políticas del mundo andino*. Lima: Instituto de Estudios Peruanos, 1975.

Noonan, John T. *The Power to Dissolve: Lawyers and Marriages in the Courts of the Roman Curia*. Cambridge, Mass.: Harvard University Press, 1972.

Outhwaite, R. B., ed. *Marriage and Society: Studies in the Social History of Marriage*. London: Europa Publications, 1981.

Ozment, Steven. *Magdalena and Balthasar*. New York: Simon and Schuster, 1986.

Partner, Peter. *Renaissance Rome, 1500–1559*. Berkeley: University of California Press, 1976.

Pastor, Ludwig von. *The History of the Popes*. 40 vols. London: Routledge & Kegan Paul; St. Louis: Herder, 1891–1953.

Pérez Moreda, Vicente. *Las crisis de mortalidad en la España interior (siglos XVI–XIX)*. Madrid: Siglo Veintiuno, 1980.

Pérez de Tudela Bueso, Juan, ed. *Crónicas del Perú*. 5 vols. Madrid: Atlas, 1963–65.

———, ed. *Documentos relativos a don Pedro de la Gasca y a Gonzalo Pizarro*. 2 vols. Madrid: Real Academia de la Historia, 1964.

Pierson, Peter. *Commander of the Armada: The Seventh Duke of Medina Sidonia*. New Haven, Conn.: Yale University Press, 1989.

Pike, Ruth. *Aristocrats and Traders: Sevillian Society in the Sixteenth Century*. Ithaca, N.Y.: Cornell University Press, 1972.

Pizarro, Pedro. *Relación del descubrimiento y conquista del Perú*. Lima: Universidad Católica, 1978.

Pocock, H. R. S. *The Conquest of Chile*. New York: Stein and Day, 1967.

Porras Barrenechea, Raúl, ed. *Cartas del Perú (1524–1543)*. Lima, 1959.

Prescott, William H. *History of the Conquest of Peru*. 2 vols. New York: Harper and Brothers, 1851.

Ribot García, Luis Antonio, et al. *Valladolid, corazón del mundo hispánico, siglo XVI*. Valladolid: Ateneo de Valladolid, 1981.

Rivera, Julius. *Latin America: A Sociocultural Interpretation.* New York: Meredith, 1971.

Rodríguez y Fernández, Ildefonso. *Historia de la muy noble, muy leal y coronada villa de Medina del Campo.* Madrid: San Francisco de Sales, 1903–1904.

Rostworowski de Diez Canseco, María. "La tasa ordenada por el Licenciado Pedro de la Gasca (1549)." *Revista Histórica* 34 (1985): 53–102.

Ruiz Almansa, Javier. *La población de Galicia, 1500–1945.* Madrid: Consejo Superior de Investigaciones Científicas, 1948.

Salas Ausens, José Antonio. *La población en Barbastro en los siglos XVI y XVII.* Zaragoza: Institución "Fernando el Católico," 1981.

Sandoval, Prudencio de. *Historia del Emperador Carlos V.* 3 vols. Madrid: Atlas, 1955–56.

Santo Tomás, Domingo de. *Gramática o arte de la lengua general de los indios de los reinos del Perú.* Lima: San Marcos, 1951.

———. *Lexicón, o vocabulario de la lengua general del Perú.* Lima: San Marcos, 1951.

Sanz, Eufemio Lorenzo, ed. *Historia de Medina del Campo y su tierra.* 3 vols. Valladolid: Andrés Martín, 1986.

Schafer, Ernesto. *El Consejo Real y Supremo de las Indias.* 2 vols. Seville: M. Carmona, 1935–47.

Seaver, Henry Latimer. *The Great Revolt in Castile: A Study of the Comunero Movement of 1521–1522.* New York: Octagon Books, 1966.

Seed, Patricia. *To Love, Honor, and Obey in Colonial Mexico: Conflicts over Marriage Choice, 1574–1821.* Stanford, Calif.: Stanford University Press, 1988.

Silverblatt, Irene. "Andean Women under Spanish Rule." In *Women and Colonization: Anthropological Perspectives,* ed. Mona Etienne and Elenor Leacock, pp. 149–85. New York: Praeger, 1980.

———. *Moon, Sun, and Witches: Gender Ideologies and Class in Inca and Colonial Peru.* Princeton, N.J.: Princeton University Press, 1987.

Simpson, Lesley B. *The Encomienda in New Spain: The Beginnings of Spanish Mexico.* Rev. ed. Berkeley: University of California Press, 1966.

Solano, Francisco de. "El conquistador hispano: señas de identidad." In *Proceso histórico al conquistador,* ed. Francisco de Solano, pp. 15–36. Madrid: Alianza Editorial, 1988.

Solano, Francisco de, ed. *Proceso histórico al conquistador.* Madrid: Alianza Editorial, 1988.

Stone, Lawrence. *The Family, Sex and Marriage in England 1500–1800.* Abridged ed. New York: Harper Torchbooks, 1979.

Sweet, David G., and Gary B. Nash, eds. *Struggle and Survival in Colonial America.* Berkeley: University of California Press, 1981.

TePaske, John Jay, ed. *Research Guide to Andean History: Bolivia, Chile, Ecuador and Peru.* Durham, N.C.: Duke University Press, 1981.

Thayer Ojeda, Tomás. *Los conquistadores de Chile.* 3 vols. Santiago, 1908–13.

Trelles Arestegui, Efraín. *Lucas Martínez Vegazo: Funcionamiento de una encomienda peruana inicial.* Lima: Universidad Católica, 1983.

Ulloa, Modesto. *La Hacienda Real de Castilla en el reinado de Felipe II.* Madrid, 1977.

Urrea Fernández, Jesús, and José Carlos Brasas Ejido. *Antiguo partido judicial de Villalón.* Valladolid: Diputación Provincial de Valladolid, 1981.

Vargas Ugarte, Rubén. *Historia del Perú: Virreinato (1551–1600)*. Buenos Aires: A. Baiocco, 1949.

Varón Gabai, Rafael, and Auke Pieter Jacobs. "Peruvian Wealth and Spanish Investments: The Pizarro Family during the Sixteenth Century." *Hispanic American Historical Review* 67 (1987): 657–95.

Vassberg, David E. *Land and Society in Golden Age Castile*. New York: Cambridge University Press, 1984.

Vovelle, Michel, with Gaby Vovelle. *Vision de la mort el de l'au-delá en Provence du XVe au XXe siècle*. Paris: A. Colin, 1970.

Wheaton, Robert, and Tamara K. Hareven, eds. *Family and Sexuality in French History*. Philadelphia: University of Pennsylvania Press, 1980.

Zárate, Agustín de. *Historia del descubrimiento y conquista del Perú*. Lima: Miranda, 1944.

Zavala, Silvio. *La encomienda indiana*. Madrid: Centro de Estudios Históricos, 1935.

Index

About the Authors

Noble David Cook, Professor of History, is the author of *The People of the Colca Valley: A Population Study* and *Demographic Collapse: Indian Peru, 1520–1620*, as well as numerous Latin American publications. He is a Guggenheim Fellow for 1990–91.

Alexandra Parma Cook, a native of Czechoslovakia, has studied history and conducted historical research in archives throughout Spain and Peru, and has coauthored "Epidemics in the Parish of Santa Ana de Triana: 1665–1850." The Cooks have worked together for many years and this is their first joint book.

Library of Congress Cataloging-in-Publication Data
Cook, Alexandra Parma.
Good faith and truthful ignorance: a case of
transatlantic bigamy / Alexandra Parma Cook and
Noble David Cook.
Includes bibliographical references and index.
ISBN 0-8223-1222-0
1. Nogueral de Ulloa, Francisco, 16th cent.—Trials,
litigation, etc. 2. Bigamy—Spain—History.
3. Latin America—History—To 1600. I. Cook,
Noble David. II. Title.
KKT174.N64C66   1991
980'.013'092—dc20
[B]   90-36173 CIP